CONTEMPORARY MONETARY ECONOMICS THEORY & POLICY

by

Chaman L. Jain, Ph.D.

Professor of Economics & Finance
St. John's University

 **Graceway Publishing Company**

Manufactured in the United States of America

Library of Congress Catalog Card No.: 79-055682
ISBN 0-932126-02-2   Hardcover
ISBN 0-932126-03-0   Softcover

Published by:

Graceway Publishing Company
P.O. Box 159, Station "C"
Flushing, N.Y. 11367

Dedicated

to

My mother, Pritam Dai Jain, and my
brother, Des Raj Jain, who have
been a great source of inspiration
in all my endeavors.

PREFACE

This book is the result of my frustration to find a suitable book to teach a course in monetary economics. I wanted a book which was descriptive and easy to follow and covered fully all the major topics of monetary economics in the light of contemporary thoughts. Since Keynesians and Monetarists, two major groups of economists, disagree vehemently on many issues, I wanted the book to explain also the position of each group on each issue and its policy implications. I could not find such a book. So I wrote one. Whether or not I succeeded in offering what I expected from others, I leave it to the judgment of readers. Readers will find, though, that a number of topics, such as those discussed in Chapters VII, VIII, IX, X, XI and XVI, are either not covered at all in other textbooks on the subject or not covered as extensively as in this book.

The book deals only with domestic monetary economics. The subject of international monetary economics is equally vast. I felt that I would not be able to do justice if I attempted to cover both in one volume. The book is suitable as a textbook for a variety of courses such as monetary economics, monetary theory, monetary policy, and fiscal and monetary policies for covering monetary policy.

This book is not the result of my efforts alone. Many individuals helped in preparing it. The man to whom I would always remain indebted is Dr. Francis A. Lees who not only provided inspiration throughout eight years of my writing but also read a number of chapters and gave many helpful comments.

I wish to express my thanks to various staff members of Board of Governors as well as of District Banks who patiently answered my questions and, in many instances, provided material, not available anywhere else. Their names are listed in footnotes and/or bibliography. I am also grateful to Dr. Jerry L. Jordan, Dr. Gary H.

Stern, Dr. Joseph M. Crews, Dr. Thomas M. Humphrey, Prof. Theodore Muzio, and Dr. Bobby L. Hamm who gave many helpful comments on certain chapters.

I also wish to express my gratitude to my students of the course, "Fiscal and Monetary Policies," who for many years helped me refine the material as I tested it in many class room situations. I also thank them for their many wonderful ideas for improving the manuscript.

I will never be able to pay my debt to my friend, Mr. Al Migliaro, who spent many days and nights in editing different drafts of the manuscript. His knowledge of the subject matter and skill as a writer and editor were invaluable in bringing clarity to the text.

A special word of thanks to my teachers, Prof. William O. Thweatt of the Vanderbilt University and Dr. Frank M. Tamagna of The American University, who have been a great source of inspiration for me to study monetary economics.

I also wish to express my thanks to Peter Harmantas and Alan Weber for their help in research and to Rosemarie Realmuto, for typing this manuscript.

Although all of these people made important contributions to the preparation of this book, I assume all responsibility for its content, especially any flaws. It was I who made the final decisions about the material that appears and the manner in which it is presented.

Finally, I must thank my wife and family for their continuing support, without which the writing of this book would have been very difficult. Perhaps impossible.

Chaman L. Jain

TABLE OF CONTENTS

PART I
MONETARY THEORY

PART 2
MONETARY POLICY

xiii

Part I

MONETARY THEORY

CHAPTER I

Introduction

In recent years no branch of economics has become as much a topic of controversy as monetary economics. Much of the controversy arises from positions taken by Monetarists, a new group of economists who have challenged many of the established principals of monetary economics. To appreciate this controversy, one must have a full understanding of monetary economics. This book attempts to explain the basic tenets of contemporary monetary theory and monetary policy, the major ingredients of monetary economics.

ORGANIZATION OF THIS BOOK

The book is divided into two parts. Monetary Theory is covered in Part I and Monetary Policy in Part II. Monetary economics revolves around money. There is no consensus about its definition. Therefore, the book begins with a discussion on the definition of money. Chapter II explains various definitions of money both on theoretical and policy levels. Money is discussed on the policy level because it is used by policymakers not as money per se but as a means of regulating the economy. The best definition is the one that provides the best control over income, employment and prices. This chapter also points out various money stock series prepared by the Federal Reserve. Chapter III discusses various determinants of money supply and factors affecting them. It also describes those determinants that are under the control of the Federal Reserve and those that are not. Chapter IV puts together all the determinants of the money supply described in the previous chapter in the form of a simplified money supply model. From the policy point of view, it is important to know not only the determinants of money supply but also of money demand because the latter helps to predict the velocity of money. Chapters V and VI describe various theories of money demand. In addition, Chapter VI gives the findings of major empirical studies on money demand. Chapter VII covers the interaction between money supply and money demand, knowledge of which is necessary for a full understanding of monetary theory. Chapter VIII explains issues pertaining to the linkage between money and economic activity. Chapter IX describes the theory of the monetary indicator and targets, as well as the pros and cons of various candidates for the indicator and operating and intermediate targets. Chapter X covers the theory of inflation, explaining its causes, transmission mechanism and cure. Chapter XI highlights policy issues currently debated by economists.

Part II begins with a chapter (Chapter XII) on goals of monetary policy and the conflicts among them. Chapter XIII discusses the organization of the Federal Reserve System and its relationship to the Congress, the Treasury, the Administration and the commercial banking community. Chapters XIV and XV discuss instruments that are used, or have been used, at one time or another, to implement monetary policy. Since the effectiveness of a policy depends, among other things, on how a decision is made, Chapter XVI explains the decision making process as used in the United States with respect to all monetary instruments. The final chapter (Chapter XVII) discusses, in detail, the problems of monetary policy.

ISSUES OF CONTROVERSY

Although the objective of this book is to explain the major aspects of contemporary monetary economics, the issues that divide economists into two groups, Keynesians and Monetarists, are emphasized throughout. The Keynesian group refers to John M. Keynes and neo-Keynesian economists. The Monetarist group, under the leadership of Milton Friedman, emerges from the traditional school associated with the quantity theory of money. Major issues that divide them are:

1. How elastic is the demand for money with respect to the interest rate?
2. How is the effect of a change in the money supply transmitted to GNP?
3. Is the relation between money and GNP stable?
4. Does the money supply in the long run affect both prices and output?

5. Is the money supply an endogenous or exogenous variable?
6. How much and how quickly does GNP respond to a change in the money supply?
7. What causes inflation?
8. How does the transmission mechanism of inflation work?
9. How can inflation be cured?
10. How are expectations formed?
11. What causes stagflation?
12. Should the monetary authority use rules or discretion in conducting policy?
13. How powerful are fiscal and monetary policies?
14. Should the monetary authority use monetary aggregates or money market conditions or both as a policy guide? Among different money stock series (M-1A, M-1B, M_2, etc.) which one should be used?
15. Should the monetary authority opt for fixed or flexible exchange rates?
16. Is there a trade-off between inflation and unemployment?
17. Should macroeconomic models be built by following the structural model or single equation (reduced form) approach?

The book covers these and other questions and specifies, as clearly as possible, the position of both Monetarists and Keynesians on each issue. Although many of the issues raised by Monetarists are still widely debated, there are some issues on which they have received acceptance. Keynesians are in complete agreement with Monetarists that expectations have an important influence in the determination of wages, interest rates and prices. They are also in full agreement that inflation cannot go too far unless it is accommodated by an increase in the money supply. Keynesians accept that the "crowding out effect" exists, though they don't share with Monetarists that almost all or a large part of the effect resulting from a fiscal action is offset. Keynesians now recognize that money is more important than what John M. Keynes was willing to accept. In the past, Keynesians advocated the use of only money market conditions as a policy guide. But now they seem to accept that monetary aggregates should also be used. Regarding foreign exchange rates, Monetarists have shifted the position of Keynesians from completely-fixed exchange rates to somewhat-flexible exchange rates.

Recently a new group of economists has emerged under the name of "Rationalists," who provide new ideas in support of some of the Monetarist views of policymaking. Their views are discussed in Chapters X and XI.

CHAPTER II

Definition of Money Supply

Monetary policy works through the regulation of the money supply which, in turn, affects the economic life of a nation. A restrictive action is called for when money expansion threatens to cause total demand to outrun productive capacity, and an easy money policy is used when a deficiency in total demand threatens a decrease in income, output and employment. In order to understand how monetary policy works, one needs to know its theory. Monetary theory cannot be discussed without first defining the money supply.

THEORETICAL APPROACHES

There is no consensus as to the definition of money supply. On a theoretical level, definitions which are most frequently debated are:
1. Conventional definition
2. Definition of Friedman and Meiselman
3. Definition of Gurley and Shaw

Conventional Definition

The conventional definition of money supply is also called "money supply narrowly defined." The money supply, under this definition, is expressed as:

Money Supply = Currency in Circulation + Demand Deposits ... 2-1

This definition is based upon the principle that a nation's stock of money should include only those assets that are generally accepted as a means of payment. Currency is legal tender and is immediately accepted for any kind of payment. Demand deposits are included in the money supply because checks drawn against demand deposits are widely accepted as a means of payment. It is estimated that more than 85% of all payments in the United States are made by checks drawn against demand deposits in commercial banks. Though demand deposits do not have legal tender status, banks have a legal obligation to pay a depositor on demand in legal tender, i.e., money.

Definition of Friedman and Meiselman

Some economists feel that the medium-of-payment concept is not altogether meaningful in defining the money stock. Assets which serve as a temporary reservoir of purchasing power should also be regarded as part of the money supply. All these assets do not perform the function of a medium of payment but they can be converted into one. For example, time deposits serve as a temporary reservoir of purchasing power and not as a means of payment. If a holder of such deposits wants to use them he can convert them into demand deposits or cash.

All the assets that can be used as temporary reservoirs of purchasing power are not equally liquid. Some assets can be easily converted into money while others can be converted with varying degrees of difficulty. Considering this problem, Milton Friedman and David Meiselman suggest that only time deposits should be added to the conventional definition of money supply because they are highly liquid.[1] The money supply then becomes:

Money = Currency in + Demand Deposits + Time Deposits ... 2-2
Supply   Circulation

This definition is called "money supply broadly defined." Critics of this definition argue that time deposits are not as highly liquid as claimed by its proponents. Certain time deposits such as certificates of deposit (CDs) have definite maturity schedules and thus cannot be redeemed except at maturity dates. Other time deposits, such as certain types of savings accounts ("Passbook Accounts", for example), require advance notice before they can be converted into cash. In practice, however, banks do not operate that way. They redeem certificates of deposit before maturity with some penalty and seldom impose the advance notice requirements in withdrawing money from savings accounts.

Definition of Gurley and Shaw

John G. Gurley and Edward S. Shaw further broadened the definition of money supply. In a series of articles, they developed a theoretical framework to show that claims against nonbank financial intermediaries are, in most cases, close substitutes for money and, thus, should be regarded as part of the money supply. The major nonbank financial intermediaries are mutual savings banks, savings and loan associations, life insurance companies and finance companies. Professor Johnson argues for the inclusion of claims against nonbank financial intermediaries on the ground that they affect the money people hold. If people have claims against financial intermediaries, they hold less money in cash or demand deposits.[2] Incorporating these claims with the definition of Friedman and Meiselman, the definition of money supply becomes:

Money   = Currency in + Demand   + Time   + Claims Against...2-3
Supply   Circulation   Deposits   Deposits   Nonbank Financial
                                                                      Intermediaries

This definition of money supply, like the one of Friedman and Meiselman discussed earlier, is based on the concept of a temporary reservoir of purchasing power. The difference between them is that this definition includes, in addition to time deposits, many more assets that serve as a temporary reservoir of purchasing power.

Recognizing the possibility that even claims against nonbank financial intermediaries could be classified as part of the money supply, Gurley suggested a definition of money supply comprising currency in circulation, demand deposits, time deposits and claims against nonbank financial intermediaries, with weights assigned to each on the basis of the degree of substitutability.[3] A weight of one can be assigned to currency and demand deposits and weights between zero and one can be given to other financial assets, depending upon how easily they can be converted into money.

MONETARY AGGREGATES

Monetary aggregates (money stock series) were redefined in 1980 in the wake of numerous changes in the payment system, and of innovation of certain financial instruments and increasing use of others.

These developments reduced the significance of old monetary measures. The money stock series that the Federal Reserve currently prepares are: M-1A, M-1B, M_2, M_3 and L (See Table 2-1). The series, M-1A and M-1B, are based on the conventional definition of money supply (money supply narrowly defined). Any asset that can be used as a medium of payment should be included in the money stock. If an asset qualifies in this regard, it is a transaction balance. The M-1A and M-1B replace the old M_1 (See Table 2-2 for old money stock series).

Changes in the payment system has occurred in two important ways: (1) Payment accounts have been extended to new institutions, e.g., NOW accounts, credit union share drafts and thrift-institution checking accounts. (2) Savings accounts can be used for the third party payments, e.g., automatic transfer system (ATS). These accounts serve as transactions balances but they are not included in the old M_1. A NOW account is an interest bearing deposit on which withdrawal can be made by a negotiable order. Credit union share draft account is usually interest bearing, from which funds can be transferred with a check like instrument called a share draft. ATS permits a bank to cover overdrafts by automatically transferring funds from savings to checking accounts.

The new M_2 is based on the definition of Friedman and Meiselman, that is, assets that do not perform the function of medium of payment but can be easily converted into one (criterion of reservoir of purchasing power) should also be included in the money stock. This series replaces the old M_2. It includes assets such as overnight repurchase agreements at commercial banks (RPs), selected overnight Eurodollars, money market mutual fund shares and time deposits at thrift institutions. These assets are as liquid as time and savings deposits at commercial banks but were not included in the old M_2. A security repurchase agreement is an arrangement whereby a bank sells a security in its portfolio—usually a Treasury or Federal agency security—to a customer and agrees to repurchase it at a specified price at some future date. Though RPs were originally created in the 1930's, they grew rapidly only in late 1970's. Eurodollars are interest bearing and they resemble large CDs issued in the United States. Money market mutual funds are a financial innovation of the 1970's. These funds maintain a portfolio of high-yielding Treasury bills, commercial paper and large CDs. With these funds, small investors, like large ones, can obtain high returns at low transaction costs. Since most

TABLE 2-1

NEW MONEY STOCK SERIES

M-1A = M_0 (currency in circulation) + adjusted demand deposits at commercial banks[1]

M-1B = M-1A + NOW accounts + ATS (automatic transfer system) + credit union share drafts + demand deposits at mutual savings banks - consolidation component[2]

M_2 = M-1B + time and savings deposits at all depositary institutions other than large negotiable CDs + overnight RPs (repurchase agreements) at commercial banks[3] + overnight Eurodollars held by U.S. residents, other than banks, at Caribbean branches of member banks[3] + money market mutual fund shares - consolidation component[4]

M_3 = M_2 + large negotiable CDs at all depositary institutions[3] + term RPs (repurchase agreements) at commercial banks and savings and loan associations[3]

L = M_3 + term Eurodollars held by U.S. residents other than banks[3] + bankers' acceptances[3] + commercial paper[3] + Treasury bills[3] + other liquid Treasury securities [3 & 5] + U.S. savings bonds

    [1] Adjusted demand deposits at commercial banks equal gross demand deposits at commercial banks, minus interbank deposits, minus items in process of collection, minus Federal Reserve float, minus United States Treasury deposits and minus deposits held by foreign banks and official institutions

    [2] Consolidation component equals demand deposits of thrift institutions that are held to service checkable deposits

    [3] Net of those held by money market mutual funds
    [4] Demand deposits of thrift institutions that are held to service demand and savings deposits, other than those deducted from M-1B

    [5] Treasury securities with a maturity up to 18 months, other than Treasury bills

Source: 1. "The Redefined Monetary Aggregates," **Federal Reserve Bulletin** (February 1980), pp. 97-122.

mutual funds offer a check writing option (usually a $500 minimum) and the same-day wire transfer service into a preauthorized deposit account, these funds are considered highly liquid.

The new series, M_3 and L, are prepared along the line of definition

TABLE 2-2

OLD MONEY STOCK SERIES

M_1 = M_0 (currency in circulation) + Adjusted demand deposits at commercial banks[1]

M_1+ = M_1 + Savings deposits at commercial banks + NOW accounts at banks and thrift institutions + credit union share draft accounts + demand deposits at mutual savings banks

M_2 = M_1 + Time and savings deposits at commercial banks other than large negotiable CDs

M_3 = M_2 + Mutual savings bank deposits + savings and loan association shares + credit union shares

M_4 = M_2 + Large negotiable CDs

M_5 = M_3 + Large negotiable CDs

M_6 = M_5 + Short-term marketable U.S. Government securities + savings bonds

M_7 = M_6 + Short-term commercial paper

[1] Adjusted demand deposits at commercial banks equal gross demand deposits at commercial banks, plus foreign deposits held at Federal Reserve Banks, minus interbank deposits, minus items in process of collection, minus Federal Reserve float and minus United States Treasury deposits.

Sources: 1. Alfred Broaddus, "Aggregating the Monetary Aggregates: Concepts and Issues," **Economic Review: Federal Reserve Bank of Richmond** (November/December, 1975), p. 4.

2. **Federal Reserve Bulletin** (July 1979), p. A3.

of Gurley and Shaw. They include many other assets that are considered fairly liquid but were not incorporated in any of old money stock series.

In addition to the criteria of medium of exchange and reservoir of purchasing power, the decision, whether or not to include a given asset in a new money stock series, is based on how well it is linked to ultimate targets such as prices, output and employment; how well the Federal Reserve can control its size; and how quickly its data become available. Monetary policy works through the money stock. Policy will be most effective if components that comprise the money stock are highly related to ultimate targets and their size can be controlled by the Federal Reserve. Furthermore, if policy is to be guided by the money stock, its data must become quickly available.

M-1A equals currency in circulation plus adjusted demand deposits at commercial banks. Currency in circulation represents only that portion of the total currency that is held by the public. Currency held by the United States Treasury, Federal Reserve Banks and commercial banks is not considered part of the currency in circulation. Currency in the possession of the Treasury and Federal Reserve Banks is not considered part of the currency in circulation because both can issue currency. The money supply includes only that currency that is actually in use and not that which might at some future date be placed into circulation by these agencies. To avoid double counting, cash reserves (currency) held by commercial banks are not included in the currency in circulation. The banks' cash reserves are primarily maintained to support demand deposits. If both are included in the supply of money, banks' cash reserves would be counted twice because they are already reflected in demand deposits.

Adjusted demand deposits at commercial banks represent the total amount held in checking accounts at these banks, less interbank deposits, items in process of collection, Federal Reserve float, United States Treasury deposits (also called tax and loan accounts), and deposits held by foreign banks and official institutions.

Interbank deposits are excluded because they are maintained for certain purposes that tend to freeze them. Some banks use interbank deposits for clearing checks, which makes it necessary for them to maintain adequate funds in such deposits. Those banks that are not members of the Federal Reserve System used a portion of their interbank deposits for the reserves required by the Federal Reserve and/or by state laws. (The Monetary Act of 1980, however, requires all banks and other depository institutions having transactions accounts and/or nonpersonal time deposits to adhere to reserve requirements of the Federal Reserve. But, unlike member banks, nonmember banks can fulfill their requirements by maintaining a significant portion of their required reserves with other banks.) In some cases, interbank accounts support correspondent relationships among banks.

To avoid double counting, checks in process of collection are excluded from total demand deposits because during this period they appear as deposited funds on the books of all banks involved. Suppose John Doe receives a check in the amount of $100 drawn on First

National City Bank and deposits it in his own bank, Chase Manhattan Bank. The $100 will appear on the books of Chase Manhattan Bank as a deposited fund because it was deposited there. It will also remain on the books of First National City Bank as a deposited fund until such time as the check is cleared.

The Federal Reserve float represents Federal Reserve credit given to a bank in the check collection process. At any given time float is equal to cash items (checks) in process of collection minus deferred availability of those items. The Federal Reserve has a schedule showing how much time is required to clear a check between two points—the point where the check originated and the point where it was deposited. After this time, it automatically credits the amount of checks to the account of depositing banks. Suppose that Mr. "A" gives a check of $10,000 to Mr. "B" drawn on Bank of Chicago, Chicago, Illinois. Mr. "B" deposits it in his own bank, Chase Manhattan Bank, New York City. Suppose further that the Federal Reserve schedule calls for one calendar day to clear a check between these two points. But, due to a snow storm, the Federal Reserve takes three days to clear this check. Then Federal Reserve float will be as follows:

Number of Days After the Check is Dispatched by a Depositing Bank	Federal Reserve Float		Items in Process of Collection		Deferred Availability of Cash
First Day	0	=	$10,000	-	$10,000
Second Day	$10,000	=	$10,000	-	0
Third Day	$10,000	=	$10,000	-	0
Fourth Day	0	=	0	-	0

As shown above, on the second day the depositing bank receives the credit even though the check has not cleared. But $10,000 remains listed under items in process of collection until it does clear. In practice, the moment the Federal Reserve gives credit to a depositing bank against an uncollected check its amount is excluded from items in process of collection, even though it is still in demand deposits of both banks involved. Therefore, to adjust for double counting, both items in process of collection and Federal Reserve float are deducted from total demand deposits. Items in process of collection adjust for double counting arising from uncollected items for which credit has not been given and Federal Reserve float, for those for which credit has been given.

Treasury deposits are excluded for the same reason as currency in possession of the Treasury is excluded. Within certain limits, the Treasury can create money. It is argued that money in the hands of a money creating agency is not in any significant respect different from money that it can bring into being. The line is drawn between money actually in use and money that may be used in the future.

Deposits held by foreign banks and official institutions are excluded because they are not used to a significant extent for payments of goods, services and securities in the United States. Foreign banks include foreign central banks and foreign commercial banks. Foreign central banks hold deposits at U.S. banks primarily for the purpose of clearing balances of international transactions and international reserves. Banks abroad hold deposits at U.S. banks primarily to clear their Eurodollar transactions, and secondarily to settle foreign exchange transactions (of which only a small percentage involves the foreign commerce of the United States). Official institutions include organizations such as the United Nations.

M-1B equals M-1A plus NOW accounts, plus ATS (automatic transfer system), plus credit union share drafts, plus demand deposits at mutual savings banks, and minus consolidation component. Consolidation component is demand deposits of thrift institutions that are held for servicing checkable deposits. They are excluded because they are maintained for clearing checks and, thus, do not serve as a transaction balance.

M_2 equals M-1B plus time and savings deposits at all depositary institutions other than large negotiable CDs, plus overnight RPs at commercial banks other than those held by money market mutual funds, plus overnight Eurodollars held by U.S. residents other than banks and money market mutual funds at Caribbean branches of member banks, plus money market mutual fund shares and minus consolidation component. Large negotiable CDs are in denominations of $100,000 or over. They are excluded because they are money market instruments, issued by banks to attract funds. Eurodollars are interest bearing and they resemble large CDs issued in the United

States. The reason for including only overnight Eurodollars held at Caribbean Islands is the speed of completing a transaction. Caribbean Islands are in the same time zone and thus the transaction of Eurodollars is completed on the same day. However, transaction from the account in Europe will be completed on the same day if information to this effect reaches there by 11 A.M. Otherwise, it will be completed on the next days. Consolidation component represents demand deposits of thrift institutions that are held to service demand and savings deposits, other than those deducted from M-1B. They are deducted to avoid double counting. Again, to avoid double counting, overnight Eurodollars and overnight RPs are included net of those held by money market mutual funds. Money market mutual funds hold these assets in their portfolio. If they are not netted, they will be counted twice, once in the total of money market mutual fund shares and the other time in the total of overnight Eurodollars and overnight RPs.

M_3 equals M_2 plus large negotiable CDs at all depositary institutions and term RPs at commercial banks and savings and loan associations. Both large CDs and term RPs are net of those held by money market mutual funds, which is done to avoid double counting for the reason explained earlier.

L equals M_3 plus term Eurodollars held by U.S. residents other than banks, bankers' acceptances, commercial paper, Treasury bills and other liquid Treasury securities and U.S. savings bonds. Bankers' acceptances is a time draft, essentially an "order to pay" a specified sum of money at a specified date, drawn on and accepted by a bank. Commercial paper refer to short-term unsecured promissory notes sold by large businesses at a discount to dealers, institutional investors and other corporations. Other liquid Treasury securities are securities other than Treasury bills with a maturity up to 18 months. All assets added to M_3 are net of those held by money market mutual funds. The purpose here again is to avoid double counting.

EMPIRICAL APPROACHES

Since the theoretical approach to define money has failed to produce a consensus, economists have tried to settle the issue empirically. Money is important to policymakers not as money per se but as a means to regulate the economy. The best definition of money is the one which provides the best control over income, employment and prices.

In the last two decades or so a number of empirical studies have been made to determine the appropriate definition of money. Since monetary aggregates were revised in 1980, most of the studies, thus far, have been done with old money stock series. Feige's study suggests the superiority of old M_1 over other old money stock series.[4] Studies of Friedman-Meiselman and Schadrack[5] conclude that the old M_2 is a preferable money stock series. Findings of Lee seem to suggest that a broader definition such as the old M_3 might be a better choice.[6]

According to Arthur F. Burns, no single definition is appropriate. In conducting monetary policy, the Federal Reserve takes into account numerous money stock series because no money stock series alone is a perfect guide to monetary ease or restraint.[7] For example, in periods of declining economic activity, a weak demand for private credit tends to slow the growth of a money supply conventionally defined. During such periods market rates of interest usually decline and thereby stimulate individual savings deposits at commercial banks and thrift institutions (intermediation). Savings deposits are not a part of a conventionally defined money supply.

During periods of economic expansion, the behavior of a money supply conventionally defined may be misleading. At such times, large demands for credit are likely to strengthen their growth. (More demand for credit normally means more money will be lent by banks. As will be explained in the next chapter, the more money banks lend to the public the more money they create.) Furthermore, at such times, open-market interest rates generally rise. High open market rates cause funds to shift out of savings deposits (disintermediation). Thus, if, during periods of expansion, monetary policy is based upon conventional definition alone, it would ignore the pressure of disintermediation and damage the mortgage market.

The recent study of the Federal Reserve shows that new money stock series, in general, are better than old ones in predicting GNP as well as the demand for money.[8]

SUMMARY

There is no consensus as to the appropriate definition of money. Three main definitions which are widely discussed in economic literature are: (1) the conventional definition, (2) the definition of Friedman and Meiselman and (3) the definition of Gurly and Shaw. The conventional definition is based on the concept of money as a medium of payment. It is composed of currency in circulation and demand deposits. Money stock series that come close to this definition are M-1A and M-1B. The definition of Friedman and Meiselman is based on the concept of money as a temporary reservoir of purchasing power. It adds time deposits to the components of the conventional definition. The money stock series that the Federal Reserve prepares along this line is M_2. The definition of Gurley and Shaw, which is also based on the concept of a temporary reservoir of purchasing power, broadens the definition of Friedman and Meiselman by adding claims against nonbank financial inter-mediaries. Money stock series that come close to this one are M_2 and M_3. Some economists further broaden the definition along the line of L.

Since theoretical approaches have failed to produce a consensus, many economists have attempted to settle this question empirically. Unfortunately, their findings are also contradictory and inconclusive.

FOOTNOTES

[1]Milton Friedman and David Meiselman, "The Relative Stability of Monetary Stability and the Investment Multiplier in the United States, 1897-1958," in **Commission On Money and Credit: Stabilization Policies** (Englewood Cliffs, New Jersey: Prentice-Hall, Inc., 1963), p. 182.

[2]Harry G. Johson, "Monetary Theory and Policy," **American Economic Review** (June 1962), p. 353.

[3]John G. Gurley, **Liquidity and Financial Institutions in the Postwar Period: Study Paper #14** (Washington, D.C.: Joint Economic Committee, Congress of the United States, 1960), p. 8.

[4]Edgar L. Feige, **The Demand for Liquidity Assets: A Temporal Cross Section Analysis** (Englewood Cliffs, New Jersey: Prentice-Hall, Inc., 1964), p. 43.

[5]Frederick C. Schadrack, "An Empirical Approach to the Definition of Money," in **Monetary Aggregates and Monetary Policy** (New York: Federal Reserve Bank of New York, 1974), p. 34.

[6]Tong Hun Lee, "Substitutability of Non-Bank Intermediary Liabilities For Money: The Empirical Evidence," **Journal of Finance** (September 1966), p. 455.

[7]Arthur F. Burns, "Statement Before the Committee on Banking, Housing, and Urban Affairs, U.S. House of Representatives: July 24, 1975," **Federal Reserve Bulletin** (August 1975), pp. 494-495.

[8]"A Proposal for Redefining the Monetary Aggregates," **Federal Reserve Bulletin** (January 1979), pp. 24-32.

QUESTIONS FOR REVIEW

1. Define the conventional definition of money supply.
   What is the principle on which this definition is based?
2. Describe how Friedman and Meiselman justify the inclusion of time deposits in the definition of money supply.
3. Explain why currency in the possession of the U.S. Treasury, Federal Reserve Banks and commercial banks is not included in the definition of money supply.
4. Describe why interbank deposits of domestic banks, items in process of collection and Treasury deposits are excluded from gross demand deposits in the computation of M-1A.
5. Explain Gurley and Shaw's definition of money supply. In what ways does it deviate from the other two definitions?
6. "Different measures of money stock do not act as substitutes for one another." Critically evaluate this statement.
7. Explain what M-1A, M-1B, M_2 and M_3 series of money stock specifically include.
8. Discuss whether or not compensating balances and travelers' checks should be included in the measurement of M-1A.
9. Explain in what ways the old M_2 differs from the new M_2.
10. What is meant by nonbank financial intermediaries? Discuss sources of funds of four nonbank financial intermediaries.

SUGGESTED FURTHER READING

1. Broaddus, Alfred. "Aggregating the Monetary Aggregates: Concept and Issues." **Economic Review: Federal Reserve Bank of Richmond.** November/December 1975, pp. 3-12.
2. Edwards, Franklin R. "More on Substitutability Between Money and Near-Monies." **Journal of Money, Credit and Banking.** August 1972, pp. 551-571.
3. Federal Reserve Bank of Chicago. "What Is Money?" **Business Conditions: Federal Reserve Bank of Chicago.** June 1971, pp. 9-15.
4. Friedman, Milton and Meiselman, David. "The Relative Stability of Monetary Velocity and the Investment Multiplier in the United States, 1897-1958," in **Commission on Money and Credit: Stabilization Policies.** Englewood Cliffs, New Jersey: Prentice-Hall, Inc., 1963, pp. 165-268.
5. Gurley, John G. **Liquidity and Financial Institutions in the Postwar Economy: Study Paper #14.** Washington, D.C.: Joint Economic Committee, U.S. Congress, 1960.

6. _____& Shaw, Edward S. "Financial Intermediaries and the Saving-Investment Process." **Journal of Finance.** May 1956, pp. 257-276.

7. Hall, Charles W. "Defining Money: Problems and Issues." **Economic Review: Federal Reserve Bank of Cleveland.** October 1971, pp. 3-12.

8. Hamburger, Michael J. "Behavior of the Money Stock: Is There a Puzzle?" **Journal of Monetary Economics.** July 1977, pp. 265-288.

9. Hunt II, Lacy H. "Attention to Series Increases as Link to Economy Discussed." **Business Review: Federal Reserve Bank of Dallas.** September 1972, pp. 1-11.

10. **Improving the Monetary Aggregates: Report of the Advisory Committee on Monetary Statistics.** Washington, D.C.: Board of Governors of the Federal Reserve System, 1976.

11. Mason, W.E. "The Empirical Definition of Money: A Critique." **Economic Inquiry.** August 1976, pp. 67-81.

12. Rutner, Jack L. "A Time Series Analysis of Income and Several Definitions of Money." **Monthly Review: Federal Reserve Bank of Kansas City.** November 1974, pp. 9-16.

13. Shaw, Edward S. "Financial Intermediaries," in Volume 5 of **International Encyclopedia of the Social Sciences.** New York, New York: The MacMillan Company & The Free Press, 1968, pp. 432-439.

14. Tatom, John A. & Lang, Richard W. "Automatic Transfers and the Money Supply Process." **Review: Federal Reserve Bank of St. Louis.** February 1979, pp. 2-10.

15. "The Redefined Monetary Aggregates." **Federal Reserve Bulletin.** February 1980, pp. 97-122.

16. Veazey, Edward E. "A Changing Relationship Between Money and Income." **Review: Federal Reserve Bank of Dallas.** April 1977, pp. 1-7.

CHAPTER III

Determinants Of Money Supply

The theory of money supply deals with two things: (1) the determinants of money supply. (2) How these determinants together affect the money supply. This chapter discusses the first; the next chapter deals with the second.

To understand the determinants of money supply one needs to know how commercial banks create money. Commercial banks influence directly or indirectly the effect of each determinant.

Commercial banks create money on the basis of a fractional reserve system, i.e., they need to maintain only a fraction of total deposits as a reserve against deposit liabilities. Money in excess of required reserves can be invested in the form of loans to the public and purchase of securities. Banks create money when they make such investments.

Assume that the supply of money, consisting of currency in circulation and demand deposits, of a country at any point in time is as follows:

Money Supply		Currency in Circulation		Demand Deposits	
$200,000	=	$50,000	+	$150,000	... 3-1

Suppose that an individual deposits $10,000 in cash in a checking account with Bank "A". Such a deposit has no effect on the total supply of money until the bank puts the money to some use. However the composition of the money supply changes. Currency in circulation decreases by $10,000 and demand deposits increase by the same amount. The composition of money supply becomes:

10,000 deposit into checking → No effect on total M.S
But ∆'s composition

20

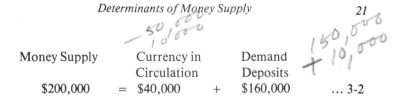

Money Supply		Currency in Circulation		Demand Deposits	
$200,000	=	$40,000	+	$160,000	... 3-2

The deposit increases the bank's excess reserves by a sum in excess of the required reserves. The maximum amount a bank can lend or otherwise invest is limited by its excess reserves. (Excess reserves are defined as total reserves minus required reserves.) If the reserve requirement is 20 per cent, the excess reserves of the bank in which $10,000 has been deposited is $8,000 ($10,000 - $2,000). This bank can, at the most, lend $8,000. Assume the full $8,000 is lent and the money is given to the borrower in cash, the supply of money becomes:

Money Supply		Currency in Circulation		Demand Deposits	
$208,000	=	$48,000	+	$160,000	...3-3

Currency in circulation increases by $8,000 because the money is given to the borrower in cash. Demand deposits remain unchanged. If the bank added the $8,000 to the borrower's checking account, the money supply would also have increased by the same amount. However, the composition would have changed. Demand deposits would have increased by $8,000 and currency in circulation would have remained unchanged.

Though a single bank cannot create money by more than its excess reserves, the banking system as a whole can create money up to several times that amount because of a multiplier effect. Each time a bank loans money, a portion of it finds its way to another bank in the form of a deposit. Each deposit provides a base for further money expansion. How much money a banking system can create from a given deposit can be determined by making the following assumptions:

1. The reserve requirement ratio of all banks is 20 percent of demand deposits.
2. Excess reserves are kept at a zero level, meaning that banks lend out every dollar they acquire over and above required reserves.
3. There is no cash drain, implying that the borrowed money is not drained away from banks; persons who receive money deposit it in one bank or another.

Assume that an individual deposits $10,000 in cash in his checking account at Bank "A". With a reserve requirement of 20 percent, the bank needs only $2,000 (20 percent of $10,000) to back up the deposit, leaving an excess reserves of $8,000 (Table 3-1, Column 4). Since it is assumed that banks do not hold excess reserves, this bank lends the entire $8,000. Bank "A" creates $8,000 in new money by the loan. The borrower spends the $8,000 by writing a check. The person receiving the check deposits it in his bank, Bank "B". This increases demand deposits of Bank "B" by $8,000. Since the reserve requirement for "B" is also 20 percent, it keeps $1,600 in required reserves and lends the rest — $6400. The person who borrows $6,400 from Bank "B" spends it. The person receiving the $6,400 deposits it in his bank, Bank "C". This increases the demand deposits of bank "C" by $6,400. Like other banks, Bank "C" keeps $1,280 (20 percent of $6,400) in required reserves and lends the rest. This process continues until the excess reserve of the last bank reaches zero. After this cycle is completed, the banking system as a whole has created new money in the amount of $40,000 (sum total of excess reserves of all the banks involved) from an initial deposit of $10,000 (Table 3-1, Column 4).

TABLE 3-1

MONEY EXPANSION BY THE BANKING SYSTEM

Banks (1)	Demand Deposits (2)	Required Reserves (3)	Excess Reserves or Money Loaned (4)
A	$10,000	$ 2,000	$ 8,000
B	8,000	1,600	6,400
C	6,400	1,280	5,120
D	5,120	1,024	4,096
E	4,096	819	3,277
---	---	---	---
---	---	---	---
Total	$50,000	$10,000	$40,000

The money expansion multiplier is used to determine how much money a banking system creates from a given demand deposit. The money expansion multiplier is expressed as:

$$M = \frac{1}{r} \qquad \qquad \text{... 3-4}$$

Where "M" stands for money expansion multiplier and "r" for reserve requirement. Assuming that the reserve requirement of each bank is 20 percent, the money expansion multiplier is:

$$M = \frac{1}{.20} = 5 \qquad \qquad \text{...3-5}$$

To determine how much new money a banking system creates from a given deposit, the money expansion multiplier is applied to the excess reserve of the bank where the deposit is initially made.

Most of the factors that determine the money supply affect, directly and indirectly, the ability of commercial banks to create money.

The most important factors which determine the money supply are:
A. Reserve Requirement Ratio (q)
B. Ratio of Currency in Circulation to Private Demand Deposits (k)
C. Ratio of Time to Private Demand Deposits (t)
D. Ratio of Government to Private Demand Deposits (g)
E. Monetary Base (B).

RESERVE REQUIREMENT RATIO (q)

The reserve requirement ratio is defined as total reserves divided by total deposits. Total reserves are equal to total cash in the hands of commercial banks plus balances on deposit with Federal Reserve Banks. Total deposits are equal to time deposits plus private demand deposits plus Treasury deposits (commonly known as tax and loan accounts). A rise in the reserve requirement ratio (q) tends to reduce the money supply, and vice versa. For example, when the legal reserve requirements are raised by the Federal Reserve, banks need more money in their total reserves to support deposit liabilities. In order to obtain the needed funds banks can sell their securities and/or restrict loans. Either of these increases the "q" ratio and diminishes the ability of banks to create money. However, banks with excess reserves can meet the higher reserve requirements from their own reserves. To the extent that they do, the "q" ratio does not go up but the bank's ability to create money is still adversely affected.

The major factors which determine the reserve requirement ratio (q)

TABLE 3 - 2

RESERVE REQUIREMENTS OF THE FEDERAL RESERVE
(In effect December 31, 1979)

	Type of Deposits	Reserve Requirement (In Percent)
Basic Reserve Requirements	Net demand deposits[1]	
	A. $2 million or less	 7
	B. Over $2 million but up to $10 million	...... 9½
	C. Over $10 million but up to $100 million	......11¾
	D. Over $100 million but up to $400 million	......12¾
	E. Over $400 million	......16¼
	Time Deposits	
	A. Regular saving deposits	 3
Marginal Reserve Requirements	Other time deposits[2]	
	A. Less than $5 million maturing in:	
	30 - 179 days	 3
	180 days to 4 years	...... 2½
	4 years or more	 1
	B. Over $5 million, maturing in:	
	30 - 179 days	 6
	180 days to 4 years	...... 2½
	4 years or more	 1

[1] Net demand deposits are equal to gross demand deposits less cash items in process of collection and demand balances due from domestic banks.

[2] The average of reserves on savings and other time deposits must be at least 3 percent, the minimum specified by law. Bank-related commercial paper are treated like "other time deposits."

Source: 1. **Federal Reserve Bulletin** (January 1980), p. A9.

are: (1) the legal reserve requirement, (2) banks' need for cash to support deposit liabilities, (3) transfers by the public of funds from time to demand deposits and from banks with smaller total deposits to ones with larger total deposits, and (4) demand for loans by the public.

The "q" ratio rises with a rise in the legal reserve requirements. (The legal reserve requirements of the Federal Reserve, in effect December 31, 1979, are given in Table 3-2.)

Due to seasonality in the demand for cash, banks may, in certain months of the year, need more reserves to meet the needs of their depositors than the amount required by law. When such a need arises, total reserves rise and so does the "q" ratio.

Transfer of funds from time to demand deposits raises total reserves and consequently the "q" ratio because demand deposits are subject to higher reserve requirements than time deposits. Reserve requirements among different banks vary with the size of total deposits (See Table 3-2), with the result that transfer of funds among banks affects the "q" ratio.

When the public demand for loans increases, excess reserves decrease causing a decline in the "q" ratio. A decline in loan demand results in a rise in the "q" ratio as excess reserves build up.

RATIO OF CURRENCY IN CIRCULATION TO PRIVATE DEMAND DEPOSITS (k)

An increase in currency in circulation (cash in the hands of the public) coupled with a decline in demand deposits, reduces the banking system's ability to create money since, as pointed out earlier, demand deposits contribute to the bank's ability to make loans or otherwise invest funds. The "k" ratio reflects the relationship between demand deposits and currency in circulation.

The ratio increases when currency in circulation rises relative to demand deposits, and vice versa. As the value of "k" rises the money supply declines.

The main factors which determine the "k" ratio are: (1) urbanization, (2) income growth, (3) easy access to credit cards, (4) availability of banking services, (5) fear of bank failures, (6) desire to evade taxes, (7) bank service charges, (8) market interest rates and (9) foreign transactions. Urbanization tends to reduce the use of cash because it provides familiarity with the advantages of checking accounts. Growth in real per capita income and credit cards tend to reduce demand for currency since, with higher incomes, people switch to more expensive items for which payment is made more often by check or charged to credit card accounts, which are paid by check. An expansion in the geographical availability of banking services and a reduction in the fear of bank failure enhances bank deposits. The desire to evade taxes raises demand for currency because it encourages cash transactions. Bank service charges levied on checking accounts tend to encourage the use of cash.

Changes in market interest rates also affect the "k" ratio. It declines when market rates rise far above the rates offered on time deposits because such a phenomenon causes funds to shift out of time deposits (disintermediation). When people withdraw funds from time deposits to invest in open securities, funds normally land in demand deposits. Furthermore, a rise in market interest rates induces the public to economize on the holding of currency.

The effect of foreign transactions on the "k" ratio depends on how transactions occur. When, for example, the U.S. balance of payments is in deficit, the "k" ratio will move up or down depending on what foreigners do with their surplus dollars. If they maintain those funds in U.S. banks without affecting the distribution between time and demand deposits, the "k" ratio remains unchanged. If, however, the distribution increases time deposits at the expense of demand deposits, "k" rises, and vice versa.

RATIO OF TIME TO PRIVATE DEMAND DEPOSITS (t)

The "t" ratio is inversely related to the conventionally defined money supply (currency in circulation plus demand deposits). The ratio changes when funds shift from time to demand deposits or the other way around.

As an illustration of this point, assume:

1. Deposits of $10 million of a certain bank shift from time to demand deposits.
2. Reserve requirements for time and demand deposits for all banks are 10 and 20 percent, respectively.
3. Excess reserves are maintained at a zero level, meaning banks loan every dollar of excess reserves they acquire. [Bank has to lend all

4. There is no currency drain, each dollar loaned by a bank goes back to the banking system in the form of a demand deposit.

With a 20 percent reserve requirement for demand deposits, the money expansion multiplier will be 5 (1/.20). Therefore, an increase in demand deposits of $10 million will generate $40 million in new money. [Eight million (excess reserve of the bank where the deposit was initially made) times 5 (money expansion multiplier)]. However, the total money supply resulting from this deposit will be $50 million ($40 million in newly created money plus the increase in demand deposits of $10 million resulting from the initial transfer from time to demand deposits). The reduction of $10 million in time deposits, on the other hand, will decrease the supply of money by $45 million [$9 million (initial excess reserves based upon 10 percent legal reserve requirement on time deposits) times 5 (money expansion multiplier)]. The original $10 million of time deposits are not added to the total because time deposits are not considered as part of the conventionally defined money supply. The expansion multiplier of 5 is also used in conjunction with time deposits because the money loaned from time deposits is used the same way as money loaned from demand deposits. Thus, a transfer of $10 million from time to demand deposits will result in a net increase in the money stock of $5 million ($50 million - $45 million). However, such a shift in funds would have decreased the overall money supply if time deposits were included in the definition of money supply—definition of Friedman and Meiselman.

The main factors that determine the "t" ratio are the maximum interest rates commercial banks are permitted to pay on time deposits and interest income available from alternative earning assets such as stocks and bonds. Under the Federal Reserve Act, the Federal Reserve is given the power to set the maximum interest rates member banks can pay on time deposits. These rates limit the ability of commercial banks to compete effectively with alternative investments. When the returns from other investment alternatives rise far above bank ceiling rates, the public tends to move its funds away from time deposits. As a result, the ratio of time to demand deposits declines. The opposite is true if the alternative opportunities yield less income than the investment in time deposits. During a period of recession, time deposits generally rise because at that time such deposits are considered a good investment.

RATIO OF GOVERNMENT TO PRIVATE
DEMAND DEPOSIT (g)

Government demand deposits refer to demand deposit accounts the United States Treasury maintains at various commercial depositaries. Such deposits accumulate primarily from the revenue collected from taxes and the sale of Treasury securities. The "g" ratio is inversely related to the money supply. The transfer of funds from private to Government demand deposits increases the "g" ratio and reduces the money supply because Government deposits are not considered a part of the money supply.

Legislation enacted in 1977 has caused a number of changes with respect to Government deposits. In addition to commercial banks, the Treasury can now maintain deposits at savings and loan associations, credit union and mutual savings banks. It can draw interest on balances held at depositaries. The Treasury offers two options to institutions that wish to serve as Government depositaries: (1) Note Option and (2) Remittance Option. Under Note Option, the depositary credits deposits to its tax and loan account (non-interest bearing demand deposits) at the time of receipt. The next day it transfers funds equal to the amount of the previous day's Treasury deposits to an interest-bearing note account. The note is callable on demand without prior notice. Under Remittance Option, the depositary does not purchase funds from the Treasury but acts only as a channel to transfer funds from private accounts to the tax and loan account. At the end of each day, it sends an advice of credit to the Federal Reserve Bank in the amount of the previous day's Treasury deposits. Upon receipt of the advice of credit, the Federal Reserve Bank withdraws funds from the reserve account of that institution. New legislation has also permitted the Treasury to invest its cash balances in its own securities or those of Federal Government agencies. The Treasury reimburses depositaries for their services on a per item basis.

The main factors affecting the "g" ratio are: (1) tax collection dates, (2) sale of Government securities to the public, (3) general level of economic activity and (4) the amount of funds the Government needs for expenditures. The Treasury balances usually increase at or around tax collection dates because most individuals and businessmen wait until the last moment to pay their taxes.

The sale of U.S. Treasury securities to the public (not to be confused with the Federal open market operation) increases Government deposits and decreases private demand deposits because almost all the proceeds from such sales are deposited in Treasury accounts at commercial depositaries. Government deposits generally increase by a substantial amount when funds are raised by a new security offering. The level of general economic activity also influences Government deposits and consequently the "g" ratio.

Government deposits increase when the economy is in high gear because at such times tax revenues rise. The opposite will be the case when the economy slows down. Almost all U.S. Treasury payments are made from its account at the Federal Reserve.[1] The Treasury maintains a certain balance at this account. Whenever this balance declines, the Treasury replenishes it by withdrawing from commercial depositaries. By doing this, the Treasury reduces the destabilizing effect that changes in Government deposits may have on the reserves of commercial depositaries.

MONETARY BASE (B)

The monetary base (also called high power money) is an important monetary aggregate through which the Federal Reserve can regulate the supply of money.

The monetary base is defined in two ways: in terms of uses of the base and sources of the base. Both uses and sources of the base are derived from a consolidated monetary balance sheet of the Federal Reserve System and the United States Treasury. Table 3-3 gives the monetary base derived both ways.

The monetary base in terms of uses is expressed as:

$$\text{Monetary Base} = \underset{\text{Reserves}}{\text{Member Bank}} + \underset{\text{Circulation}}{\text{Currency in}} \qquad \dots 3\text{-}6$$

Member bank reserves consist of money that member banks have on deposit at the Federal Reserve plus their own vault cash. (Since such reserves include only those assets that member banks may count to meet their legal reserve requirements, demand balances held with other banks are not added to the total of member bank reserves.) Currency in circulation is that portion of the total currency held by the public.

The monetary base in terms of sources is expressed as:

TABLE 3-3

MONETARY BASE[1]

Sources of Funds		Amount (Millions)
Sources Supplying Member Bank Reserves		
1. Federal Reserve holdings of U.S. Government and Federal Agency Securities and Prime Bankers' acceptances	+	$123,719
2. Federal Reserve discounts & advances	+	1,908
3. Federal Reserve float	+	6,119
4. Other Federal Reserve assets	+	4,950[2]
5. Gold stock	+	11,159
6. Special Drawing Rights Certificate account	+	1,800
7. Treasury currency outstanding	+	12,828
Sources Absorbing Member Bank Reserves		
1. Treasury cash holding	-	397
2. Treasury deposits with Federal Reserve Banks	-	3,050
3. Foreign deposits with Federal Reserve Banks	-	353
4. Other deposits with Federal Reserve Banks	-	294
5. Other Federal Reserve liabilities and capital accounts	-	$ 4,894
Monetary base		$153,495

Uses of Funds		Amount (Millions)
1. Member bank reserves	+	$ 32,098
2. Currency in Circulation	+	121,397
		$153,495

[1]Based upon November 1979 data.

[2]Other Federal Reserve assets include buildings, fixtures, equipment, etc.

Source: 1. Board of Governors of the Federal Reserve System, **Federal Reserve Bulletin** (January 1980), p. A4.

Monetary = Sources Supplying   Sources Absorbing ... 3-7
Base   Member Bank Reserves   Member Bank Reserves
                                      Excluding Currency
                                      in Circulation

The sources supplying member bank reserves tend to increase member bank reserves. The sources absorbing member bank reserves, on the other hand, tend to decrease member bank reserves.

The sources supplying member bank reserves are: *GNMA*

1. Federal Reserve holdings of U.S. Government and Federal agency securities and prime bankers' acceptances
2. Federal Reserve discounts & advances
3. Federal Reserve float
4. Other Federal Reserve assets
5. Gold stock
6. Special Drawing Rights certificate account
7. Treasury currency outstanding

The sources absorbing member bank reserves (other than currency in circulation) are:

1. Treasury cash holdings
2. Treasury deposits with Federal Reserve Banks
3. Foreign deposits with Federal Reserve Banks
4. Other deposits with Federal Reserve Banks
5. Other Federal Reserve liabilities and capital accounts

To understand how the monetary base affects the supply of money, one needs to know the way in which each of these sources influences member bank reserves.

Here is how each of the sources supplying member bank reserves affects those reserves:

Federal Reserve Holdings of U.S. Government and Federal Agency Securities and Prime Bankers' Acceptances

An increase in the Federal Reserve holdings of these securities increases member bank reserves because when a bank presents a check received from a seller for collection, the Federal Reserve increases the bank's reserve balance by the same amount. The opposite is true when the Federal Reserve sells securities. Changes in such holdings come solely at the discretion of the Federal Reserve. (Bankers' acceptance is a time draft, essentially an "order to pay" a specified sum of money at a specified date, drawn on and accepted by a bank.)

Federal Reserve Discounts & Advances

Discounts and advances are loans made by the Federal Reserve to member banks. They occur at the initiative of member banks. An individual bank is usually prompted to borrow from the Federal Reserve to avoid a deficiency in its legal reserve requirement. When a loan is granted, the bank's reserve deposit rises. The reverse occurs when the loan is paid back. Under the Depository Institutions Deregulation and Monetary Control Act of 1980, the Federal Reserve is permitted to extend loans even to nonmember banks and other qualified depository institutions.

Federal Reserve Float

Float represents Federal Reserve credit given to banks' reserve accounts in the check collection process. At any given time the float is equal to the cash items (i.e., checks) in process of collection minus the deferred availability of those cash items. The Federal Reserve has a schedule showing how much time is required to clear checks. After this time, it automatically credits the amount of checks to the account of depositing banks. Any delay experienced by the Federal Reserve in collecting any part of these funds gives the depositing banks float equal to the uncollected amount. The float thus created increases total bank reserves by an amount equal to the credit given to the depositing banks, since the banks against which the check items are drawn still have the same amount in their reserve accounts. From the way float arises it is apparent that the Federal Reserve has no control over it.

There are different types of float. The most important among them are:

  i.   **Holdover float** that arises from unexpected peaks in items presented for collection, unusually high staff absences and computer malfunctions.
 ii.   **Transportation float** that results from transportation problems caused by bad weather, strikes, mechanical breakdowns and fuel shortages.
iii.   **Rejected items float** that arises from rejection of an item by a high-speed computer sorting equipment, necessitating

handling on a slower-manual operating machine. For example, a badly crumpled check cannot be processed on a high speed computer.

iv. **Delayed presentation float** that arises because the bank on which the check is drawn is not open on a given day. All banks do not follow the same holidays. Some Illinois banks close regularly on Wednesday and remain open on Saturday. Furthermore, on certain days, Federal Reserve offices are closed in one district while open in others.

Other Federal Reserve Assets

Other Federal Reserve assets include such items as buildings, fixtures and equipment. An increase in any of these assets increases member bank reserves. For example, when a Federal Reserve Bank buys a building, fixtures or equipment, it isssues a check to cover the purchase. The person who receives the check deposits it with his own bank. When the bank presents it for collection, the Federal Reserve credits its account, thereby increasing member bank reserves.

Gold Stock

Gold stock consists of monetized and nonmonetized gold. Monetized gold is that against which gold certificates have been issued by the Treasury. Nonmonetized gold is that against which no gold certificates have been issued. Since January 1, 1975, every ounce of gold held by the Treasury has been monetized.[2]

Gold stock increases when the U.S. Treasury buys gold. The Treasury can purchase gold from domestic producers and foreign holders. When a domestic producer sells gold to the Treasury, he receives a check drawn on the Federal Reserve. The producer deposits this check with his own bank which, in turn, deposits it with the Federal Reserve for clearance. When the check is cleared, the reserve balance of the depositing bank rises, thereby, increasing member bank reserves.

When a foreign authority sells gold, the effect on member bank reserves depends upon how the accounts are settled. The Federal Reserve holds deposit accounts of foreign governments. If the Federal Reserve makes the payment by transferring the amount from the Treasury account to the account of a foreign government, there will be no change in member bank reserves. However, member bank reserves will increase when a foreign authority draws on its deposit account at the Federal Reserve to provide funds for goods and services its people bought on the American markets, to invest in American financial assets or to transfer funds to commercial banks in the U.S. for other reasons.

Special Drawing Rights Certificate Account

Special Drawing Rights (SDRs) are, in effect, a line of credit allowed to member nations by the International Monetary Fund (IMF). Nations use their allocation to obtain the currencies of other member nations to settle their balance-of-payments deficits. They can also use it to obtain loans from other countries. They exercise their line of credit when they ask countries with strong balance of payments and reserve positions to convert their SDRs into a foreign exchange they need.

When the U.S. Treasury issues SDR certificates to the Federal Reserve against its allocation of SDRs from the IMF, it receives an equal amount of dollars credited to a "special cash account of the Exchange Stabilization Fund" at the Federal Reserve. Issuance of SDR certificates to the Federal Reserve by the Treasury is referred to as "monetizing the SDR allocation."

The SDR certificates are used to acquire additional foreign exchange reserves in the following manner: Assume the United States has a deficit in the balance of payments with Great Britain, implying that Great Britain has earned a surplus of U.S. dollars. Great Britain can do a number of things with this dollar surplus. It can hold it at U.S. commercial banks or invest it in U.S. securities. Such action will present no problem to the United States because it will settle its deficit without any difficulty. A problem may arise, however, if Great Britain decides to convert dollars into pounds because their sale in the foreign exchange market may lower the value of the dollar. One way the United States can avoid this is by exchanging its SDRs for pounds and then using the pounds to redeem its dollars. According to the procedure set by the IMF, the United States can obtain pounds against SDRs either from a country designated by the IMF or from a country willing to do so through mutual agreement. Let us say that it obtains pounds against SDRs from West Germany. This reduces the

Federal Reserve holdings of SDR certificates. When the United States redeems its dollars by giving pounds to Great Britain, the deposits of Great Britain in U.S. commercial banks decline. As a result, member bank reserves decline. Thus, when the Federal Reserve holdings of SDR certificates drop, member bank reserves drop also. (It is assumed here that Great Britain had deposited its newly acquired dollar surplus in U.S. commercial banks. If it had deposited these dollars in its accounts at the Federal Reserve, the redemption of dollars by the United States would not have affected member bank reserves. Member bank reserves were affected at the time when Great Britain shifted funds from commercial banks to its account at the Federal Reserve.)

Conversely, if the United States acquires SDRs from other countries in exchange for foreign currency, the Federal Reserve holdings of SDR certificates may or may not increase, depending upon whether or not the Treasury issues certificates against these SDRs. The Treasury is not required to issue a certificate against every SDR it requires.[3] Member bank reserves also may or may not increase. They increase if the Treasury provides the foreign currency from the market. If it provides the foreign currency from its own holdings or from those of the Federal Reserve, member bank reserves do not rise.

Treasury Currency Outstanding

Treasury currency outstanding consists of coins and currency that are legal obligations of the U.S. Treasury held by the public, commercial banks, Federal Reserve Banks and the Treasury itself. The larger part of this item is coin.

When new coins are minted member bank reserves increase because the Treasury issues checks to pay for the cost of producing them. For example, U.S. Mint employees deposit their paychecks in their own banks, who present them to the Federal Reserve Bank of their district for collection. The result of such transactions is an increase in member bank reserves, since the money comes from the Treasury's account at the Federal Reserve.

The amount of coins in circulation is determined to a great extent by the public since they are minted to meet people's needs. Hence, neither the Treasury nor the Federal Reserve has much control over Treasury currency outstanding.

Here is how each of the sources absorbing member bank reserves affects those reserves:

Treasury Cash Holdings

In addition to deposit balances at commercial and Federal Reserve Banks, the Treasury holds some cash in its own vaults. When the Treasury increases this cash by withdrawing it from its accounts at commercial banks, member bank reserves fall.

Treasury Deposits With Federal Reserve Banks

As described earlier, the Treasury has a demand deposit account with the Federal Reserve. The amount of this account goes down when the Treasury pays bills because most of the payments are made by checks drawn on its account at the Federal Reserve. When the checks are presented for collection, member bank reserves rise. Conversely, member bank reserves go down when the Treasury transfers funds from commercial banks to its account at the Federal Reserve.

Foreign and Other Deposits With Federal Reserve Banks

Foreign central banks and international institutions also maintain deposit accounts with the Federal Reserve. In general, the balances in these accounts are built up out of funds transferred from member banks. Because of this, when the balances in these accounts rise, they absorb member bank reserves, and vice versa.

Other Federal Reserve Liabilities and Capital Accounts

Capital accounts comprise the bulk of the amount under this heading. These accounts include capital paid in (the amount paid by member banks for the capital stock of Federal Reserve Banks), surplus (retained net earnings of Federal Reserve Banks) and other capital accounts (unallocated net earnings of Federal Reserve Banks for the year to the date of statement). When the capital accounts increase, member bank reserves decline, and vice versa.

It is quite clear that the monetary base is affected by numerous sources (supplying and absorbing member bank reserves), many of which are outside the control of the Federal Reserve. The only source over which the Federal Reserve has complete control is holdings of U.S. Government and Federal agency securities and prime bankers' acceptances. The Federal Reserve, by forecasting changes in other sources, can use these holdings to achieve a desired change in the level of the monetary base. For example, if it wishes to achieve a growth of $1 billion in the monetary base in any given week and a net increase of $0.4 billion is expected from other sources in that week, the Federal Reserve will purchase securities worth $0.6 billion to make up the difference.

SUMMARY

The major factors that determine the money supply are: (A) reserve requirement ratio (inversely related to the money supply), (B) ratio of currency in circulation to private demand deposits (inversely related to the money supply), (C) ratio of time to private demand deposits (inversely related to the conventionally defined money supply), (D) ratio of Government to private demand deposits (inversely related to the money supply) and (E) monetary base (positively related to the money supply).

The monetary base is defined in terms of uses as well as sources of the base. In terms of uses, the monetary base is equal to member bank reserves plus currency in circulation. In terms of sources, the monetary base is equal to sources supplying member bank reserves minus sources absorbing member bank reserves. Among all the sources that determine the monetary base, the Federal Reserve has complete control only over its own holdings of U.S. Government and Federal agency securities and bankers' acceptances.

FOOTNOTES

[1]Federal Reserve Bank of Cleveland, "The Role of U.S. Government Demand Deposits in the Monetary Process," **Economic Review: Federal Reserve Bank of Cleveland** (June 1969), p. 7.

[2]Albert E. Burger, "Monetary Effects of the Treasury Sale of Gold," **Review: Federal Reserve Bank of St. Louis** (January 1975), p. 21.

[3]Letter from T. Page Nelson, Director, Office of International Gold and Foreign Exchange Operations, Department of Treasury, Washington, D.C., November 9, 1972.

QUESTIONS FOR REVIEW

1. What are the major determinants of money supply? Take any three determinants and discuss how a change in each affects the money supply.

2.   Discuss in detail the effect of a transfer of funds from time to demand deposits on the supply of money.

3.   What are the factors which determine the ratio of Government to private demand deposits? How would a rise in this ratio affect the supply of money?

4.   What is the money expansion multiplier? What factors determine the size of this multiplier?

5.   What is the monetary base? What part does it play in the determination of money supply?

6.   Distinguish between sources supplying and sources absorbing member bank reserves. What would be the net effect on member bank reserves of each of the following:
    i.   Shifting of funds from a nonmember bank to the Treasury accounts at Federal Reserve Banks?
    ii. Sale of Government securities to the public?
    iii. An increase in legal reserve requirements?
    iv. A decrease in foreign deposits with the Federal Reserve?

7.   Discuss the Special Drawing Rights certificate account. What purpose does it serve? Suppose the Exchange Stabilization Fund acquires SDRs from another country in exchange for lira. How would it affect the Special Drawing Rights certificate account?

8.   Describe in detail the effect of an increase in U.S. exports over imports on the "k" ratio.

9.   "The amount of money a single bank can create is limited by its excess reserve whereas the banking system as a whole can do so to some multiple of the excess reserve of a single bank." Explain.

10. How does the "k" ratio affect the supply of money? What are the factors which determine the value of this ratio?

SUGGESTED FURTHER READING

1.   Andersen, Leonall C. **A Study of Factors Affecting the Money Stock: Phase I: Staff Economic Studies.** Washington, D.C.: The Federal Reserve System, 1965.

2.   Anderson, Jane and Humphrey, Thomas. "Determinants of Change in the Money Stock: 1960-1970." **Monthly Review: Federal Reserve Bank of Richmond.** March 1972, pp. 2-8.

3.   Barrett, Martin. "Activation of the Special Drawing Rights Facility in the IMF." **Monthly Review: Federal Reserve Bank of New York.** February 1970, pp. 40-46.

4.   Beck Jr., William E. "Determinants of the United States Currency - Demand Deposit Ratio." **Journal of Finance.** March 1975, pp. 57-74.

5. Board of Governors of the Federal Reserve System. "SDR's in Federal Reserve Operations and Statistics." **Federal Reserve Bulletin.** May 1970, pp. 421-424.

6. Brewer, Elijah. "Treasury to Invest Surplus Tax and Loan Balances." **Economic Perspectives.** November/December 1977, pp. 14-20.

7. Burger, Albert E. and Balbach, Anatol. "Measurement of the Domestic Money Stock." **Review: Federal Reserve Bank of St. Louis.** May 1972, pp. 10-23.

8. Burger, Albert E. **The Money Supply Process.** Belmont, California: Wadsworth Publishing Company, Inc., 1971.

9. Cagan, Philip. **Determinants and Effects of Changes in the Stock of Money: 1875-1960.** New York: National Bureau of Economic Research, 1965.

10. Cox, William N. "Changes in the Treasury's Cash Management Procedures." **Economic Review: Federal Reserve Bank of Atlanta.** January/February 1978, pp. 14-16.

11. Federal Reserve Bank of Cleveland. "The Role of U.S. Government Demand Deposits in the Monetary Process." **Economic Review: Federal Reserve Bank of Cleveland.** June 1969, pp. 3-11.

12. Federal Reserve Bank of Dallas. "Interest Authorized on U.S. Treasury Demand Deposits at Commercial Banks." **Voice: Federal Reserve Bank of Dallas.** January 1978, pp. 5-6.

13. Friedman, David H. **Glossary: Weekly Federal Reserve Statements.** New York: Federal Reserve Bank of New York, October 1975.

14. Hoel, Arline. "A Primer on Federal Reserve Float." **Monthly Review: Federal Reserve Bank of New York.** October 1975, pp. 245-253.

15. Jordan, Jerry L. "Elements of Money Stock Determination." **Review: Federal Reserve Bank of St. Louis.** October 1969, pp. 10-19.

16. Nichols, Dorothy M. **Modern Money Mechanics: A Work Book on Deposits, Currency, and Bank Reserves.** Chicago, Illinois: Federal Reserve Bank of Chicago, June 1975.

17. Rea, John D. "Sources of Money Growth in 1970 and 1971." **Monthly Review: Federal Reserve Bank of Kansas City.** July-August 1972, pp. 3-13.

18. Timberlake Jr., Richard H. "The Supply of Money in the United States." **Monthly Review: Federal Reserve Bank of Richmond.** February 1971, pp. 12-15.

19. Zanzi, Aldo W. "Second Amendment of Fund Articles in Force: Changes Made in Powers and Organization." **Finance & Development.** June 1978, pp. 4-41.

CHAPTER IV
Money Supply Model

In the previous chapter, we discussed how various determinants individually affect the supply of money. In this chapter, a money supply model is developed to show how these determinants together affect the supply of money.

GENERAL MONEY SUPPLY MODEL

There are many models of money supply but here a general money supply model, as outlined by Jerry L. Jordan, will be discussed.[1]

The money supply as conventionally defined is:

$$M = C + D \qquad \qquad ... 4\text{-}1$$

Where

M	=	Supply of money as conventionally defined
C	=	Currency in the hands of public
D	=	Private demand deposits

Monetary base is equal to:

$$B = C + R \qquad \qquad ... 4\text{-}2$$

Where

B	=	Monetary base
R	=	Member bank reserves

Member bank reserves are equal to:

$$R = q(D + T + G) \qquad \qquad ... 4\text{-}3$$

Where

G	=	Government deposits with commercial banks
q	=	Weighted-average reserve ratio against all bank

deposits (private demand, time, and government deposits). It is computed directly by dividing total reserves by total deposits.

T   =   Time deposits

Currency in circulation in terms of private demand deposits can be expressed as:

C   =   kD   ... 4-4

Where

k   =   C/D---ratio of currency in circulation to private demand deposits.

Time deposits in terms of private demand deposits can be written as:

T   =   tD   ... 4-5

Where

t   =   T/D---ratio of time to private demand deposits.

Government deposits in terms of private demand deposits can be expressed as:

G   =   gD   ... 4-6

Where

g   =   G/D---ratio of government to private demand deposits.

Substituting (4-3) and (4-4) into (4-2), we get:

B   =   kD + q (D + T + G)   ... 4-7

Substituting (4-5) and (4-6) into (4-7), we obtain:

B   =   kD + q (D + tD + gD)   ... 4-8

or

B   =   [q(1 + t + g) + k] • D   ... 4-9

From the above equation, we can express demand deposits in terms of monetary base as below:

$$D = \frac{1 \cdot B}{q(1 + t + g) + k} \qquad \text{... 4-10}$$

Using (4-4) and (4-10) to define C in terms of the base:

$$C = \frac{k}{q(1 + t + g) + k} \cdot B \qquad \text{... 4-11}$$

Substituting (4-10) and (4-11) into (4-1), we get:

$$M = \frac{k}{q(1 + t + g) + k} \cdot B + \frac{1}{q(1 + t + g) + k} \cdot B \qquad \text{...4-12}$$

or

$$M = \frac{1 + k}{q(1 + t + g) + k} \cdot B \qquad \text{... 4-13}$$

Let

$$m = \frac{1 + k}{q(1 + t + g) + k}$$

Then (4-13) becomes:

$$M = m \cdot B \qquad \text{... 4-14}$$

The "m" is called the monetary multiplier and is based upon the conventional definition of money stock. Knowing the monetary multiplier, one can determine how much the money supply will change in the monetary base. Suppose g = .023, k = .296, q = .068 and t = 1.606, then the monetary multiplier will be:

$$m = \frac{1 + .296}{.068 (1 + 1.606 + .023) + .296} = 2.73 \qquad \text{...4-15}$$

This means that a one dollar increase in the monetary base will result in a $2.73 increase in the money supply, and vice versa.

This model would prove fairly reliable as a predicting device if "g", "k", "q" and "t" ratios did not change over time and the monetary base and monetary multiplier were not affected by each other. In the real world, neither of these conditions prevails. These ratios change over a period of time. For example, the "k" ratio was .304 in 1947. Thereafter, it started declining. It reached a trough in 1959/1960 (.252). Since then it has been rising, though gradually and erratically.

The monetary base and monetary multiplier are affected by each other. For example, when the Federal Reserve purchases Treasury bills on the open market in an attempt to achieve an increase in the base, the increased demand tends to increase their prices and reduce their yields. As the yields of Treasury bills decline relative to yields on time deposits, Treasury bill holders tend to convert their assets from bills to time deposits, thereby, raising the "t" ratio and causing a change in the monetary multiplier. The "q" ratio may also rise if banks respond to the decline in yields of Treasury bills by holding a larger proportion of bank assets in the form of excess reserves. Since ratios used in the model do change, and the monetary base and the monetary multiplier are affected by each other, the estimates of changes in the money supply derived from a change in the base should be interpreted as nothing more than rough approximations.

SUMMARY

To predict the money supply from a given change in the monetary base, a money supply model was developed. This would be a good predictive model if various ratios used in it did not change and the monetary base and the monetary multiplier were not affected by each other. In the real world, neither of these conditions prevails. Therefore, the prediction of the money supply made by it should be considered nothing more than a rough approximation.

FOOTNOTES

[1]Jerry L. Jordan, "Elements of Money Stock Determination," **Review: Federal Bank of St. Louis** (October 1969), pp. 15-16.

[2]If the money supply is defined to include time deposits ($M = C + D + T$), then the monetary multiplier will be:

$$m \quad = \quad \frac{1 + k + t}{q\,(1 + t + g) + k}$$

QUESTIONS FOR REVIEW

1. Explain in brief a general money supply model. How is this model used to estimate a change in the money supply from a given change in the monetary base? In your judgment, is it a reliable model?
2. What is the monetary multiplier? What factors determine the size of this multiplier?
3. Suppose the monetary base in a given period is $2 billion. If the Federal Reserve wants to raise the money supply to the level of $10 billion, by how much should it increase the monetary base? The monetary multiplier is here assumed to be 1.5.
4. In your judgment, which one — currency in circulation or private demand deposits — is the major component of the money supply in the United States. Why?
5. Describe in detail why the ratios "t" and "q" are not independent of each other.

SUGGESTED FURTHER READING

1. Andersen, Leonall C. "Three Approaches to Money Stock Determination." **Review: Federal Reserve Bank of St. Louis.** October 1967, pp. 6-13.
2. Burger, Albert E. "Money Stock Control." **Review: Federal Reserve Bank of St. Louis.** October 1972, pp. 10-16.
3. Hoffman, Stuart G. "Component Ratio Estimation of the Money Multiplier." **Economic Review: Federal Reserve Bank of Atlanta.** September/October 1977, pp. 120-124.
4. Jordan, Jerry L. "Elements of Money Stock Determination." **Review: Federal Reserve Bank of St. Louis.** October 1969, pp. 10-19.
5. Rasche, Robert H. "A Review of Empirical Studies of the Money Supply Mechanism." **Review: Federal Reserve Bank of St. Louis.** July 1972, pp. 11-19.

CHAPTER V

Money Demand Models: From Fisher To Keynes

The theory of money supply has been covered in the previous three chapters. In this and the next chapter, we turn our attention to the theory of money demand.

DEFINITION OF MONEY DEMAND

The money demand refers to money that individuals and businessmen hold in demand deposits and/or cash. Suppose a person has take-home pay of $3,000 a month and is paid on the first of each month. Let us assume that he pays his bills on the first of each month in the amount of $2,000 and holds the balance. Then, on the first of each month, his demand for money will be $1,000 ($3,000-$2,000). If he spends $500 on the 15th day and another $500 on the 30th, his demand for money will be $500 on the 15th and zero on the 30th. In other words, whatever money people physically hold at any one time is the quantity of money demanded. This explains the demand for money of an individual. The aggregate demand for money will be the sum total of money held by all individuals and businesses combined. People hold money to buy things during periods when their income is cut off or reduced, to meet emergencies, to speculate in securities and for numerous other purposes.

Knowledge about the factors controlling the demand for money plays an important role in the conduct of monetary policy. The understanding of these factors helps to predict the velocity of money because the velocity is a reciprocal of demand. The number of times a given dollar changes hands (velocity) enables policymakers to determine the quantity of money needed to accomplish a desired goal, since if the velocity is high, a small quantity of money supply can serve the purpose of a larger quantity. For example, if the velocity of money is 2 a money supply of $1 billion will serve the purpose of $2 billion. Policymakers—whether they want to control inflation or deflation—have to decide upon the level of money supply required to achieve a set of objectives.

Certain properties of the demand function influence the effects of a policy action. Especially important are: (1) the interest elasticity of the demand for money (responsiveness of the quantity of money demanded to changes in interest rates) and (2) the stability of the functional relationship between the quantity of money demanded and independent variables such as interest rates and income. If the quantity of money demanded is significantly interest elastic, monetary policy may be powerless to stimulate the economy because, in this case, the slightest fall in the interest rate resulting from an expansionary action would simply induce money holders to absorb all the new money into idle hoards. As a result, no increase in expenditure would occur. (For more detail, read Fiscal vs. Monetary Policy in Chapter XI.) The instability in the money demand function makes it difficult to predict the impact of policy induced changes in the money supply. An erratically shifting demand function might offset the effect of a controlled shift in the money supply at one time and accentuate it at another.

VELOCITY OF MONEY

The concept of velocity of money gained popularity when Professor Irving Fisher used it in his famous equation of exchange. The exact meaning of this concept depends upon the type of velocity.

There are three types of velocity:
    A.   Income Velocity
    B.   Transaction Velocity
    C.   Sector Velocity

Income Velocity

Income velocity is the ratio of national income to total money stock. It shows how many times an average dollar becomes income during a year. If, in any given year, national income and money stock are $400 and $200 billion, respectively, income velocity will be 2 ($400 ÷ $200). This means that an average dollar became income two times in that year.

Transaction Velocity

Transaction velocity is the ratio of total expenditures (or total amount of transactions) to total money stock. It measures the intensity of the use of money stock. It tells us the number of times the average dollar is used.

Sector Velocity

Sector velocity refers to the velocity of money of one sector of the economy such as the trading sector, manufacturing sector, etc. It differs from one sector to another. The study of Richard Selden shows that transaction velocity is higher in larger cities than in small; it is higher in trade than in manufacturing; and finally, it is higher in small than in large firms.[1]

MONEY DEMAND MODELS

In the last sixty years or so economists have developed various models of money demand. Each model emphasizes different determinants of the money demand. Among all models, the most important are:

A. Fisher's Model
B. Cambridge Model
C. Liquidity Preference Model
D. Inventory Approach Model
E. Friedman's Model
F. Risk Aversion Model
G. Portfolio-Balance-Approach Model

The first three models will be discussed in this chapter and the remaining models in the next chapter.

Fisher's Model

Fisher's theory of money demand stems from his equation of exchange. Though his equation was designed to describe the relationship between money supply and prices, its results can be readily transformed into a model of money demand. Fisher's equation of exchange is:

$$M_s.V \quad = \quad P.T \qquad \qquad \dots \quad 5\text{-}1$$

Or $$M_s \quad = \quad \frac{P.T}{V} \qquad \qquad \dots \quad 5\text{-}2$$

Where M_s =   Supply of money

           P =   Price Level

           V =   Number of times an average dollar changes hands (or transaction velocity—Fisher calls it velocity of circulation of money)

           T =   Total quantity of goods and services sold

In equilibrium, the demand for money must be equal to its supply. Thus, at the point of equilibrium:

$$M_d \quad = \quad M_s \qquad \qquad \dots \quad 5\text{-}3$$

Where M_d =   Demand for money

Substituting (5-2) into (5-3), we get Fisher's model of money demand:

$$M_d \quad = \quad \frac{P.T}{V} \qquad \qquad \dots \quad 5\text{-}4$$

$$\frac{\triangle M_d}{\triangle P} \quad \rangle \, O \qquad \frac{\triangle M_d}{\triangle T} \quad \rangle \, O \qquad \frac{\triangle M_d}{\triangle V} \quad \langle \, O$$

The above model shows that the demand for money is a function of price level (P), quantity of goods and services sold (T) and velocity of money (V). The amount of money demanded varies directly with P and T and inversely with V.

In the short run, according to Fisher, the price level is the main determinant of money demand because, during such a period, velocity of money and quantity of goods and services traded remain constant. Fisher says that the velocity of money is determined by institutional factors, which do not change significantly over a short period of time. Institutional factors include payment habits, extent of the use of credit cards, and speed of transportation and communication. How do these institutional factors affect the velocity of money? If people start paying bills faster, the quantity of money demanded will fall and the velocity of money will rise. Suppose an individual has take home pay of $1,000 which he receives on the first of a month. Let us assume further that his bills, amounting to $1,000, are due for payment on the first of a month but he pays them on the 10th. Then his demand for money will be $1,000 on the first of each month. If he speeds up his payments by paying all bills on the first of a month, his demand for money on that day will drop to zero. The use of credit cards reduces the demand for money and increases the velocity of money because, with credit cards, less money is needed to cover day-to-day transactions. Regarding speed of communication and transportation, if funds are transmitted by telephone and telegraph, less money will be needed in comparison with a system where messages concerning the transfer of funds are sent by mail. The volume of trade is determined by the supply of natural resources and technical conditions of production and distribution. Such factors, according to Fisher, do not change much over a short period of time. If the volume of trade (T) and velocity of money (V) remain unchanged in short periods, the quantity of money demanded, as discussed earlier, will vary directly and proportionately with a change in the price level. For example, a 10 per cent increase in the price level will be accompanied by a 10 per cent increase in the quantity of money demanded, and vice versa. The quantity of money demanded rises with a rise in the price level because at a higher price level more money is needed to buy the same amount of goods and services.

Though Fisher's model was quite influential in stimulating further discussion in the area of money demand, his thesis of proportionality (the quantity of money demanded varies proportionately with a change in the price level) received a considerable amount of criticism. It is argued that V and T do not remain constant even in short periods. Therefore, the thesis of proportionality does not hold. The V, in addition to institutional factors (which change over the long run), is also determined by psychological factors, which change in short periods. The psychological factors include such things as public desire to hold or not to hold money, to hold a small or a large amount of money, etc. The amount of goods and services traded (t) also changes in short periods.

Cambridge Model

The Cambridge model may be regarded as the first comprehensive model developed expressly to explain the theory of money demand. As described earlier, Fisher's model did not originate as a model of money demand. It came out as an equation of exchange which was later transformed into a model of money demand.

The Cambridge model states that the demand for money arises because people want to hold a portion of their assets in the form of money. Why do people hold money? They hold money because it is a convenient asset. It is readily accepted as a means of payment. Pigou, the major architect of this model, says that everybody is anxious to hold enough resources in money form in order to carry on the ordinary transactions of life and secure themselves against unexpected expenditures. [2]

The Cambridge model is expressed as:

$$M_d = k.\Pi.R. \qquad \qquad .... \quad 5\text{-}5$$

$$\frac{\triangle M_d}{\triangle \Pi} \rangle 0 \qquad \frac{\triangle M_d}{\triangle R} \rangle 0 \qquad \frac{\triangle M_d}{\triangle k} \rangle 0$$

Where Π = Average price of assets
           R = Total quantity of assets (or resources) held by the public
           k = Proportion of total assets people want to hold in money form

Since Π is average price of all assets and R, quantity of assets, $\Pi.R$ will be total assets expressed in current dollars.

The model shows that the demand for money is a function of Π, R and k. Their relationship with the demand for money is direct but not proportional. The relationship will be proportional if one determinant changes while the others remain constant. The Cambridge economists believe that all these determinants are subject to change. The k depends upon preferences as well as expectations and thus it can be expected to vary significantly even during short periods. Preferences include such things as desire to spend money now or at a later date. Expectations here pertain to changes in prices of goods, services and earning assets. An expected rise in prices will reduce k because more money will be spent now than at a later date. The opposite will be the case if prices are expected to fall. The Π is closely tied to the money supply and thus it can change with a change in the money supply. The R does not remain constant either. According to Pigou, it can increase with an increase in efficiency either through mechanical inventions or through innovations in business organizations.[3]

Cambridge economists improved upon Fisher's model in four ways:

i. They challenged the thesis of proportionality, that is, the relation between the money demand and the price level (average price of assets) is not proportional. Fisher's thesis was based upon the assumption that when π changed k and R remained constant. According to Cambridge economists, other variables, particularly k, do not remain constant.

ii. In Fisher's model, the demand for money was linked to transactions (or expenditures). The Cambridge model improved upon this model by linking the demand for money to a broader base, that is, public asset holdings (or wealth).

iii. To Cambridge economists, V depends not only on institutional factors but also on psychological factors such as preferences and expectations. The inclusion of psychological factors into the determinants of k emphasizes the public volition which, according to Pigou, is the ultimate cause of money demand. Some economists believe that V is not really a determinant but it is determined by the money demand. When the demand for money increases V declines, and vice versa. The V may be just a residual brought in by Fisher to insure identity in his equation of exchange. Pigou, at one place, says that V, at first sight, appears to be accidental and arbitrary.[4]

iv. Finally, Fisher assumes that V and T are independent of the money supply. Cambridge economists made their model more pragmatic by saying that k and R (counterparts of V and T) were not independent of the money supply. When the money supply increases marginal utility of money declines. As a result, k will decline. The opposite will be the case if the money supply falls. The R is also affected by the money supply, particularly, when an increase in the money supply comes from an increase in gold production.

Though the Cambridge model is not complete, it intitiated development in the theory of money demand in many directions. The emphasis on uncertainty about the future led to the development of the idea of holding money for precautionary and speculative motives as described by Keynes in his Liquidity Preference model. Friedman made use of the Cambridge wealth variable in his model of money demand. Cambridge economists hinted at the role of interest rates in the determination of money demand but they left it to their successors to investigate it in detail. In the last two decades or so, various empirical studies have been made to determine the effect of interest rates on the demand for money.

Liquidity Preference Model

The Liquidity Preference model of money demand was developed by Keynes. Algebraically, it can be expressed as follows:

$$M_d = L_1 (Y) + L_2(i_e-i) \qquad \dots\ 5\text{-}6$$

$$\frac{\triangle L_1}{\triangle Y} \gt 0 \qquad\qquad \frac{\triangle L_2}{\triangle(i_e-i)} \gt 0$$

Where

L_1	=	Liquidity preference (or amount held) for transaction and precautionary motives.
L_2	=	Liquidity preference (or amount held) for speculative motive
i	=	Current interest rate
i_e	=	Expected interest rate
(i_e-i)	=	Expected change in the interest rate

The above equation shows that the demand for money is the sum total of L_1 and L_2 where L_1 is a function of Y, and L_2, of (i_e-i).

According to Keynes, people hold money or prefer to keep their assets in liquid form for three motives. They are:

i. Transaction motive
ii. Precautionary motive
iii. Speculative motive

Transaction motive

The transaction motive refers to the desire to hold money to meet day-to-day transactions. This is similar to what classical economists described as holding money for bridging the time gap between known receipts and known expenditures. Suppose a person is paid every Friday. He spends $1.40 a day on bus fare for going to and from work and $2 a day on lunch. He eats lunch outside on the days he works. This means that every Friday when he receives his pay check he has to hold $17 to take care of expenses for transportation and lunch for the next week, assuming he works 5 days a week. The holding of this $17 is what Keynes calls holding money for transaction motive.

According to Keynes, holding money for the transaction motive is a function of income. When income increases more money is held for the transaction motive, and vice versa. In the above example, if income of that person rises he may prefer to take a cab instead of a bus to and from work. He may eat lunch at a fancy restaurant. As a result, his demand for money for the transaction motive will rise.

Businessmen also hold money for the transaction motive. They do so for such things as meeting payrolls, paying rents, etc. The amount of money they hold for this purpose is also a function of income. When their business expands (meaning, their income rises), they have to hire more people. As a result, their demand for money for the transaction motive rises.

Precautionary motive

Individuals and businessmen hold money to protect themselves against emergencies. Keynes calls it holding money for the precautionary motive. This is similar to what Pigou calls holding money for security against unforseen events.

According to Keynes, money held for the precautionary motive is also a function of income. It increases when income increases. This is probably due to the fact that when a person's income rises the magnitude of its emergency expressed in dollars also rises. A rich man's emergency generally calls for more money than that of a poor man. The same is true with businessmen. Big businessmen need more money for an emergency than small businessmen.

Speculative motive

The speculative motive refers to holding money for the purpose of making a profit by predicting better than the average about the future market trend. When a speculator expects a decline in prices of bonds to a point where capital loss will outweigh his gains from yields, he will sell bonds in the current period with a plan to buy again when prices decline. The speculator will profit if his expectations come true.

Cash balances held during the period when bonds are liquidated and before they are bought again reflect the demand for money for the speculative motive.

What causes fluctuations in bond prices? Bond prices are inversely related to the market interest rate. When the market interest rate rises, prices of bonds fall, and vice versa. Example: The price of a perpetual bond is $1,000 with a yield of $30 per year. This is equivalent to a return of 3 per cent—the rate at which one can lend money with no more risk than the money invested in the bond. Let us assume that the market interest rate rises from 3 to 3.75 per cent. This means that it will pay bondholders to liquidate their bonds and invest their funds in the lending markets. When bondholders sell their bonds, the price of bonds will fall until it reaches a point where it is no longer advantageous to transfer funds from bonds to the lending markets. This point will be reached when the bond price declines to $800 because at this price the return on investment in bonds will be equal to 3.75 per cent. Thus, we see that when the market interest rate goes up prices of bonds decline, and vice versa.

What determines the demand for money for the speculative motive? According to Keynes, it depends upon expected change in the interest rate (i_e-i). If a person expects a rise in the market interest rate he expects a decline in prices of bonds. To avoid capital losses, he will liquidate his bond holdings. As a result, his demand for speculative cash will rise. Conversely, if he expects a decline in the market interest rate (or rise in price of bonds) he will purchase bonds in order to take advantage of anticipated capital gains. As a result, his demand for speculative cash balance will fall.

The Liquidity Preference model has been criticized on three major points:

i. Many economists have demonstrated that the demand for money for transaction and precautionary motives is a function not only of income as Keynes visualized but also of the market interest rate. Whalen, Baumol and Tobin agree that the demand for transaction balance is inversely related to the market interest rate.[5] When the interest rate rises, the cost of holding cash also rises. Under this condition, it will pay individuals and businessmen to hold down transaction and precautionary balances to a bare minimum and invest idle funds in banks or short term bonds. However, if alternative cost (interest or yield rate) is very low it may not be worth the effort to invest the funds. Baumol says that cash users, particularly large ones, can be expected to economize transaction balances when the interest rate rises.[6] Cash will be employed even more economically where payments are lumpy and can be determined ahead of time with accuracy.

According to Whalen, the demand for money for the precautionary motive is also affected by the interest rate (opportunity cost for holding precautionary balances).[7] Other factors which determine precautionary balances are cost of illiquidity and uncertainty about the future. The cost of illiquidity refers to consequences which one will face in case of a failure to come up with sufficient cash to meet an emergency. Failure to acquire adequate funds for necessary disbursement can result in bankruptcy. The cost of illiquidity will be low if a person or firm has a line of credit with one or more banks, has assets which can be easily liquidated or has access to other avenues which can provide funds without any problem at the time of emergency. A low level of illiquidity accompanied by a small degree of uncertainty with regard to future need causes precautionary balances to respond strongly but inversely to changes in the interest rate.

ii. Harry Johnson criticizes the Liquidity Preference model on the ground that it fails to distinguish clearly the precautionary motive from the speculative one.[8] The precautionary motive seems to be included in the speculative motive because both are based upon uncertainty. The speculative motive for holding cash in a period of uncertainty about the future interest rate is really a precautionary motive in disguise. However, there is a difference between them. Precautionary balances are maintained to protect against uncertainty while speculative balances to profit from them.

iii. The Liquidity Preference theory states that holding securities is the only relevant alternative to holding money, that is, people hold money either in cash or in securities. In reality, however, money can be invested in many other assets such as real estate, inventory, etc. Moreover, Keynes lumped all securities together yielding a single interest rate. By doing this, he overlooked the existence of a wide variety of equities and fixed-interest yielding securities of different maturity. According to Harry G. Johnson, once we recognize the existence of short term securities such as Treasury notes which are highly liquid, the demand for money for the speculative motive will cease to exist.[9] If a person does not want to hold long term securities, he will hold short term securities instead of cash because short term securities yield income and cash yields no income at all. Furthermore, the precautionary demand can be satisfied not only by cash balances but also by financial assets which are readily marketable with a minimum of potential loss.

Despite all this, the Liquidity Preference model has made important contributions. It described for the first time the mechanism through which the market interest rate affects the demand for money. It stimulated interest in the further development of the theory of money demand. The Inventory Approach model, Risk Aversion model, Friedman's model and Portfolio-Balance Approach model were all influenced by it.

SUMMARY

The demand for money is the amount of money people hold in demand deposits and/or cash to buy things when they won't be receiving income, to protect against future emergencies, to speculate in securities markets, or for numerous other reasons.

To develop a proper course of action for a monetary policy, the monetary authority needs to know not only the supply of money but also the demand for money because the knowledge about the demand for money enables the authority to predict the effect of changes in the money supply on inflation, income and employment.

Fisher's model states that the demand for money is a function of price level (P), number of times an average dollar changes hands (V), and total quantity of goods and services sold (T). According to Fisher, the quantity of money demanded changes directly and proportionately with a change in the price level because V and T change only over the long run.

Cambridge economists challenged the thesis of proportionality by saying that k (counterpart of V) and R (counterpart of T) do not remain constant even during short periods.

Keynes' model stated that the demand for money is the sum total of

L_1 (amount held for transaction and precautionary motives) and L_2 (amount held for speculative motive), where L_1 is a function of income and L_2 of expected change in the interest rate. He was the first economist to explain in detail the mechanism through which the market interest rate affected the demand for money.

FOOTNOTES

[1]Richard T. Selden, "The Postwar Rise in the Velocity of Money: A Sectoral Analysis," **Journal of Finance** (December 1961), p. 530.

[2]A.C. Pigou, "The Value of Money," **Quarterly Journal of Economics** (November 1917), p. 41.

[3]**Ibid.**, p. 43.

[4]**Ibid.**, p. 54.

[5]Edward L. Whalen, "An Extension of the Baumol-Tobin Approach to the Transactions Demand for Cash," **Journal of Finance** (March 1968), p. 124.

[6]William J. Baumol, "The Transactions Demand for Cash: An Inventory Theoretical Approach," **Quarterly Journal of Economics** (November 1952), p. 554.

[7]Edward L. Whalen, "A Rationalization of the Precautionary Demand for Cash," **Quarterly Journal of Economics** (May 1966), p. 315.

[8]Harry Johnson, "The General Theory After Twenty-Five Years," **American Economic Review** (May 1961), p. 8.

[9]Harry G. Johnson, **Essays in Monetary Theory** (Cambridge, Mass.: Harvard University Press, 1967), p. 93.

QUESTIONS FOR REVIEW

1. What do we mean by the demand for money? What role does it play in monetary policy?
2. What do we mean by the velocity of money? How do the income velocity, transaction velocity and sector velocity differ from each other?
3. Describe in brief Fisher's model of money demand.
4. Explain in brief the Cambridge model of money demand. In what way does it deviate from Fisher's model?
5. Explain transaction, precautionary and speculative motives for holding money.
6. Describe how security prices are related to the market interest rate.
7. Explain in detail how the market interest rate affects the demand for money.
8. "The demand for money for transaction and precautionary motives is a function of income." Critically evaluate this statement.
9. Discuss three major grounds on which the Liquidity Preference model has been criticized.

10. In what ways does the Liquidity Preference model deviate from classical models (Fisher's and Cambridge models) and in what ways does it support them?

SUGGESTED FURTHER READING

1. Anderson, Paul S. "Behavior of Monetary Velocity." **New England Economic Review.** March/April 1977, pp. 8-20.
2. Fisher, Douglas. "The Speculative Demand for Money: An Empirical Test." **Economica.** May 1973, pp. 174-179.
3. Garvy, George and Blyn, Martin R. **The Velocity of Money.** New York: Federal Reserve Bank of New York, 1969.
4. Higgins, Bryon. "Velocity: Money's Second Dimension." **Economic Review: Federal Reserve Bank of Kansas City.** June 1978, pp. 15-31.
5. Humphrey, Thomas M. "Evolution of the Concept of the Demand for Money." **Monthly Review: Federal Reserve Bank of Richmond.** December 1973, pp. 9-19.
6. Johnson, Harry G. "A Note on the Theory of Transactions Demand for Cash." **Journal of Money, Credit and Banking.** August 1970, pp. 383-384.
7. **Essays in Monetary Theory.** Cambridge, Mass., Harvard University Press, 1967, pp. 91-96.
8. Keynes, John M. **The General Theory of Employment, Interest, and Money.** New York: Harcourt, Brace and Company, 1935, pp. 165-185.
9. Laidler, David E. **The Demand for Money: Theories and Evidence.** New York: Dun-Donnelley & Harper & Row, Publishers, 1977, pp. 49-98.
10. McGoluldrick, Paul F. "A Sectoral Analysis of Velocity." **Federal Reserve Bulletin.** December 1962, pp. 1557-1570.
11. Pigou, A.C. "The Value of Money." **Quarterly Journal of Economics.** November 1917, pp. 35-65.
12. Rousseas, Stephen W. **Monetary Theory.** New York: Alfred A. Knopf, 1972, pp. 93-115.
13. Spitzer, J.J. "The Keynesian Demand for Money Function Revisited." **Journal of Monetary Economics.** July 1976, pp. 381-387.
14. Weinrobe, Maurice D. "A Simple Model of the Precautionary Demand for Money." **Southern Economic Journal.** July 1972, pp. 11-18.
15. Whalen, Edward L. "An Extension of the Baumol-Tobin Approach to the Transactions Demand for Cash." **Journal of Finance.** March 1968, pp. 113-134.

CHAPTER VI

Models of Money Demand: From Baumol To Gurley and Shaw

The Liquidity Preference model stimulated more interest in the theory of money demand than anything that came before it. Models appearing since Liquidity Preference arrived have taken either of two directions: direct attacks upon it, as in the case of Friedman's model, or attempts to improve upon it by expanding certain aspects, as in the case of the Portfolio-Balance-Approach model.

MONEY DEMAND MODELS

This chapter covers the major models of money demand (labelled from D to G in the previous chapter) that have appeared since the development of the Liquidity Preference model.

Inventory Approach Model

This is a model of money demand developed by William J. Baumol in 1952.[1] It is an extension of the Liquidity Preference model. In the Liquidity Preference model people hold money for transaction, precautionary and speculative motives. The Inventory Approach model assumes that people hold money for transaction purposes only. Baumol calls this an Inventory Approach because a stock of cash is like an inventory of a commodity that is given up at the appropriate time in return for profit.

The model is built on these assumptions:

i. An individual or firm spends a certain amount of money in a steady stream during a given period. By steady stream Baumol means that money is spent at a constant amount and at a constant interval. A person with expenditures of $12,000 a year, spends either $6,000 semi-annually or $3,000 quarterly or $1,000 monthly or in any other similar combination.

ii. A person obtains cash by disinvesting. For example, a person needing $100 acquires it by selling securities. Two costs are incurred by disinvesting: loss of interest income (or yield on investment) which one would otherwise earn, and a brokerage fee for converting a security into cash.

iii. Money is withdrawn in lots of equal amount spaced evenly throughout the period. In the example discussed in assumption (i), a person may decide to spend $1,000 monthly. This means that, at the beginning of each month, a cash balance of at least $1,000 is required to meet this need, withdrawals from investments are made in the amount required at specific intervals— $1,000 a month, $2,000 every other month, $3,000 every three months or in any other combination.

iv. Brokerage fee is fixed. It varies neither with the size of lot nor with time. The interest rate is also assumed to be fixed.

Based upon these assumptions, the total cost to an individual (or firm) to obtain funds in any given period will be:

$$Q = \frac{b(T)}{(C)} + \frac{i(C)}{(2)} \qquad \qquad .... \quad 6\text{-}1$$

C = Size of lot (or the amount a person disinvests at a given time)

Q = Total cost of disinvesting

T = Total amount a person spends during a given period (or value of total transactions)

b = Brokerage fee

i = Interest rate

(T/C) gives the number of times a person disinvests money. Total brokerage cost in a given period is brokerage fee multiplied by the number of times a person disinvests (b • T/C). An average cash balance a person holds or demand for money is (C/2). Suppose a person disinvests $1,000 a month and spends it in equal amounts, say, $250 a week. Under these conditions, the person holds money as follows:

Week	Money Held at the Beginning of a Week	Money Held at the End of a Week	Average Amount of Money Held During a Week
1st	$1,000	$750	$875
2nd	750	500	625
3rd	500	250	375
4th	250	---	125
			Total $2,000

The holder starts the first week with a cash balance of $1,000 and ends it with $750, holding an average balance of $875 in that week, starts the second week with a cash balance of $750 and ends it with $500, holding an average balance of $625 in that week, and so on. Thus, on the average, he winds up holding $500 (2,000/4) per week—one half of $1,000. The total loss of interest income for holding money will be the interest rate times the average cash balance held ($i \bullet C/2$).

If a person disinvests the amount on the day he wants to spend it, the loss of interest income would be minimum and brokerage cost, maximum. Brokerage cost would be maximum because the investor would be withdrawing money a maximum number of times. On the other hand, disinvesting an amount equal to all the money needed once a year, loss of interest income would be maximum and the cost of brokerage fee, minimum. The loss of interest income would be maximum because the investor would be holding a maximum amount of idle cash balances during a year. A person can optimize his position by minimizing total cost. There is a certain value of C that minimizes total cost. We arrive at that value using simple calculus, that is, by taking a derivative of the equation (6-1) with respect to C, and then equate it with zero. By doing this, we get:

$$\frac{-b \bullet T}{C^2} + \frac{i}{2} = 0 \qquad \dots \ 6\text{-}2$$

$$\text{Or} \qquad C = \sqrt{\frac{2 b \bullet T}{i}} \qquad \dots \ 6\text{-}3$$

If b, i and T are \$1, 5% and \$1,000, respectively, then total cost will be minimum when:

$$C = \sqrt{\frac{(2)\,(1)\,(1,000)}{.05}} \qquad \text{....} \qquad 6\text{-}4$$

Or

$$C = \$200$$

The above result implies (assuming T corresponds to a one year period) that a person will minimize his total cost by disinvesting five times a year at the rate of \$200 each time. The validity of this answer can be checked by plugging this value of C in equation (6-1) and then comparing its result with any other value.

As discussed earlier, in this model the demand for money or an average cash balance a person holds is:

$$M_d = \frac{C}{2} \qquad \text{....} \qquad 6\text{-}5$$

Substituting (6-3) into (6-5), the final form of the Inventory Approach model becomes:

$$M_d = \frac{1}{2} \cdot \sqrt{\frac{2\,b \cdot T}{i}} \qquad \text{....} \qquad 6\text{-}6$$

This model brings out three interesting points:

i. The demand for transaction balance is a function not only of income as Keynes visualized but also of the interest rate. The relation between the money demand and the interest rate is negative. In this model, T, value of total transactions, is a proxy for income.

ii. The transaction demand changes less than the proportionate change in the level of total expenditures (t). In the equation (6-6), if T rises M_d will increase but less than the increase in T. Particularly with large expenditures, people do find ways to economize cash.

iii. If the cost of converting nonmonetary investment into cash is zero (i.e., b = 0), there will be no demand for transaction motive because, under this condition, it will pay an individual (or firm) to disinvest at the time of spending. On the other hand, if investment does not yield any income (i.e., i = 0), people will hold all their investments in money form.

Nevertheless, it is an oversimplified model of money demand. It assumes that an individual (or firm) disburses its funds in a steady stream and that the interest rate and brokerage fee remain constant over a period of time. In reality, such assumptions are not true. Moreover, the model excludes the consideration of cash receipts that do not require disinvestment and neglects the demand for money for precautionary and speculative motives.

Friedman's Model

Friedman's model of money demand developed out of an attack on the Keynesian model. Keynes claims that it is not the price level but the market interest rate that is the principal determinant of money demand. Friedman deemphasizes the role of the interest rate and argues that the price level, among other things, is an important determinant of money demand. His original model of money demand appeared in 1956[2] but was revised somewhat over time. His latest model of money demand can be summed up as follows:[3]

$$M_d = f(P_p, R_m, R_b, R_e, G_p, Y_p, w, U) \qquad \ldots \quad 6\text{-}7$$

$$\frac{\triangle M_d}{\triangle P_p} > 0 \qquad\qquad \frac{\triangle M_d}{\triangle R_b} < 0$$

$$\frac{\triangle M_d}{\triangle R_m} > 0 \qquad\qquad \frac{\triangle M_d}{\triangle R_e} < 0$$

$$\frac{\triangle M_d}{\triangle Y_p} > 0 \qquad\qquad \frac{\triangle M_d}{\triangle G_p} < 0$$

$$\frac{\triangle M_d}{\triangle U} \quad 0 \qquad\qquad \frac{\triangle M_d}{\triangle w} < 0$$

Where

G_p =   Expected rate of change in P_p

P_p =   Permanent price level (or long-term price level)

R_b =   Expected rate of return on bonds. Return includes yield plus capital gains or losses associated with a change in prices of bonds

R_e =   Expected rate of return on equities. Return includes dividend plus capital gains or losses associated with a change in prices of equities

R_m =   Expected rate of return on money

U   =   Tastes and preferences of people holding money

w   =   Ratio of nonhuman wealth (tangible or marketable capital) to total wealth (human plus nonhuman wealth). (Friedman holds that a human being represents a form of wealth because he generates income over time like other income producing assets.)

Y_p =   Permanent income — an average income which a person expects to receive over several years to come.

When the permanent price level (P_p) rises, the amount of money demanded by the public rises because a rise in the price level reduces the value of money.

Other things being equal, an expected decline in return on money (R_m) reduces the quantity of money demanded, and vice versa. Factors that reduce the return on money include service charges for holding money in demand deposits, decline in money value associated with a rise in the price level, etc. Factors that yield positive return on money include money held in savings accounts, convenience and security associated with cash holdings, etc.

An increase in return on bonds (R_b) or equities (R_e) decreases the amount of money demanded because it encourages the public to reduce its cash balances to a bare minimum.

An expected rise in the permanent price level (G_p), other things being equal, reduces the quantity of money demanded because, to take advantage of present lower prices, people increase current spending.

The empirical findings of Friedman show that the amount of money demanded rises proportionately more than the rise in permanent income (Y_p). This, according to Friedman, may be due to the fact that money is just like a luxury item whose quantity demanded generally increases proportionately more than the increase in income.[4].

A decline in the ratio of nonhuman to total wealth (w) increases the amount of money demanded, and vice versa. The w ratio falls when human wealth rises. A rise in human wealth presumably increases permanent income which, as discussed earlier, increases the amount of money demanded.

Tastes and preferences (U) also affect the demand for money. According to Friedman, people's preference for cash balances rise when they travel more frequently and when they are subject to unusual uncertainty about the future.[5]

Friedman's model of money demand has been criticized on three main counts:

i. His idea that money is just like a luxury product and, therefore, the amount of money demanded increases or decreases proportionately more than an increase or decrease in permanent income does not apply to business firms, which hold most of the money stock. It would be strange if management of a large corporation decides to increase its firm's cash holdings proportionately more than the rise in real profits.

ii. Some of the variables such as return on money associated with convenience and security, human wealth, etc. are not directly measurable. Friedman was aware of this problem. This is why in his empirical study he either completely ignored such variables or took them into account in an indirect way. In his study he excluded the variable, return on money associated with convenience and security. He also excluded the wealth variable. Friedman's concept of wealth consists of tangible wealth, which is directly measurable and human wealth, which is not directly measurable. He claims that the effect of the wealth variable is not totally lost by its exclusion; it is picked up by the permanent income variable since, in his view, the source of permanent income is wealth.

iii. Friedman's study concludes that interest rates (returns on bonds and equities) play an insignificant role in the demand for money. However, many studies, as will be discussed in the next section, refute that view.

Despite these criticisms, Friedman deserves the credit for expanding on the Keynesian demand function. In the words of Don Patinkin, "-- Milton Friedman provides us in 1956 with a most elegant and sophisticated statement of modern Keynesian theory—misleadingly entitled, "The Quantity Theory of Money—A Restatement."[6] According to Stephen Rousseas, Friedman expanded on the Keynesian demand function in five ways:[7] (i) he broadened the concept of wealth to include human wealth; (ii) included time deposits in the definition of money supply; (iii) replaced money income and prices with permanent income and prices; (iv) interpreted the return on money in terms of expected change in the price level, convenience and security associated with money holdings, etc.; and (v) emphasized the role of price in the determination of money demand. According to Thomas M. Humphrey, nobody prior to Friedman had thought to incorporate the anticipated rate of inflation into the demand function.[8]

Risk Aversion Model

The Risk Aversion model is another offshoot of the Liquidity Preference model. The Liquidity Preference model demonstrates that speculators hold wealth either in money form or in bonds. Those who expect a fall in the interest rate (or a rise in prices of bonds) will hold all their wealth in bonds, and those who expect a rise in the interest rate (or a fall in prices of bonds) will hold all their wealth in money form. Whether Keynes realized it or not, it is assumed here that each speculator is pretty certain about the future, no matter whether he expects an increase or decrease in the prices of bonds. Otherwise, he would not hold all his wealth in either of these two assets. In reality, no one is absolutely certain about the future. Of course, one may be more certain than another. Because of this, each speculator tries to hold a diversified portfolio made up of both money and nonmoney assets. The Risk Aversion model of James Tobin attempts to describe diversification between money and bonds.[9]

The Risk Aversion model can be written as follows:

$$Md_s \quad = \quad f(R_b, R_r) \qquad \qquad \dots \quad 6\text{-}8$$

$$\frac{\triangle Md_s}{\triangle R_b} \; \langle \; 0 \qquad \qquad \frac{\triangle Md_s}{\triangle R_r} \; \rangle \; 0$$

Where

Md_s = Demand for speculative balance
R_b = Expected income from bonds
R_r = Amount of risk involved in investment in bonds

According to Tobin, the demand for speculative balance (Md_s) depends upon two things: (i) expected income from bonds (R_b) and (ii) amount of risk involved in investment (R_r). Expected income includes interest payments, which are fairly certain, and capital gains, which are not certain. Expected income rises with a rise in investment in bonds. It will be maximum where a portfolio includes bonds only and zero where it includes money only. Tobin assumes that the only alternative to money asset is bonds. Risk, on the other hand, is related to capital losses which might result from an unexpected decline in prices of bonds. It increases with an increase in investment in bonds. It will be maximum where a portfolio contains bonds only.

A speculator likes income and dislikes risk. But they go together. Under these circumstances, how does a speculator determine the composition of a portfolio? According to Tobin, income yields utility and risk yields disutility. The speculator divides a portfolio between money and bonds in such a way as to maximize total utility. Though income yields utility, marginal utility associated with income decreases with an increase in investment in bonds. This is because additional investment in bonds is expected to yield less income. Marginal disutility associated with risk, on the other hand, increases with each dollar of additional investment in bonds because risk is expected to rise with a rise in such an investment . Total utility will be maximum where marginal utility associated with income is equal to marginal disutility associated with risk. The demand for money for an individual is the amount of speculative balance held where total utility is at maximum.

Tobin divides speculators into two categories: (i) risk lovers and (ii) risk averters. A risk lover is one who is willing to take a risk even for a small chance of large capital gains. A person with this kind of behavior holds a large portion of wealth in bonds. Thus, the risk taker's demand for money is low. A risk averter, on the other hand, requires a fair amount of compensation for each unit of additional risk. Because of this type of behavior, the averter's demand for money is generally higher.

Though the Risk Aversion theory is one of individual behavior and deals only with speculative balances, it explains fairly well how a speculator arrives at a diversified portfolio. Moreover, it is a precursor to the Portfolio Balance Approach, which introduced the idea of many different financial assets and many different interest rates.

Portfolio Balance Approach Model

The Portfolio Balance Approach to the demand for money is another extension of the model of Liquidity Preference. Keynes' explanation of how a change in the interest rate affects the demand for money led to the examination of the effect of return from other assets. This model points out that there is not just one interest rate as visualized by Keynes, but as many different interest rates as there are imperfect substitutes among earning assets.[10] It further indicates that holding of cash balances also yields interest, which is called implicit deposit rate.

The implicit deposit rate, according to Gurley and Shaw, depends upon transaction costs of buying and selling securities, types of bonds, chances of debtors' default, prospects of business profit, etc. If transaction costs of buying and selling securities are high, the implicit deposit rate is also high because high transaction costs encourage people to hold more assets in money form. Investment in long term securities raises the implicit deposit rate because such securities do not have as much moneyness as short term securities. The implicit deposit rate is high where the chances of debtors' default are high because, in such a situation, people prefer to hold money rather than invest it. Prospects of business profits also affect the implicit-deposit rate. It is high where prospects of business profits are bleak, and vice versa.

The model of Portfolio Balance Approach can be expressed as follows:

$$M_d = f(R_1, R_2, \ldots R_n; R_m) \qquad \ldots 6\text{-}9$$

$$\frac{\triangle M_d}{\triangle R_1} \langle \, 0 \qquad\qquad \frac{\triangle M_d}{\triangle R_m} \rangle \, 0$$

$$\frac{\triangle M_d}{\triangle R_2} \langle \, 0$$

$$\text{-- -- -- --}$$
$$\text{-- -- -- --}$$
$$\text{-- -- -- --}$$

$$\frac{\triangle M_d}{\triangle R_n} \langle \, 0$$

$R_1, R_2, \ldots R_n =$ Expected rate of return (or interest rate) from asset 1, 2, ..., n, excluding money

$R_m =$ Implicit deposit rate or expected rate of return on money

Other things being equal, an expected rise in return on an asset other than money (R_1, R_2, ... or R_n) reduces the amount of money demanded because it encourages the public to cut down its money balances to a bare minimum. This also results in a reallocation of investment funds among different assets. Individuals expand their investment in assets where the return is expected to be high and reduce it where it is expected to be low. Other things being constant, an increase in the implicit deposit rate (R_m) increases the quantity of money demanded because it provides incentive to hold assets in money form. At equilibrium, the marginal expected rate of return from each asset, including money, will be the same.

Though the Portfolio Balance Approach describes beautifully the demand for money, it gets into trouble when "certain" or "almost certain" investments are introduced. Why should a person hold money, particularly, for precautionary and speculative purposes when he knows that a certain portion of his financial assets can be converted into cash with a minimum amount of loss at any time? In the words of

Franco Modigliani, "As long as there exists any interest-bearing obligations that are issued by credit-worthy borrowers, and are of sufficiently short maturity--it is impossible to explain why any portion of the portfolio should be held in the form of money, yielding less or nothing at all--except by explicit analysis of transaction costs."[11] Nevertheless, even if there is one or more certain investments in a multi-asset portfolio, it is possible that people may hold a portion of their assets in money form not because of any economic justification but because of convenience and/or plain fear.

Besides what has been discussed in various models of money demand, there are many other factors such as the size of individual financial assets and promotional efforts of savings institutions, which affect the demand for money. The demand for money is generally high where the size of individuals' financial assets is small because, to small asset holders, it does not pay to invest. They have to pay more for transaction costs and receive a lower return. They receive a lower return because they cannot afford to hire professional services for investing their funds. Moreover, in time of emergency, it is difficult for small asset holders to obtain credit.

The promotional efforts of savings institutions also affect the demand for money. Other things being equal, the more money they spend on promotion, the less will be the demand for money, and vice versa. Savings institutions, through promotional efforts such as free gift offers, attract funds not only from time and demand deposits of other insitutions but also from the public's cash balances.

Changes in payment system also affect the demand for money. In recent years, the introduction of NOW accounts, automatic transfer to cover overdrafts, electronic transfer system, etc., have contributed to the reduction in the desire to hold funds in checking accounts.

EMPIRICAL FINDINGS

Different economists use different definitions of money, a variety of methodologies and/or different data to measure money data. Consequently, their findings are not in agreement as to the importance of various determinants and their effect on the demand for money. Empirical findings of some economists, which are discussed in this section, shed some light on the subject.

There appears to be a consensus on the subject of interest rate. With the exception of Friedman and Andersen,[12] all of the major studies [Latane (1954),[13] Meltzer and Brunner (1963),[14] Meltzer (1963),[15] Teigen (1964),[16] Laidler (1966),[17] Lee (1967),[18] and Campbell and Falero (1971)[19]] demonstrate that the quantity of money demanded is closely and inversely related to one type of interest rate or another.

Although many economists agree that the interest rate is an important variable, they differ on the question of which type of interest rate—short-term interest rate as measured by yield on short term bonds or long-term interest rate as measured by yield on long term bonds (e.g., yield on equities and savings and loan shares)—exerts the most significant influence on the demand for money. Lee[20] and Hamburger[21] conclude that long term rates are significant determinants of the money demand. However, studies of Heller[22] and Laidler[23] conclude just the opposite.

Empirical studies on wealth and income center on a controversy over whether the money demand depends upon wealth or income, or both. Some economists assert that the demand for money is a function of wealth while others conclude that it is a function of income. Those who favor wealth are Lydall, [24] Bronfenbrenner and Mayer,[25] Meltzer and Brunner,[26] and Laidler.[27] The study of Chow showed clearly that permanent income is a better variable than wealth.[28] Heller summed up his findings by saying that wealth is more important as a constraint when money is broadly defined, and income is the appropriate constraint when money is narrowly defined.[29]

Between permanent and current incomes, Chow,[30] and Laumas[31] and Petersen[32] assert that permanent income is a better variable in affecting the demand for money. However, studies by Taylor and Newhouse[33] and Kilman[34] reached the opposite conclusion.

Regarding the price level, almost all the empirical studies took it for granted that the demand for nominal money balances (value of money expressed in current dollars) is proportional to the price level, meaning that a one per cent increase in the price level can be expected to increase the demand for nominal money balances by the same percentage. In practically every case, data on wealth, income and money supply were converted into real dollars before they were used in the study on the demand for money. Meltzer was not willing to take the thesis of proportionality between nominal money balances and the price level for granted. He statistically investigated this matter and confirmed what the indirect evidence suggested, i.e., that the demand for nominal money balances was proportional to the price level.[35] Goldfeld also directly investigated this matter and arrived at the same conclusion.[36]

There is a fair amount of evidence that the expected rate of change in prices has an important effect on the quantity of money demanded particularly when a nation is passing through a major and long period of inflation (Deaver, Chile[37] ; Diz, Argentina[37]; Campbell, South Korea and Brazil[37]; Hu, China[38]; and Valentine, Australia[39]).

The stability of the functional relationship between the quantity of money demanded and a few macroeconomic variables is one of the factors determining the effectiveness of monetary policy. A stable money demand function enables the monetary authority to predict with a reasonable amount of accuracy the effect of changes in the money supply on inflation, income and employment. There is some evidence that the money demand funciton is stable [Clinton (1973)[40], Kahn (1974),[41] Laumas and Mehra (1976)[42] and Foot (1977)[43]]. Laumas and Mehra claim that the function becomes stable when short and intermediate term rates and the real income (current or permanent) are used as explanatory variables. Kahn concludes that that is true, especially when a long term rather than a short term rate is used as an explanatory variable along with per capita income. Clinton and Foot find stability in the function when the money demand is conventionally defined. However, Mullineaux claims that the function loses its stability when monthly data are used.[44] All the studies that concluded stability in the function used either quarterly or annual data. It is possible that the instability is masked by time aggregation of the data.

Recent experience has also led some researchers to question the stability in the money demand function. One of the elements that alters the function is the quickened pace of financial innovations such as the introduction of NOW accounts, electronic transfers and automatic transfer to cover overdrafts. Business and state and local government units are now authorized to hold some of their funds in savings deposits. These developments have contributed to a reduced desire to hold funds in checking accounts. Many empirical studies find that velocity in recent years cannot be explained by the traditional money demand function. A great deal of additional work is needed to resolve what Goldfeld calls "The Case of the Missing Money." Some new determinants have to be incorporated into the function to yield a reasonably stable function. Hamburger, however, claims that he has solved the problem.[45] But it is yet to be seen whether his money demand function will remain stable on the basis of future data.

SUMMARY

All of the models of money demand discussed in this and the previous chapter can be summarized as follows:

$$M_d = f[A, G_p, P, P_p, (R_1, R_2,..., R_n), R_m, R_r, S, U, W, Y, Y_p, b, (i_e - i), w] \qquad ...6\text{-}10$$

Other things being equal, the amount of money demanded rises with a rise in either of these variables: Price level (P), permanent price level (P_p), return on money (R_m), amount of risk involved in investment (R_r), taste and preferences (U), nonhuman wealth—tangible or marketable capital—(W), income (Y), permanent income (Y_p), brokerage fee (b) and expected interest rate ($i_e - i$). The opposite will be the case when any of these variables declines. Variables which are inversely related to the quantity of money demanded are: Advertising expenditure of savings and loan associations (A), expected change in the price level (G_p), expected rate of return from assets 1, 2, ..., n excluding money ($R_1, R_2, ..., R_n$), individuals' size of financial assets (S) and ratio of nonhuman wealth to total wealth (w).

All of the major empirical studies, except of Andersen and Friedman, are in virtual agreement that the quantity of money demanded is closely and inversely related to the market interest rate. However, there is no agreement as to the type of interest rate (short or long term) that exerts the most significant influence. There is no consensus whatsoever about whether the demand for money depends upon wealth, income or both. Almost all of the studies have taken for granted that the demand for nominal money balances is proportional to the price level. There is some evidence to indicate that the money demand function is stable particularly when quarterly or annual data are used.

FOOTNOTES

[1]William J. Baumol, "The Transactions Demand for Cash: An Inventory Theoretical Approach," **Quarterly Journal of Economics** (November 1952), pp. 545-556.

[2] Milton Friedman, "The Quantity Theory of Money—A Restatement," in **Studies in**

the Quantity Theory of Money, ed. Milton Friedman (Chicago, Illinois: The University of Chicago Press, 1956), pp. 3-21.

³Milton Friedman, "Money: Quantity Theory," in Volume 10 of **International Encyclopedia of the Social Sciences** (New York: The MacMillan Company & The Free Press, 1968), p. 440.

⁴Milton Friedman, "The Demand for Money: Some Theoretical and Empirical Results," **Journal of Political Economy** (August 1959), p. 349.

⁵Friedman, "The Quantity Theory of Money—A Restatement," p. 9.

⁶Don Patinkin, "The Chicago Tradition, The Quantity Theory, and Friedman," **Journal of Money, Credit and Banking** (February 1969), p. 61.

⁷Stephen W. Rousseas, **Monetary Theory** (New York: Alfred A. Knopf, 1972), p. 179.

⁸Thomas M. Humphrey, "Evolution of the Concept of the Demand for Money," **Monthly Review: Federal Reserve Bank of Richmond** (December 1973), p. 16.

⁹James Tobin, "Liquidity Preference as Behavior Towards Risk," **Review of Economic Studies** (February 1958), pp. 65-86.

¹⁰John G. Gurley and Edward S. Shaw, **Money in Theory of Finance** (Washington, D.C.: The Brookings Institution, 1960), pp. 150-190.

¹¹Franco Modigliani, "Liquidity Preference," in Volume 10 of **International Encyclopedia of the Social Sciences** (New York: The MacMillan Company and The Free Press, 1968), p. 398.

¹²Leonall C. Andersen, "Observed Income Velocity of Money: A Misunderstood Issue in Monetary Policy," **Review: Federal Reserve Bank of St. Louis** (August 1975), p. 14.

¹³Henry A. Latane, "Cash Balance and the Interest Rate—Pragmatic Approach," in **Monetary Theory and Policy**, ed. Richard S. Thorn (New York: Random House, 1966), p. 126.

¹⁴Allan H. Meltzer and Karl Brunner, "Predicting Velocity: Implications for Theory and Policy," **Journal of Finance** (May 1963), p. 350.

¹⁵Allan H. Meltzer, "The Demand for Money: The Evidence from Time Series," **Journal of Political Economy** (June 1963), p. 244.

¹⁶Ronald L. Teigen, "Demand and Supply Functions for Money in the United States: Some Structural Estimates," **Econometrica** (October 1964), p. 506.

¹⁷David E. Laidler, "The Rate of Interest and the Demand for Money—Some Empirical Evidence," **Journal of Political Economy** (December 1966) p. 544.

¹⁸Tong H. Lee, "Alternative Interest Rates and the Demand for Money: The Empirical Evidence," **American Economic Review** (December 1967), p. 1169.

¹⁹Donald L. Campbell and Frank Falero Jr., "Additional Evidence on the Demand for Money," **Quarterly Review of Economics and Business** (Summer 1971), p. 15.

²⁰Tong Hun Lee, "Alternative Interest Rates and the Demand for Money: Reply," **American Economic Review** (June 1969), p. 417.

²¹Michael J. Hamburger, "The Demand for Money by Households, Money Substitutes, and Monetary Policy," **Journal of Political Economy** (December 1966), p. 608.

²²Henry R. Heller, "The Demand for Money: The Evidence from the Short-Run Data," **Quarterly Journal of Economics** (May 1965), p. 300.

²³Laidler, p. 547.

²⁴H.F. Lydall, "Income, Assets, and the Demand for Money," **Review of Economics**

and Statistics (February 1958), p. 11.

[25]M. Bronfenbrenner and T. Mayer, "Liquidity Functions in the American Economy," **Econometrica** (October 1960), p. 834.

[26]Meltzer and Brunner.

[27]David E. Laidler, **The Demand for Money: Theories and Evidence,** (Scranton Pennsylvania: International Textbook Company, 1970), p. 102.

[28]Gregory Chow, "On the Long-Run and Short-Run Demand for Money," **Journal of Political Economy** (April 1966), p. 127.

[29]Heller, p. 294.

[30]Chow.

[31]G.S. Laumas, "The Permanent Rate of Interest and the Demand for Money," **Southern Economic Journal** (April 1970), pp. 460-461.

[32]Richard Petersen, "A Cross Section Study of the Demand for Money: The United States, 1960-62," **Journal of Finance** (March 1974), p. 87.

[33]Lester D. Taylor and Joseph P. Newhouse, "On The Long-Run and Short-Run Demand for Money: A Comment," **Journal of Political Economy** (September/October 1969), p. 854.

[34]M.L. Kliman, "Aggregative and Sectoral Hypotheses on the Demand for Money: Comparative Tests for the Business Sector," **Journal of Finance** (December 1972), p. 1175.

[35]Meltzer, p. 227.

[36]Stephen M. Goldfeld, "The Demand for Money Revisited," **Brookings Papers on Economic Activity: 3** (1973), p. 625.

[37]David Meiselman (ed.) **Varieties of Monetary Experience** (Chicago, Illinois: The University of Chicago Press, 1970), pp. 34 (J.V. Deaver), 123 (A.C. Diz) and 372 (C.D. Campbell).

[38]T.W. Hu "Hyperinflation and the Dynamics of the Demand for Money in China, 1945-1949," **Journal of Political Economy** (January/February 1971), p. 186.

[39]T.J. Valentine, "The Demand for Money and Price Expectations in Australia," **Journal of Finance** (June 1977), p. 747.

[40]Kevin Clinton, "The Demand for Money in Canada 1955-1970: Some Single-Equation Estimates and Stability Tests," **Canadian Journal of Economics** (February 1973), p. 61.

[41]Mohsin S. Kahn, "The Stability of the Demand-for-Money Function in the United States: 1901-1965," **Journal of Political Economy** (December 1974), p. 1217.

[42]G.S. Laumas and Y.P.Mehra, "The Stability of the Demand for Money Function: The Evidence From Quarterly Data," **Review of Economics & Statistics** (November 1976), p. 468.

[43]David Foot, "The Demand for Money in Canada; Some Additional Evidence," **Canadian Journal of Economics** (August 1977), p. 484.

[44]Donald J. Mullineaux, **The Stability of the Demand for Money: Some Adaptive Regression Tests on Monthly Data,** Philadelphia Fed Research Papers No. 25 (Philadelphia: Federal Reserve Bank of Philadelphia, 1977), p. 2.

[45]Michael J. Hamburger, "The Behavior of the Money Stock: Is There a Puzzle?" **Journal of Monetary Economics** (July 1977), p. 285.

QUESTIONS FOR REVIEW

1. Evaluate critically the Inventory-Approach model.
2. Explain Friedman's model of money demand. In what ways did he expand on the Keynesian model?
3. Discuss briefly the Risk-Aversion model. In what ways does it deviate from the Liquidity Preference model?
4. A. What do we mean by implicit deposit rate?
   B. How does it affect the demand for money?
   C. Describe the main factors which determine the size of implicit deposit rate.
5. Discuss the role of interest rate in the theory of money demand as demonstrated by various empirical studies.
6. Distinguish between income and wealth. What part do they play in the theory of money demand?
7. "The demand for nominal balances is proportional to the price level." Evaluate this statement.
8. What does Tobin mean by "risk averter" and "risk lover"? How does the demand for money of these two types of individuals differ from each other?
9. Distinguish between "W" and "w". How do they affect the demand for money?
10. Evaluate critically the Portfolio-Balance-Approach model.

SUGGESTED FURTHER READING

1. Baumol, William J. "The Transactions Demand for Cash: An Inventory Theoretical Approach." **Quarterly Journal of Economics,** November 1952, pp. 545-556.
2. Boonekamp, C.F.J. "Inflation, Hedging, and the Demand for Money." **American Economic Review.** December 1978, pp. 821-833.
3. Chetty, V.K. "On the Long-Run and Short-Run Demand for Money: Some Further Evidence." **Journal of Political Economy.** November/ December 1969, pp. 921-931.
4. Courch, R.L. "Tobin vs. Keynes on Liquidity Preference." **Review of Economics and Statistics.** November 1971, pp. 368-371.
5. Duesenberry, James S. "The Portfolio Approach to the Demand for Money and Other Assets." **Review of Economics and Statistics.** February 1963, pp. 9-24.
6. Eden, Benjamin. "On the Specification of the Demand for Money: The Real Rate of Return Versus the Rate of Inflation." **Journal of Political Economy,** December 1976, pp. 1353-1359.

7. Enzler, Jared, Johnson, Lewis & Paulus, John. "Some Problems of Money Demand." **Brookings Papers on Economic Activity.** 1976: 1, pp. 261-282.

8. Fisher, Douglas. "Real Balances and the Demand for Money." **Journal of Political Economy.** November/December 1970, pp. 1340-1354.

9. Friedman, Milton. "Money: Quantity Theory," in Volume 10 of **International Encyclopedia of the Social Sciences.** New York: The Macmillan Company and The Free Press, 1968, pp. 432-447.

10. Goldfeld, S.M. "The Demand for Money Revisited." **Brookings Paper on Economic Activity.** 1973:3, pp. 577-638.

11. Gurley, John G. & Shaw, Edward S. **Money in a Theory of Finance.** Washington, D.C.: Brookings Institution, 1960, pp. 150-190.

12. Hicks, John. **Critical Essays in Monetary Theory.** Oxford: The Clarendon Press, 1967, pp. 103-125.

13. Higgins, Bryon. "Velocity: Money's Second Dimension." **"Economic Review: Federal Reserve Bank of Kansas City.** June 1978, pp. 15-31.

14. Jacobs, Rodney L. "Estimating the Long-Run Demand for Money from Time-Series Data." **Journal of Political Economy.** November/December 1974, pp. 1221-1237.

15. Johnson, Harry G. "A Note on the Theory of Transactions Demand-for-Money Function: Another Look and Some Additional Evidence." **Journal of Money, Credit and Banking.** August 1970, pp. 383-384.

16. Konstas, Panos and Khouja, Mohamed W. "The Keynesian Demand-for-Money Function: Another Look and Some Additional Evidence." **Journal of Money, Credit and Banking.** November 1969, pp. 765-777.

17. Laidler, David E.W. **The Demand For Money: Theories and Evidence.** New York: Dun Donnelly & Harper & Row, Publishers, 1977.

18. Meyer, Paul A. and Neri, John A. "A Keynes-Friedman Demand Funtion." **American Economic Review.** September 1975, pp. 610-623.

19. Park, Yung Chul. "The Variability of Velocity: An International Comparison." **IMF: Staff Papers.** November 1970, pp. 620-637.

20. Rousseas, Stephen W. **Monetary Theory.** New York: Alfred A. Knopf, 1972, pp. 155-279.

21. Sastry, A.S. Rama. "The Effect of Credit on Transactions Demand for Cash." **Journal of Finance.** September 1970, pp. 771-781.

22. Saving, Thomas R. "Transactions Costs and the Demand for Money." **American Economic Review.** June 1971, pp. 407-420.

23. Stevens, Stanley C. "The Negative Precautionary Demand for Money Reconsidered." **Journal of Finance.** June 1971, pp. 749-755.

CHAPTER VII

Interaction Between The Supply Of And Demand For Money

A change in the money supply affects the demand for money, and vice versa. The extent to which one impacts the other is important to the monetary authority since it helps to determine the appropriate action required to achieve a desired objective. When the monetary authority wants to determine the increase required in the size of the monetary base to raise the level of the money supply to a certain value, it is in a better position to do so if it can measure the interaction between money supply and money demand.

An increase in the money demand increases the supply of money as follows: An increase in the money demand causes the interest rate to rise. A rise in the interest rate encourages banks to economize on their reserves and expand their loans and investments. The supply of money increases when banks expand loans and investments.

An increase in the money supply causes an increase in the demand for money as follows: When the money supply is increased, the interest rate falls. A fall in the interest rate causes the demand for money to go up. The demand for money will further rise when lower interest rate stimulates income, output and employment. As explained in the previous chapter, other things being equal, an increase in income causes an increase in the demand for money. The interaction between the supply of and demand for money can also be shown graphically.

EFFECT OF THE MONEY DEMAND ON THE SUPPLY OF MONEY

In Figure 7-1, D and S are demand and supply curves of money balances, respectively. The D curve slopes downward toward the right implying that more money is demanded at a lower interest rate, and vice versa. At a lower interest rate the public has less incentive to loan money and more to hold it. (Friedman claims that the demand for money is relatively inelastic with respect to the interest rate.) The S curve, on the other hand, slopes upward toward the right implying that more money is supplied at a higher interest rate, and vice versa. This is because when the interest rate rises, the opportunity cost of banks for holding excess reserves rises. As a result, banks tend to reduce their excess reserves by investing or lending them. When banks invest or lend money they create money.

FIGURE 7-1

EFFECT OF A CHANGE IN THE MONEY DEMAND

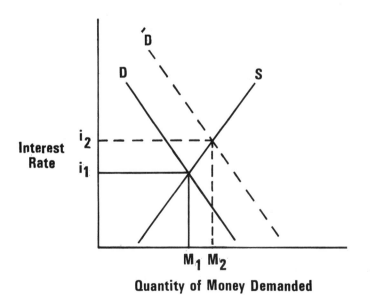

Quantity of Money Demanded
& Money Supplied

When the money demand increases, i.e., the D curve shifts upward to $\acute{D}$ (Figure 7-1), the interest rate and, consequently, the money stock rises—the interest rate from i_1 to i_2 and the money stock from M_1 to M_2. Albert Burger and Neil Stevens call this increase in the money stock, demand determined, since it stems completely from an increase in the money demand.[1] The opposite is the case when the curve shifts downward.

EFFECT OF THE MONEY SUPPLY ON THE DEMAND FOR MONEY

Suppose that the Federal Reserve shifts the supply curve to $\acute{S}$ by raising the monetary base (Figure 7-2). Assuming there is no change in the demand curve, the interest rate will fall from i_1 to i_2,

FIGURE 7-2

EFFECT OF A CHANGE IN THE MONEY SUPPLY

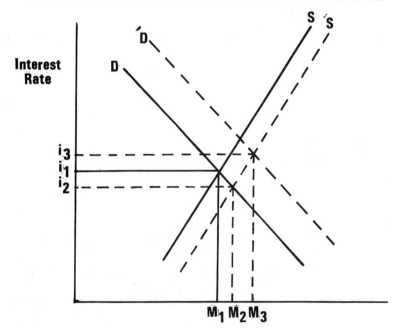

Quantity of Money Demanded & Money Supplied

and the quantity of money demanded will rise from M_1 to M_2. Furthermore, a rise in the money supply will cause income, wealth and the price level to rise, which will, in turn, cause an upward shift in the demand curve. (An increase in the money supply stimulates economic activity and, consequently, income and wealth of the people. Also, as will be explained in the next chapter, an increase in the money supply generally puts upward pressure on the price level.) An upward shift in the demand curve will increase the quantity of money demanded to M_3—from M_1 to M_2, supply determined, and from M_2 to M_3, demand determined.

SUMMARY

Knowledge of the extent of the interaction between the supply of and demand for money helps the monetary authority determine the appropriate action required to accomplish a set goal.

An increase in the money demand raises the interest rate which, in turn, raises the supply of money. An increase in the money supply, on the other hand, lowers the interest rate, which, in turn, raises the demand for money.

FOOTNOTE

[1]Albert E. Burger and Neil A. Stevens, "Monetary Expansion and Open Market Committee Operating Strategy in 1971," **Review: Federal Reserve Bank of St. Louis** (March 1972), p. 18.

QUESTIONS FOR REVIEW

1. Explain with the help of a diagram how does an increase in the supply of money resulting from an increase in the monetary base affect the demand for money?
2. Explain with the help of a diagram how will a shift in the money demand function affect the supply of money?
3. A. Distinguish between the supply determined and demand determined increase in the supply of money.
   B. Using a diagram, show how does an upward shift in the money supply function result in an increase in the supply of money which is both supply and demand determined?
4. Describe how a change in the interest rate causes a change in the money supply.

SUGGESTED FURTHER READING

1. Brunner, Karl and Meltzer, Allan H. "Some Further Investigations of Demand and Supply Functions for Money." **Journal of Finance.** May 1964, pp. 240-283.
2. Burger, Albert E. and Stevens, Neil A. "Monetary Expansion and Federal Open Market Committee Operating Strategy in 1971." **Review: Federal Reserve Bank of St. Louis.** May 1972, pp. 11-31.

CHAPTER VIII

Linkage Between Money and Economic Activity

Between the publication of Keynes' General Theory in 1936 and 1956, the link between the money supply and economic activity (GNP) was explained pretty much in the Keynesian style. In 1956 the traditional school, associated with the quantity theory of money, reemerged under the new name of Monetarist school to offer a new explanation. The views of the two schools are presented in this chapter. How the money supply is linked to economic activity has a bearing on policy making.

The Keynesian school refers to both Keynes and neoKeynesian group. Principal members of this school, in addition to John M. Keynes, are: Paul Samuelson, James Tobin, James Duesenberry, Walter Heller, Franco Modigliani, Gardner Ackley and Arthur Okun. Principal members of the Monetarist school are: Milton Friedman, Karl Brunner, Allan Meltzer, Leonall Andersen and Jerry Jordan.

The linkage is discussed in terms of (A) transmission process (how the effect of a change in the money supply is transmitted to GNP), (B) real vs. nominal GNP (whether a change in the money supply affects real or nominal GNP), (C) stable vs. unstable relation (whether the relationship between the money supply and GNP is stable or unstable), (D) exogeneity vs. endogeneity (whether the money supply is an exogenous or endogenous variable) and (E) the speed and size of response to a monetary action (how much and how quickly GNP responds to a change in the money supply).

TRANSMISSION PROCESS

The transmission process as viewed by Keynesians is summarized as follows:

A change in the money supply causes a change in interest rates, which, in turn, changes aggregate demand. When aggregate demand changes, GNP (aggregate spending) changes. A change in interest rates affects aggregate demand (or aggregate spending) via interest rate effect, wealth effect and credit availability effect.

Interest rate effect describes the reaction of borrowers to a change in market interest rates. When they fall in response to an increase in the money supply, individuals, businessmen, and local and state governments increase spending with low-cost borrowed funds. When market interest rates rise, borrowing is curtailed and aggregate spending (GNP) declines.

Wealth effect describes the change in household and business wealth, which occurs when prices of securities (bonds and stocks) change. Wealth goes up when prices of securities rise in the wake of lower interest rates, and vice versa. An increase in wealth increases aggregate spending.

Credit availability effect describes the degree to which credit is available at the prevailing market interest rate. GNP will not rise if enough funds are not available at that rate. Sometimes when the money supply is tight banks fail to raise interest rates sufficiently to equate the supply with demand, with the consequence that they will not be able to meet fully the borrowing needs of all their customers.

FRB-MIT Model

Keynesians have developed various models of the U.S. economy such as the Brookings, Wharton and FRB-MIT models. The most popular is the FRB-MIT model. A simplified version of the transmission process as viewed in this model is outlined in Diagram 8-1. The instruments of monetary policy used in the model are unborrowed reserves (total reserves less borrowings from Federal Reserve Banks) and the Federal Reserve discount rate. (Unborrowed reserves are regarded as a proxy for open market operations.)

Diagram 8-1 shows that a change in monetary policy first affects short-term interest rates and then long-term interest rates, which, in turn, affect consumption, investment and government expenditures, three components of GNP. Example: Assume that the Federal Reserve, in an effort to stimulate the economy, increases the money supply by purchasing government securities. The purchase of securities causes a rise in unborrowed reserves and a fall in the Treasury bill rate. In the model, it is assumed that the commercial paper rate (short term rate) depends upon the Treasury bill rate; and that the commercial loan rate (another short term rate) depends upon the commercial paper rate, bank business loans and the Aaa corporate bond rate (long-term rate).[1] Through the term structure relationship, the commercial paper rate is linked to the Aaa corporate rate, which, in turn, influences other long term rates. When the Treasury bill rate declines the commercial paper rate also declines. A fall in the commercial paper rate lowers the Aaa corporate bond rate, which, in turn, lowers other long term rates.

The effect of changes in long term rates in the FRB-MIT model spreads through the economy by way of three separate channels: (i) cost of capital, (ii) net worth of households and (iii) credit rationing.

Cost of capital

The cost-of-capital channel captures the effect of four long-term interest rates. They are: industrial bond rate, state and local bond rates, mortgage rate and stock market yield. Final expenditures, which are affected by this channel, are equipment and structures, single and multi-family housing, consumer goods, and state and local government construction.

Equipment and structures: Businessmen, before making a decision about this type of investment, determine the quasi rent, that is, what has to be earned by a piece of equipment or structure to make its purchase worthwhile. Changes in the cost of equipment or structures affect the quasi rent. Other things being equal, a decline in the cost of a piece of equipment or a structure reduces its quasi rent. Changes in the quasi rent affect the desired ratio of capital to output and, consequently, expenditure on equipment and structures. Other things being equal, a decline in the quasi rent increases the desired ratio of capital to output, which, in turn, increases capital expenditure.

Single and multi-family housing: Expenditure for single and multi-family housing (residential construction) is determined by the relationship between the mortgage rate and the rate of return on investment in houses where the former represents the cost of financing and the latter, income from such an investment. If the mortgage rate

DIAGRAM 8-1

FIRST ROUND EFFECTS OF MONETARY
POLICY AS VIEWED IN FRB-MIT MODEL

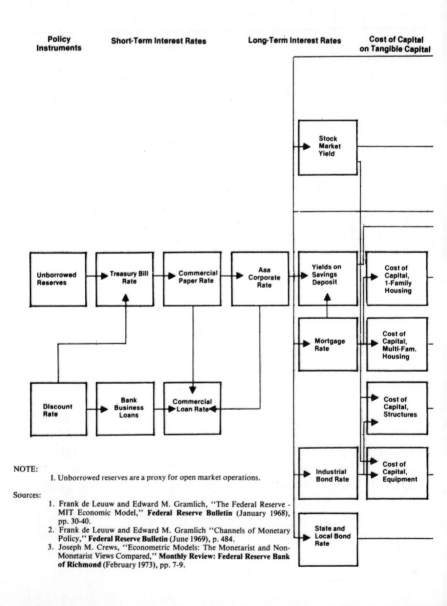

| Policy Instruments | Short-Term Interest Rates | Long-Term Interest Rates | Cost of Capital on Tangible Capital |

NOTE:

    I. Unborrowed reserves are a proxy for open market operations.

Sources:

    1. Frank de Leuuw and Edward M. Gramlich, "The Federal Reserve - MIT Economic Model," **Federal Reserve Bulletin** (January 1968), pp. 30-40.

    2. Frank de Leuuw and Edward M. Gramlich "Channels of Monetary Policy," **Federal Reserve Bulletin** (June 1969), p. 484.

    3. Joseph M. Crews, "Econometric Models: The Monetarist and Non-Monetarist Views Compared," **Monthly Review: Federal Reserve Bank of Richmond** (February 1973), pp. 7-9.

DIAGRAM 8-1 CONTINUED

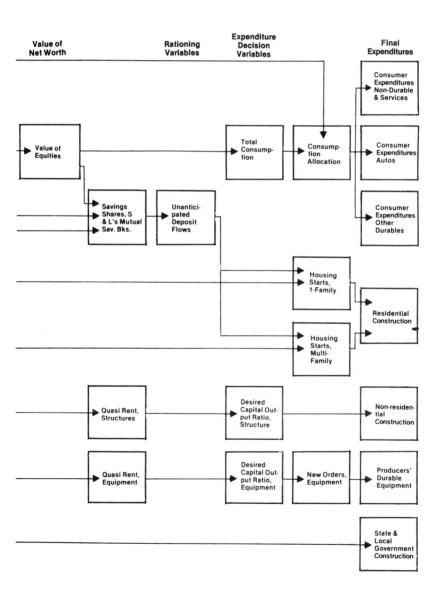

goes down relative to the rate of return, expenditure on residential construction rises.

Consumer goods: As will be discussed in the next section, changes in interest rates affect expenditure for consumer goods by the channel of net worth (wealth effect). A small portion of such expenditure is affected also by the cost-of-capital channel. Total consumption expenditure is assumed to depend upon current and lagged disposable income and net worth. The expenditure is then allocated among durable and nondurable goods and services depending upon population, the relative cost of durable and nondurable goods, existing stock of durables and, to a minor extent, interest rates.[2] A rise in interest rates reduces the consumption of durable goods and increases the consumption of nondurable goods and services.

State and local government construction: The capital stock that governments wish to hold depends, among other things, upon interest rates (state-and-local-government bond rates) because they affect their cost of financing. Construction expenditure depends upon the relation of actual and desired capital stock, together with the matching grants-in-aid of the Federal Government.[3] Other things being equal, when interest rates fall the capital stock these governments wish to hold rises, which, in turn, raises their construction expenditure.

Net worth of households

The second channel of monetary policy is the net worth of households. Here, there are two key relationships: One, the link between interest rates and the value of equities. Two, the link between household net worth (of which one component is the value of equities) and consumption. Since equities are a substitute for bonds, changes in the long-term bond rate cause a change in the value of equities in net worth. Other things being equal, when the interest rate declines the value of bonds and equities and, consequently, net worth rises. Changes in net worth cause a change in consumption expenditure. Although the marginal propensity to consume out of net worth is quite small (less than 0.04 in the consumption function currently used), consumption is so important in total final expenditures that even this small response is large enough for changes in stock prices to produce a significant effect on the economy.[4]

Credit rationing

The third channel of monetary policy is credit rationing. In the FRB-MIT model, it is confined to the link between savings institutions and the housing market because in recent years this is where it has been found to be most widely used. Credit rationing refers to a practice by which lenders ration credit by nonprice methods such as changing terms of downpayment, altering requirements for collateral balances and/or outright refusal to make loans.

Savings institutions practice credit rationing particularly at a time when the money market is tight and market interest rates are rising. At that time, they experience reductions in deposit inflows because the rates they pay to depositors rise very sluggishly partly due to an oligopolistic market structure and costliness of frequently changing advertised rates and partly due to restrictions on maximum rates they are allowed to pay. At the same time, due to state government ceilings, savings associations cannot raise rates they charge on mortgages. (They cannot divert their funds to other vehicles either because, by law, they are required to invest a high portion of their portfolio in mortgages.)

Monetarists, until now, have not sufficiently spelled out how money is linked to GNP.[5] Their writings, however, seem to suggest the transmission process as follows:

| Money Supply | → | Rates of Return | → | Aggregate Demand | → | GNP |

A change in the money supply affects rates of return of different assets, which, in turn, affect aggregate demand. When aggregate demand changes GNP changes.

When the monetary authority increases the money stock by purchasing government securities, the effect on aggregate demand depends upon whether the securities are bought from the public or commercial banks. Let us first examine a case where securities are bought from the public. The Monetarist school postulates that business and consumers allocate wealth among various assets such as consumer durables, capital goods, stocks, bonds and money in such a way that the marginal dollar invested in each asset yields the same amount of return.[6] Returns from assets are received in the form of services (as in the case of consumer durable goods), income (as in the case of investment in stocks, bonds, machine and equipment) and convenience (as in the case of money). In addition to convenience, people also hold money for a number of other reasons. For more detail, see Chapters V and VI on theories of money demand.

When the monetary authority increases the money stock, money assets of the public rise. Assuming the public is at equilibrium as to the distribution of wealth (implying that the marginal rate of return of each asset is the same), an increase in money assets will reduce their marginal rate of return and the rate will fall below the rates of return of other assets because they, like other assets, are subject to the law of diminishing returns. If the marginal rate of return of money assets is lower than those of other assets, this means that the public is holding more wealth in money assets than it would like to hold. Another way of saying it is that a situation of excess supply of money assets has developed. The excess supply of money assets will increase aggregate demand and, consequently, aggregate spending because it induces the public to optimize its position by disposing of these assets. The public can dispose of excess money assets by purchasing consumer durable goods, capital goods, bonds and stocks. Purchase of these assets causes aggregate spending to rise. Aggregate spending rises directly, if consumer durables and capital goods are bought. If stocks and bonds are purchased, aggregate spending also rises, though in an indirect way. If the public disposes of a portion or all of its excess money assets by buying stocks, prices of stocks rise. Rising stock prices may encourage investment because they make it easier for new and existing firms to raise funds by issuing new stocks. The purchase of bonds raises their prices. Since bond prices and interest rates are inversely related, a rise in bond prices reduces interest rates, which, in turn, will stimulate consumption, investment and government spendings.

Let us now assume that the monetary authority raises the money supply by buying securities from commercial banks. This also increases aggregate spending. Here the effect is transmitted in an indirect way. The purchase of securities by the monetary authority raises excess reserves of banks. Excess reserves do not yield any return. Banks, in an attempt to dispose of excess reserves, either buy securities or expand loans, depending upon expected rates of return from each type of investment. If they buy securities, prices of securities go up and interest rates go down. A fall in interest rates, as described earlier, stimulates aggregate spending. Aggregate spending also rises if banks expand loans because the proceeds of loans are almost always spent.

St. Louis Model

The St. Louis model is the most popular model of Monetarists. The transmission process as viewed in this model is outlined in Diagram 8-2. It shows that policy instruments work through the money stock, and changes in the money stock directly affect total spending. Contrary to standard practice, this model determines the change in total spending and then divides it between price change and output change. (Standard practice in econometric model building is first to determine output and prices separately and then combine them to determine total spending.) A change in the price level is a function of current and past demand pressures and anticipated price changes. Demand pressure is defined as the change in total spending minus the potential increase in output. (Potential increase in output is equal to output at full employment minus output in the previous period.) After the price component of total spending is computed, output is derived by subtracting price component from total spending.

DIAGRAM 8-2

EFFECTS OF MONETARY POLICY AS VIEWED IN THE ST. LOUIS MODEL

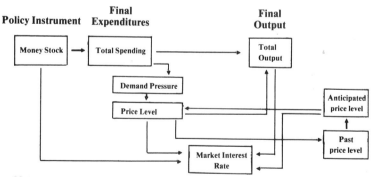

Note:
1. The money stock represents a proxy for policy instruments.
Source:
1. Leonall C. Andersen and Keith M. Carlson, "A Monetarist Model for Economic Stabilization," **Review: Federal Reserve Bank of St. Louis** (April 1970), pp. 9-10.

In this model, changes in the money stock, current and past changes in output, and current and anticipated price changes determine the market rate of interest but the market rate of interest does not exercise any direct role in the determination of spending, output and prices.

REAL VS. NOMINAL GNP

The previous section explains how a change in the money supply brings a change in GNP. But, which type of GNP—real or nominal—is affected? Real GNP changes when output changes. Nominal GNP includes the impact of both prices and output.

Both Keynesian and Monetarist schools seem to be in agreement that, in the short run, a change in the money supply generates changes both in prices and output, though the way they describe it differs somewhat. Keynesians say that if the monetary authority increases the money supply, the effect on prices and output depends first, on how aggregate demand responds to the action and second, on how output, factor prices and mark-up over cost respond to an increase in aggregate demand. The current rate of inflation also indirectly influences the price level.

How does aggregate demand respond to an increase in the money supply? John M. Keynes states that there are a number of possibilities as to how the money supply is related to aggregate demand, two of them are described here:

One, when the money supply increases, aggregate demand rises rather rapidly at first but eventually, as more money is added, its potency in raising demand becomes progressively weaker.[7] This may be due to the fact that the liquidity preference function (or money demand function) is at first interest inelastic but eventually reaches a point where it becomes interest elastic. The investment function, on the other hand, is interest elastic at first but eventually becomes interest inelastic. When the liquidity preference function is interest inelastic and the investment function is interest elastic, a fall in the interest rate (resulting from a rise in the money supply) stimulates aggregate demand. This condition is brought about because a lowered interest rate will not increase the public desire to hold more money (if the public holds money that is injected into the economy, aggregate demand will cease to rise) but it will raise investment spending. As more money is added (or as the interest rate continues declining), its potency to raise aggregate demand becomes progressively weaker because the economy approaches the threshold of an elastic range on the liquidity preference function and an inelastic range on the investment function.

Two, an increase in the money supply causes a very small amount of increase in aggregate demand. Such a situation may arise during an economic depression when the liquidity preference function is interest elastic and the investment function, interest inelastic.

How much real GNP increases depends upon how output responds to an increase in aggregate demand. Output increases when the economy is below full employment. According to Keynes, output first increases approximately in the same proportion as aggregate demand but these increases become progressively smaller as the economy approaches full employment.[8]

The rise in the price level depends upon how factor prices, output and the mark-up-over cost rule respond to a rise in aggregate demand. In the SSRC-MIT-Penn model (another version of the FRB-MIT model), the size of markup declines when business is bad and rises slightly when business is good because businessmen want to prevent the entry of new competitors.[9] The price level is also affected, though indirectly, by the current rate of inflation. Wages are important components of the cost of production. In the SSRC-MIT-Penn model, wages are assumed to rise faster as the unemployment rate falls and the cost of living rises (inflation).[10] According to Keynes, the price level rises slowly at first.[11] But when the economy approaches full employment, it starts rising rapidly relative to the increase in aggregate demand.

Like Keynesians, Monetarists state that, in the short run, changes in the money supply affect both output and prices but the extent to which they influence them depends upon the level of resource utilization and the expected rate of inflation.[12] Output increases by a small quantity, if money is expended at a time when the economy is operating at a high level of resource utilization (when the economy is near full employment). The size of a change in prices is determined by both the level of resource utilization and the expected rate of inflation. As discussed earlier, an increase in the money supply increases aggregate demand. An increase in aggregate demand puts a strong upward pressure on prices if the economy is at a high level of resource utilization (mild upward pressure, if it is at a low level of resource utilization) because at this level the supply of goods and services responds rather sluggishly to a rising demand. Pressure on prices is enhanced further if people expect a rise in the rate of inflation. According to Monetarists, price changes over a period of time generate price expectations, which serve as a separate influence on price movements.

The discussion thus far has been confined to the problem of how, in the short run, a change in the money supply affects output and prices. But such a change also has long run effects. Keynesians believe that if the economy is below the full employment level, then, even in the long run, a change in the money supply affects both prices and output.[13] Monetarists, on the other hand, believe that long run movements in output are independent of the money supply and thus, in the long run, changes in the money supply influence prices only. They further argue that long run output is determined by basic growth factors such as labor force, technology, capital stock and natural resources.[14]

STABLE VS. UNSTABLE RELATION

There is strong disagreement between the Keynesian and Monetarist schools regarding the stability of the relationship between the money supply and GNP. The Keynesian school believes that the relationship between them is unstable. The Monetarist school believes that it is stable. (If there is, in fact, a stable relationship, the monetary authority could predict with considerable accuracy how GNP changes from a given change in the money supply.) As discussed in the section on "transmission process," changes in the money supply cause changes in interest rates, which, in turn, cause changes in aggregate demand and GNP. The relationship between the money supply and GNP will be considered unstable if there exists a loose relationship between the money supply and interest rates and/or between interest rates and aggregate spending (GNP). Keynesians say that there is a loose relationship between the money stock and GNP due to the instability in the demand for money.[15] If the demand for money is unstable, a given quantity of money produces different interest rates at different times. Keynesians further assert that the relationship between the money supply and GNP is unstable also because the relationship between interest rates and GNP is unstable.[16]

The Monetarist school, on the other hand, states that there exists a stable relationship between the money supply and GNP. They support this thesis with a number of empirical studies such as one by Milton Friedman and David Meiselman.[17]

EXOGENEITY VS. ENDOGENEITY

Keynesians and Monetarists disagree over whether the money supply is an exogenous or endogenous variable. Keynesians claim that it is an endogenous variable. Many Monetarists treat it as an exogenous variable. In statistical theory a variable is endogenous when it is jointly determined with other variables in the system. Economists generally call the money supply endogenous when it has a feedback effect (reverse causation) and thus outside the direct control of the monetary authority. (The feedback effect means that the effect of a change in the money supply runs from money to economic activity and then back to money.) Some economists say that the money supply should be regarded endogenous also when the monetary authority permits changes in the money supply to offset changes in bank reserves and the demand for money resulting from forces outside its control (defensive action). In the absence of such actions, these forces can be expected to cause abrupt changes in the money market.

Whether the money supply is an endogenous or exogenous variable has an important impact on policy decisions. If it is endogenous, policymakers must take into account the feedback effect in formulating policy. This also means that statistical estimates of the relationship between money and income computed by econometric models that assume money to be an exogenous variable are not reliable.

Keynesians explain the feedback effect of the money supply as follows: When the monetary authority increases the money supply in an attempt to stimulate the economy, the resulting rise in economic activity causes a rise in the demand for money and, consequently, in interest rates. When interest rates rise, the opportunity cost of banks for holding excess reserves rises. As a result, banks tend to reduce their excess reserves to a bare minimum by investing or lending money. When banks invest or lend money they create money. Keynesians add that the money supply is endogenous also because the actions of the monetary authority are predominantly defensive in nature.[18]

Though Monetarists recognize the feedback effect, they treat the money supply as an exogenous variable for two reasons: (i) They claim that the effect running from money to economic activity is predominant.[19] (The effect running from economic activity to money is very weak.) (ii) The monetary authority can control the behavior of money and can influence economic activity without being concerned about feedback effects.[20]

SPEED AND SIZE OF RESPONSE TO A MONETARY ACTION

Controversy also exists between Keynesians and Monetarists as to how quickly and how much GNP responds to a change in the money supply. Keynesians claim that the lag between changes in the money supply and GNP is quite long. They support their position by arguing that investment and consumption expenditures, which are affected by interest rates, are responsive to long-term rather than short-term interest rates, e.g., plant and equipment expenditures respond to corporate bond rates and stock prices; housing responds to mortgage rates; consumer durables respond to consumer credit rates and construction of state and local government responds to state and local government bond rates. It takes longer for long-term interest rates to change in response to a change in the money supply. After interest rates are changed, it takes time before firms order and purchase capital goods, homeowners alter their house purchases, and local and

TABLE 8-1

MONEY MULTIPLIERS IN THE FRB-MIT AND ST. LOUIS MODELS

Elapsed Time	FRB-MIT Multiplier	St. Louis Multiplier
After 1 quarter	0.2	1.6
After 2 quarters	0.4	3.5
After 4 quarters	0.4	6.6
After 12 quarters	2.2	6.6

Source:
  1. Richard G. Davis, "How Much Does Money Matter? A Look at Some Recent Evidence," **Monthly Review: Federal Reserve Bank of New York** (June 1969), p. 123.

state governments float bonds for construction projects. In support of this claim, they refer to the results reported by the FRB-MIT model, which state that it takes about 12 quarters to realize the full impact of a change in the money supply on GNP (Table 8-1).

Monetarists claim that the lag between changes in the money supply and GNP is quite short. Their argument is that a change in the money supply, in many cases, has a direct impact on aggregate spending. An increase in the money supply increases excess money balances of individuals, who, seeking to dispose of their excess balances, may spend a portion of them on goods and services, which directly enhances aggregate spending. Monetarists support this viewpoint with the help of the St. Louis model, which indicates that the total impact of a change in the money supply on GNP is, on the average, realized within four quarters (not 12 quarters as estimated by the FRB-MIT model—see Table 8-1).

With regard to the size of response, Monetarists believe that monetary influences have a strong impact on GNP. Keynesians, on the other hand, believe that they have a weak impact on GNP. The money multipliers in the St. Louis model (an important Monetarist model) and the FRB-MIT model (an important Keynesian model) clearly support their respective positions (See Table 8-1). The money multiplier in the St. Louis model shows that a $1 billion once-and-for-all increase in the old M_1 will raise GNP after the end of 12 quarters by the amount of $6.6 billion. In the FRB-MIT model, by contrast, the same amount of increase in the money supply raises GNP only by the amount $2.2 billion over the same period.

SUMMARY

Linkage between money and economic activity has been discussed in terms of transmission process, real vs. nominal GNP, stable vs. unstable relation, exogeneity vs. endogeneity and the speed and size of response to a monetary action.

Transmission Process: According to Keynesians, a change in the money supply causes a change in interest rates. A change in interest rates causes a change in aggregate demand and, consequently, in GNP. According to Monetarists, a change in the money supply causes a change in rates of return of a broad spectrum of assets, including money, which, in turn, causes a change in aggregate demand and, consequently, in GNP.

Real vs. Nominal GNP: Both groups agree that, in the short run, a change in the money supply influences both output and prices (real and nominal GNP). They differ, however, on how it affects long run GNP. To Keynesians, it affects both prices and output until the economy reaches full employment, at which point it will affect prices only. To Monetarists, long run movements in output are independent of the money supply and thus, in the long run, a change in the money supply influences prices only.

Stable vs. Unstable Relation: Keynesians claim that the relationship between money and GNP is unstable. Monetarists claim that it is stable.

Exogeneity vs. Endogeneity: Keynesians claim that the money supply is an endogenous variable and thus, not completely under the control of policymakers. Monetarists claim that it is an exogenous variable.

Speed and Size of Response to a Monetary Action: Keynesians believe that the impact of a change in the money supply on GNP is weak and takes a while before its full effect is exerted. Monetarists assert that the impact of money on GNP is quite strong and is exerted very quickly.

FOOTNOTES

[1]Frank de Leeuw and Edward Gramlich, "The Federal Reserve-MIT Econometric Model," **Federal Reserve Bulletin** (January 1968), p. 31.

[2]Frank de Leeuw and Edward M. Gramlich, "Channels of Monetary Policy," **Federal Reserve Bulletin** (June 1969), pp. 479-480.

[3]**Ibid.**

[4]**Ibid.**, p. 481.

[5]Leonall C. Andersen, "The State of the Monetarist Debate," **Review: Federal Reserve Bank of St. Louis** (September 1973), p. 8.

[6]Leonall C. Andersen and Jerry L. Jordan, "Money in a Modern Quantity Theory Framework," **Review: Federal Reserve Bank of St. Louis** (December 1967), p. 4.

[7]Alvin H. Hansen, **Monetary and Fiscal Policy** (New York: McGraw-Hill Book Company, Inc., n.d.), pp. 134-135.

[8]**Ibid.**, p. 136.

[9]Dan M. Bechter, "Money and Inflation," **Monthly Review: Federal Reserve Bank of Kansas City** (July/August 1973), p. 5.

[10]**Ibid.**

[11]Hansen, p. 136.

[12]Leonall Andersen, "A Monetarist View of Demand Management: The United States Experience," **Review: Federal Reserve Bank of St. Louis** (September 1971), p. 6.

[13]Lawrence R. Klein, "Commentary on the State of the Monetarist Debate," **Review: Federal Reserve Bank of St. Louis** (September 1973), p. 10.

[14]Andersen, "A Monetarist View of Demand Management...," p. 4.

[15]Andrew F. Brimmer, "Monetarist Criticism and the Conduct of Flexible Monetary Policy in the United States," paper presented at the Institute of Economics and Statistics, Oxford University, Oxford, England, April 24, 1972 (Mimeographed), p. 11.

[16]**Ibid.**, p. 27.

[17]Milton Friedman and David Meiselman, "The Relative Stability of Monetary Velocity and the Investment Multiplier in the United States, 1897-1958," in **Monetary Economics: Controversies in Theory and Policy,** ed. Jonas Prager (New York: Random House, 1971), p. 215.

[18]Raymond Lombra and Raymond Torto, **Federal Reserve Defensive Behavior and the Reverse Causation: Staff Economic Studies** (Washington, D.C.: Board of Governors of the Federal Reserve System, n.d.), p. 1.

[19]Michael W. Keran, "Monetary and Fiscal Influences on Economic Activity—The Historical Evidence," **Review: Federal Reserve Bank of St. Louis** (November 1969), p. 21.

[20]Leonall C. Andersen & Jerry L. Jordan, "Monetary and Fiscal Actions: A Test of Their Relative Importance in Economic Stabilization; Reply," **Review: Federal Reserve Bank of St. Louis** (April 1969), p. 16.

QUESTIONS FOR REVIEW

1. Distinguish between the Keynesian and Monetarist views concerning the "transmission process."
2. Discuss the major differences separating the Keynesian and Monetarist schools regarding the linkage between money and economic activity.
3. "Every time a spending unit spends money in an attempt to dispose of its excess money supply it directly and indirectly increases spending and, consequently, income." Explain.
4. Does a change in the money supply influence nominal or real GNP or both? Discuss.
5. On what grounds do Keynesians argue that the relationship between the money supply and economic activity is unstable?
6. Discuss the speed and size of response to a monetary action as viewed by Keynesians and Monetarists.
7. Explain how, in the Keynesian framework, a fall in interest rates affects aggregate demand.
8. Keynes says, "As more and more money is added to the economy, its potency to raise aggregate demand becomes progressively weaker." Explain.

9. How do Monetarists explain that GNP increases by a multiple of the initial increase in aggregate spending resulting from a rise in the money supply?

10. Describe how, in the Monetarist framework, an increase in the supply of money affects rates of return of a broad spectrum of assets.

SUGGESTED FURTHER READING

1. Andersen, Leonall C. "A Monetarist View of Demand Management: The United States Experience." **Review: Federal Reserve Bank of St. Louis.** September 1971, pp. 3-11.

2. _____ "The State of the Monetary Debate." **Review: Federal Reserve Bank of St. Louis.** September 1973, pp. 2-14.

3. _____ and Carlson, Keith M. "A Monetarist Model For Economic Stabilization." **Review: Federal Reserve Bank of St. Louis.** April 1970, pp. 7-25.

4. Battenberg, Douglas, Enzler, Jared and Havenner, Arthur. "Minne: A Small Version of the MIT-PENN-SSRC Econometric Model." **Federal Reserve Bulletin.** November 1975, pp. 721-727.

5. Brimmer, Andrew F. "Monetarist Criticism and the Conduct of Flexible Monetary Policy in the United States." Paper presented at the Institute of Economics and Statistics, Oxford University, Oxford, England. April 24, 1972. (Mimeographed.)

6. Brunner, Karl and Meltzer, Allan H. "Friedman's Monetary Theory." **Journal of Political Economy.** September/October, 1972, pp. 837-851.

7. Burns, Arthur F. "Letter From Chairman Burns to Senator Proxmire." **Monthly Review: Federal Reserve Bank of New York.** November 1973, pp. 266-272.

8. Carlson, Keith M. "Monetary and Fiscal Actions in Macroeconomic Models." **Review: Federal Reserve Bank of St. Louis.** January 1974, pp. 8-18.

9. Cooper, Phillip J. & Nelson, Charles R. "The Ex Ante Prediction Performance of the St. Louis and FRB-MIT-PENN Econometric Models and Some Results on Composite Predictors." **Journal of Money, Credit and Banking.** February 1975, pp. 1-32.

10. Cooper, R.N. & Brainard, W.C. "Empirical Monetary Macroeconomics: What Have We Learned in the Last 25 Years?" **American Economic Review.** May 1975, pp. 167-175.

11. Crews, Joseph M. "Econometric Models: The Monetarist and Non-Monetarist Views Compared." **Monthly Review: Federal Reserve Bank of Richmond.** February 1973, pp. 3-12.

12. Davidson, Paul. "A Keynesian View of Friedman's Theoretical

Framework for Monetary Analysis.'' **Journal of Political Economy.** September/October 1972, pp. 864-882.

13. DeLeeuw, Frank and Gramlich, Edward M. ''The Channels of Monetary Policy.'' **Federal Reserve Bulletin.** June 1969, pp. 472-491.

14. _____. ''The Federal Reserve-MIT Econometric Model.'' **Federal Reserve Bulletin,** January 1968, pp. 11-40.

15. Dew, Kurt. ''Practical Monetarism and the Stock Market.'' **Economic Review: Federal Reserve Bank of San Francisco.** Spring 1978, pp. 39-53.

16. Elliot, J.W. ''The Influence of Monetary and Fiscal Actions on Total Spending: The St. Louis Total Spending Equation Revisited.'' **Journal of Money, Credit and Banking.** May 1975, pp. 181-192.

17. Fand, David I. ''A Monetarist Model of the Monetary Process.'' **Journal of Finance,** May 1970, pp. 275-289.

18. _____''Some Issues in Monetary Economics.'' **Review: Federal Reserve Bank of St. Louis.** January 1970, pp. 11-26.

19. Friedman, Milton. ''A Theoretical Framework for Monetary Analysis.'' **Journal of Political Economy.** March/April 1970, pp. 193-238.

20. _____''Comments on the Critics.'' **Journal of Political Economy.** September/October, 1972, pp. 906-950.

21. _____ **The Counter-Revolution in Monetary Theory.** Washington, D.C.: The Institute of Economic Affairs, 1970.

22. _____ and Meiselman, David. ''The Relative Stability of Monetary Velocity and the Investment Multiplier in the United States, 1897-1958,'' in **Monetary Economics: Controversies in Theory and Policy,** ed. Jonas Prager, New York: Random House, 1971, pp. 204-215.

23. Gramlich, Edward M. ''The Role of Money in Economic Activity: Complicated or Simple?'' **Business Economics.** September 1969, pp. 21-26.

24. Johnson, Harry G. ''The Keynesian Revolution and the Monetarist Counter Revolution.'' **American Economic Review: Papers and Proceeding of the Eighty-Third Annual Meeting of the American Economic Association.** May 1971, pp. 1-14.

25. Hamburger, Michael J. ''The Impact of Monetary Variables: A Survey of Recent Econometric Literature,'' in **Essay in Domestic and International Finance,** ed. Federal Resrve Bank of New York, New York: Federal Reserve Bank of New York, 1969, pp. 37-49.

26. Humphrey, Thomas M. ''The Monetarist Non-Monetarist Debate: Some 19th Century Controversies Revisited.'' **Monthly Review: Federal Reserve Bank of Richmond.** December 1970, pp. 2-6.

27. Hunt II, Lacy H. ''Money Stock-Attention to Series Increases as Link to Economy Discussed.'' **Business Review: Federal Reserve Bank of Dallas.** September 1972, pp. 1-11.

28. Laidler, David. ''Money and Money Income: An Essay on the Tran-

smission Mechanism." **Journal of Monetary Economics.** April 1978, pp. 151-191.

29. Mehra, Y.P. "Is Money Exogenous in Money-Demand Equation?" **Journal of Political Economy.** April 1978, pp. 211-228.

30. Modigliani, F. "Monetary Policy and Consumption: Linkages via Interest Rate and Wealth Effects in the FMP Model," in **Consumer Spending and Monetary Policy: The Linkages.** Boston, Mass.: The Federal Reserve Bank of Boston, 1971, pp. 9-84.

31. Park, Yung, C. "Some Current Issues on the Transmission Process of Monetary Policy." **IMF: Staff Papers.** March 1972, pp. 1-45.

32. Patinkin, Don. "Friedman on the Quantity Theory and Keynesian Economics." **Journal of Political Economy.** September/October 1972, pp. 883-905.

33. Pierce, James L. and Thomson, Thomas D. "Short-Term Financial Models at the Federal Reserve Board." **Journal of Finance.** May 1974, pp. 349-357.

34. Poole, William. **Money and the Economy: A Monetarist View.** Reading, Massachusetts: Addison-Wesley Publishing Company, 1978.

35. Spencer, Roger W. "Channels of Monetary Influence: A Survey." **Review: Federal Reserve Bank of St. Louis.** November 1974, pp. 8-26.

36. Tobin, James. "Friedman's Theoretical Framework." **Journal of Political Economy.** September/October 1972, pp. 852-863.

37. Teigen, Ronald L. "A Critical Look at Monetarist Economics." **Review: Federal Reserve Bank of St. Louis.** January 1972, pp. 10-25.

CHAPTER IX

Theory of Monetary Indicators And Targets

The formulation of an optimum monetary policy would be simple and straightforward for the monetary authority if it knew completely and precisely how certain economic variables are related to a nation's economy and/or if there existed a short time lag between monetary actions and their effect on the economy. If the time lag were short, the authority could experiment with various courses of action to come up with the right one.

The theory of monetary indicators and targets is an attempt to describe how the optimum monetary policy can be pursued where the monetary authority has partial knowledge of the economic structure, and monetary actions affect the economy only after a long lag.

The theory of monetary indicators and targets is outlined in terms of:

    A. Definition of Indicators and Targets
    B. Optimal Policy Under Partial Knowledge and Long Lags
    C. Review of Important Candidates for Indicators and Targets

INDICATORS

Indicators are those variables that best describe the stance of the policy, i.e., whether the current policy is having an expansionary or contractionary effect on the economy. If the interest rate is an ideal indicator, an increase will mean that the policy is contractionary, and vice versa. It is like a speedometer in a car that tells the driver the rate at which he is driving the car. An indicator, as the name implies, indicates to the monetary authority what effect its policy is producing.

One may argue, "Why does the monetary authority want to know the stance of the policy?" The monetary authority knows what its intentions are and what the Manager of the System Open Market account is doing. Intentions are not always a true reflection of the thrust of a policy. Assume that the authority wants to pursue an expansionary policy and that the money stock is rising at the rate of 5%. The authority believes that its objective can be fulfilled by raising the growth rate of the money stock to 6%. Suppose that it succeeds in hitting the target of 6%. Does it mean that the authority has achieved its objective of pursuing an expansionary policy? Not necessarily. The growth in the money stock can be caused by both policy and nonpolicy variables. A policy is considered expansionary only if the increase in the money stock is caused by policy variables. An indicator helps to make this determination. Suppose further that the interest rate is a good indicator. When the target of the money stock was hit, the interest rate rose from 8 to 9%. This means that the monetary authority failed to achieve the expansion in the economy as intended by its policy. It also reveals that the growth in the money stock would have been even higher had the Manager not intervened. This is evidenced by the rise in the interest rate in the face of a rising rate of growth in the money stock.

The monetary authority can do without an indicator if the Manager consistently (week after week) buys or sells securities because buying of securities is considered expansive and selling them, contractive. But the Manager cannot buy or sell consistently. He must change from a buyer to a seller and vice versa constantly as nonpolicy variables put targets off the intended track.

An ideal indicator satisfies the following conditions:

1. It is responsive to policy instruments (discount rate, reserve requirements, etc.) and exhibits the response within a short interval.

2. It is not affected by nonpolicy variables (variables not controlled by the monetary authority) and if affected, the effects of nonpolicy variables are amenable to separation from those of policy variables (policy instruments). Otherwise, the effect of a given policy will be misinterpreted.

3. It is associated with economic activity (or ultimate targets) in a predictable manner.

TARGETS

Targets are goals that the authority attempts to achieve in any given period. They are of three kinds: (1) operating, (2) intermediate and (3) ultimate.

Operating Targets

An operating target is an economic variable that the monetary authority attempts to control directly in its day-to-day operations and that satisfies the following conditions:

   i. Its magnitude can be accurately measured over a very short period of time.

   ii. The monetary authority can easily control it by manipulating policy instruments. If the authority cannot control an operating target variable, it cannot control intermediate and ultimate target variables either, because it uses the operating target variable to regulate the other two. The operating target variable is affected by both policy and nonpolicy variables. If nonpolicy variables produce an undesired change in the operating target variable, the authority corrects it by adjusting policy variables.

   iii. It is related to intermediate target variables in a somewhat known fashion.

Intermediate Targets

An intermediate target is an economic variable that the monetary authority attempts to control indirectly through operating target variables in order to produce certain changes in ultimate target variables. It should satisfy the following conditions:

   i. It is affected by changes in operating target variables. If nonpolicy variables cause an undesired change in it, the authority corrects it by adjusting operating target variables. (Like operating target variables, it can be affected by both policy and nonpolicy variables.)

   ii. Its magnitude can be precisely measured and is quickly affected by changes in operating target variables. An intermediate target variable is used to influence an ultimate target variable. The policy may be considered to be on the right path if the intermediate target is hit.

iii. It is related to the ultimate target variables in the sense that the policy designed to produce a certain change in an intermediate target variable must, in turn, produce a desired change in the ultimate target variable.

Ultimate Targets

An ultimate target is a final goal, such as reducing unemployment to a certain level, raising the growth rate of the economy to a certain value or maintaining balance-of-payments equilibrium. Ultimate targets are discussed in detail in Chapter XII.

OPTIMAL POLICY UNDER PARTIAL KNOWLEDGE AND LONG LAGS

The theory of monetary indicators and targets states that the best way to pursue the policy, under conditons of partial knowledge of economic structure and long lags between monetary actions and ultimate targets, is to aim policy instruments at operating targets in order to bring about certain changes in intermediate and, consequently, in ultimate targets (Diagram 9-1). By doing this, the monetary authority can observe the effectiveness of a policy at different stages of the transmission process. If policy instruments are aimed directly at ultimate targets, the authority will be operating in the dark for some time. Indicators can help to determine what effects the policy is producing on ultimate targets much before the effects are fully realized and are observable. Step-by-step, the policy can be pursued somewhat along the following lines:

DIAGRAM 9-1

WORKING OF THE POLICY VIA INDICATORS AND TARGETS

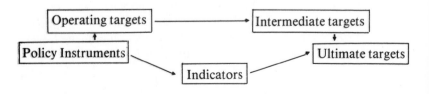

   i. Establish ultimate targets.

  ii. Based upon judgment and experience, establish appropriate values of intermediate targets required to reach desired ultimate targets.

 iii. Establish appropriate values of operating targets (again on the basis of judgment and experience) needed to hit desired intermediate targets.

 iv. Direct policy instruments toward establishing operating targets.

  v. Determine whether intermediate targets are hit precisely. If not, readjust operating targets. Before making any change, be sure enough time has elapsed to allow intermediate targets to respond to variations in operating targets.

 vi. While observing intermediate targets, determine, also, whether the policy is producing the right effect. This can be done by looking at indicators. Here, too, sufficient time must be allowed before making any determination. If indicators show that the policy is not producing the desired effect, intermediate targets have to be revised. The change in intermediate targets would, once again, require adjustment in operating targets.

Following is an example: Suppose that the current rate of economic growth of a nation is 2 percent and the monetary authority wants to raise it to a level of 4 percent. The 4 percent rate of growth becomes the ultimate target. Assume further that the rate of increase in the money stock (positively related to the growth rate) is the intermediate target; free reserves (total reserves minus borrowings from Federal Reserve Banks—positively related to the money stock), the operating target; and the interest rate (negatively related to economic growth), the monetary indicator. Based upon judgment and experience, the authority determines that the ultimate target—a 4 percent rate of economic growth—can be reached if the rate of increase in the money stock is raised from the present rate of, say, 4 percent to 6 percent. The 6 percent rate of increase in the money stock becomes the intermediate target. Again, based upon judgment and experience, the authority determines that the intermediate target will be hit if free reserves are raised from the current level of, say $1 billion to $1.5 billion. Free reserves of $1.5 billion become the operating target.

As mentioned earlier, the operating target is affected not only by policy instruments but, also, by nonpolicy variables. Free reserves, the operating target in this case, can be affected by nonpolicy variables such as float, currency in circulation and treasury balances at commercial banks. In order to hit the operating target, the monetary authority reviews forecasts of various nonpolicy variables and their possible effects on the target variable, and then lays down a week-by-week (or day-by-day) plan of buying and selling securities for a certain period. The plan calls for selling a certain amount of securities in the weeks free reserves are expected to rise above the target level and buying a certain amount in the weeks they are expected to fall below it.

After the policy is pursued for a while, the monetary authority looks at the intermediate target variable (the rate of increase in the money stock) to find out how well the policy is proceeding toward that target. Since the authority does not have complete knowledge about the relationship between the operating and the intermediate targets, it is possible it may overshoot or undershoot the intermediate target. In either event, an adjustment in the operating target is needed.

Since the monetary authority does not have perfect knowledge about the relationship between the intermediate and ultimate targets, hitting the intermediate target is no assurance that the ultimate target will be met. Ultimate targets are affected only after a long lag. Therefore, for sometime, the monetary authority will be operating in the dark without knowing whether or not the policy is generating the right effect. To avoid this, the authority will look at the interest rate (indicator in this case) to determine the thrust of the policy (or the actual effect of its policy as opposed to the intended effect). In this example, an expansionary effect is needed because the goal is to raise the economic growth.

Suppose further that after the new policy is put into effect, the interest rate, instead of declining, goes up from 7 to 8 percent. The rise in the interest rate implies that the effect of the policy is contractive and not expansive as intended. It also means that the increase in the rate of growth in the money stock has been caused by market forces and not by the action of the monetary authority.

Upon discovery that the policy is having a contractionary effect on the ultimate target variable, the authority can raise the target of the money stock to, say, 7 percent to bring about the desired expansionary effect. This also requires a readjustment of the operating target. If the authority had not used the incidator, it would not have learned that the policy is producing the undesired effect until after it had pursued it for a longer period of time. At that time, it could have been too late to correct the situation. Thus, by following the procedure outlined in the theory of monetary indicators and targets, the authority pursues the policy effectively even though the economic structure is not fully known and long lags exist between monetary actions and ultimate targets.

It should be borne in mind that it is not necessary for an indicator to be different from an intermediate target.[1] A given variable can do the job of both, provided the effect of the policy on that variable can be separated from those other variables. In this case, however, the monetary authority will eliminate the effects of nonpolicy variables before using a variable as an indicator.

The theory of monetary indicators and targets has been criticized by some economists. The main criticism is that, though indicators are useful in pursuing the optimal policy, reliable indicators are not known at the present time. Without them, critics say, the theory cannot work. The proponents of the theory recognize this problem and believe that, with further research, reliable indicators can be found. Furthermore, even without reliable indicators, the policy can be pursued better when the procedure is followed. Proponents contend that by going through operating and intermediate targets, the monetary authority does not operate completely in the dark as is the case when policy instruments are aimed directly at ultimate targets.

IMPORTANT CANDIDATES FOR INDICATORS AND TARGETS

It is difficult to find a variable that can be considered a perfect indicator or target. Each variable has points of both strength and weakness. This section reviews these points for each of the important candidates for indicators and targets.

Indicators

Variables that are widely mentioned as candidates for an indicator

are (a) money stock, (b) interest rates and (c) borrowings from Federal
Reserve Banks.

Money Stock

Its points of strength as an indicator are:
   i. It is responsive to policy instruments.
  ii. It is related to the economic activity in a predictable manner.
      Those who make this claim do so on the ground that there
      exists a close association between the money stock and econ-
      omic activity. However, there are economists who argue that
      the close association does not imply that economic activity
      can be predicted from the money stock. This may be the case
      if the effect runs only in one way, i.e., from the money stock
      to economic activity. But the effect also runs from economic
      activity to the money stock. An increase in economic activity
      can increase the demand for loans and, consequently, the
      amount of money created by banks.
The opponents of the money stock as an indicator point out its
weaknesses as follows:
   i. It is affected by nonpolicy variables such as actions taken by
      banks and the public, and their effects cannot be isolated
      from those of policy instruments.
  ii. There is a long lag between a change in operating targets and
      its effect on the money stock. Models of the Board of Gover-
      nors of the Federal Reserve System suggest that the effect of
      operating targets on the money stock may take on the order
      of six to eight months to work themselves out fully.[2] Policy-
      makers cannot afford to wait that long to know the effect of
      their policy.
 iii. The weekly, monthly and quarterly data of the money stock
      are estimates and not precise measurements.[3] This is because
      a part of the money stock consists of deposits held at non-
      member banks, which report their statistics only for two to
      four days of each year, in contrast to member banks, which
      report daily. However, Depository Institutions Deregulation
      and Monetary Control Act of 1980 will enable the Federal
      Reserve to have access to the data of deposits held at non-
      member banks the same way as it has with those of member

banks.

Interest Rates

Points of strength of interest rates as an indicator are:
  i. Interest rates are responsive to policy instruments, though long-term interest rates take a little longer to respond than short term rates.
  ii. They are related to economic activity, though their relationship is not precisely known. (Keynesians believe, as discussed in Chapter VIII, that interest rates are a crucial link between the money stock and economic activity.)
  iii. Some interest rates such as the Federal funds rate are readily observable.

Points of weakness of interest rates as an indicator are:
  i. Interest rates are influenced by nonpolicy variables such as demand for money, the effects of which cannot be isolated. At the time of revival or prosperity in a business cycle, rising interest rates reflect a growing demand for credit. If at that time interest rates are used as an indicator, the policy will be wrongly interpreted as restrictive.
  ii. Some economists such as Meltzer believe that we know very little about what causes changes in short-term interest rates.[4] Therefore, if changes in such interest rates are used to judge the stance of a policy, policymakers may be misled.
  iii. There are a large number of interest rates in any developed economy. Each interest rate exhibits the money conditon of specific institutions. For example, the Treasury bill rate is an indicator of the money position of institutions such as commercial banks, corporations and others that hold bills as liquid reserves. It is hard to determine which interest rate (or combination of them) can be used as an indicator.

Borrowing from Federal Reserve Banks

Points of strength of borrowings from the Federal Reserve as an indicator are:
  i. The data are readily available.
  ii. An increase in borrowings from the Federal Reserve is a good indication of a contractionary policy because banks typically

manage their affairs without resorting to the discount window
except for necessary contingencies and, once in debt, tend to
pay back promptly. By the same token, a decrease in borrowings is an indication of an expansionary policy.

The points of weakness as an indicator are:

i. They are affected by nonpolicy variables such as changes in
the demand for loans.

ii. There are banks that are reluctant to borrow at the discount
window even at the time of contingency and prefer to adjust
their reserve positions in other ways including, when necessary, restrictions on loans to customers. As a result, the effect
of a contractionary policy may not fully show up in borrowings at the discount window.

Targets

As explained earlier, there are three types of targets: (a) operating
targets, (b) intermediate targets and (c) ultimate targets.

Operating Targets

The important variables commonly mentioned as candidates for an
operating target are: (i) Federal funds rate, (ii) Treasury bill rate, (iii)
free reserves, (iv) RPDs and (v) monetary base.

Federal Funds rate: The Federal funds rate is the rate at which one
bank lends its funds to another, usually overnight. The loan is transac-
ted mainly through the transfer of funds from the account of the lending bank to that of the borrowing one at a Federal Reserve Bank (or
Banks).

There are many advantages in using the Federal funds rate as an
operating target. The rate is available instantaneously. Its preliminary
figure is the final figure. It is an operationally feasible target since the
Federal Reserve can easily reach it by feeding reserves into and out of
the market—feeding reserves into the market, if the rate is above the
target level, and vice versa. According to Schadrack, the Federal
Reserve has the ability to hit a target based on weekly average of the
Federal funds rate.[5]

Nevertheless, it has a disadvantage of not being related to the
money stock (an important intermediate target) in a predictable way.
It is estimated that forecasts of growth rates of the money stock from

Federal funds rates for one quarter ahead have an average absolute error of 2.1 percent which declines to 1.2 percent when forecasts are made six months ahead.[6] The relation between the Federal funds rate and long-term interest rates (other important intermediate targets) is not definitive. The reaction time—the time for long-term interest rates to respond to a change in the Federal funds rate—may be quite short or may extend over several months.

Treasury bill rate: There are certain advantages in using the Treasury bill rate as an operating target. The information on it is readily available and the Federal Reserve can control it with virtually any degree of accuracy it desires. It is closely related to short-term and intermediate-interest rates.[7] However, its relationship with the money stock and with long-term interest rates (intermediate targets) is neither precise nor predictable.

Free Reserves: Free reserves (total reserves minus borrowings from Federal Reserve Banks) are a good operating target because reliable data are available after 9 to 14 days, and the Federal Reserve has a fair amount of control over them. However, if the Federal Reserve controls free reserves it has to allow interest rates to fluctuate. The problem stemming from this is whether the benefits derived from the control over free reserves is worth the price the economy would have to pay in the way of fluctuating interest rates. Moreover, free reserves are related neither to the money stock nor to interest rates in a predictable way. According to Schadrack, forecasts of growth rates of the money stock from free reserves for three months as well as for six months have an average absolute error of 2.1 percent.[8]

RPDs: RPDs (reserves available to support private nonbank deposits) are equal to total reserves minus reserves required to support government and net interbank deposits. Like free reserves, reliable estimates of RPDs are available after 9 to 14 days. The Federal Reserve can control them better than free reserves because RPDs exclude required reserves for net interbank and U.S. Government deposits. But the relationship between RPDs and the money stock (intermediate target) is not tight and predictable. This is because large negotiable certificates of deposit (which are not included in the definition of M-1A, M-1B or M_2 but are required to be supported by reserves) and excess reserves (which are part of RPDs) vary from time to time in an unpredictable way. The relationship between RPDs and interest rates (other intermediate targets) is not definitive either.

Monetary base: Economists such as Allan Meltzer recommend the use of the monetary base as an operating target because its weekly data can be estimated with greater reliability than other operating targets such as free reserves, and the Federal Reserve can hit its weekly targets with as much accuracy as other target variables.[9] (Schadrack, however, questions the ability of the Federal Reserve to hit weekly targets of the base because of the difficulty in predicting changes in borrowings at the discount window and the volume of float.[10]) Moreover, their studies show that there exists a close relationship between the base and the money stock, implying that the latter can be predicted from the former with a reasonable degree of accuracy.

Intermediate Targets

The most widely discussed intermediate targets are (i) the money stock and (ii) interest rates. As discussed earlier, a variable can be used both as an indicator and as a target.

Money stock: There is considerable controversy regarding the use of the money stock as an intermediate target. Those who argue for it claim that the Federal Reserve can control it quite effectively by controlling the monetary base,[11] and is related to income in a fairly predictable fashion.

Those who argue against the use of the money stock as an intermediate target claim that it is difficult for the Federal Reserve to hit its short term (weekly, monthly and quarterly) targets. The Federal Reserve can do it, they claim, if such targets are allowed to average out over a period of six months or more and the Manager is willing to move operating targets sufficiently and vigorously to accomplish them.[12] They don't accept the argument that the money stock is related to income in a predictable fashion. Furthermore, they add, if the authority decides to use it, which money stock series should be used (M-1A, M-1B or any other series). At times these series diverge from each other.

Interest rates: Economists also argue over the use of interest rates as an intermediate target. Those who argue for their use claim that their data are instantly available and the effect of a monetary action is transmitted to the economy through them. They add that if the policy is focused only on the money stock there would be sharp fluctuations in interest rates, which would disrupt economic decisions. Many decision units rely heavily on the interest rate structure as a source of information about what is happening in the credit market and to the economy. Considerations of balance of payments, mortgage markets and security market speculations also require that a certain amount of attention be given to interest rates.

The group that argues against the use of interest rates as an intermediate target does so on the ground that the Federal Reserve cannot effectively control economic activity through them because data reported on them are of nominal interest rates (market interest rates) while it is real interest rates (market interest rate minus the anticipated rate of inflation) that affects economic activity.[13] Moreover, studies show that changes in real output are not as closely related to interest rates as money.[14]

SUMMARY

The theory of monetary indicators and targets shows how the optimal policy can be pursued where the monetary authority has partial knowledge of the economic structure and monetary actions affect the economy after a long lag.

Indicators are those variables that best describe the stance of the policy. Targets are objectives that the monetary authority seeks to achieve. There are three types of targets—operating, intermediate and ultimate. Operating targets are those that the monetary authority attempts to control directly in its day-to-day operation. Intermediate targets fall in the transmission process between operating and ultimate targets. The authority controls them indirectly through operating targets in order to produce certain changes in ultimate targets. Ultimate targets are final goals.

According to this theory, the best way to pursue a monetary policy is to direct policy instruments to operating targets in order to bring about certain changes in intermediate and, consequently, in ultimate targets. By doing this, the monetary authority can observe the effectiveness of its policy at different stages of the transmission process. If policy instruments are aimed directly at ultimate targets the authority, for long periods of time, will not know whether or not targets will be reached because ultimate targets are affected after a long lag. Indicators should be used to determine what effects the policy is producing on ultimate targets long before the effects have impacted fully on ultimate targets. In this way, if a policy is not producing the right effects, the authority can change it before it is too late.

FOOTNOTES

[1]William G. Dewald, "A Review of the Conference on Targets and Indicators of Monetary Policy," in **Targets and Indicators of Monetary Policy,** ed. Karl Brunner (San Francisco, California: Chandler Publishing Company, 1969), p. 322.

[2]Richard G. Davis, "Implementing Open Market Policy with Monetary Aggregate Objectives," **Monthly Review: Federal Reserve Bank of New York** (July 1973), p. 180.

[3]"Letter From Chairman Burns to Senator Proxmire," **Monthly Review: Federal Reserve Bank of New York** (November 1973), p. 269.

[4]Allan H. Meltzer, "The Role of Money in National Economic Policy," in **Controlling Monetary Aggregates** (Boston, Mass.: Federal Reserve Bank of Boston, 1969), p. 27.

[5]F.C. Schadrack, "Some Issues in Monetary Control," New York: Federal Reserve Bank of New York, April 1974, p. 7. (Mimeographed.)

[6]**Ibid.,** pp. 12-13.

[7]Warren Smith, "A Neo-Keynesian View of Monetary Policy," in **Controlling Monetary Aggregates,** p. 122.

[8]Schadrack, pp. 12-13.

[9]Allan H. Meltzer, "Controlling Money," **Review: Federal Reserve Bank of St. Louis** (May 1969), pp. 18 and 20.

[10]Schadrack, p. 6.

[11]David I. Fand, "Some Issue in Monetary Economics," **Review: Federal Reserve Bank of St. Louis** (January 1970), p. 15.

[12]Richard G. Davis, "Implementing Market Policy With Monetary Aggregate Objectives," **Monthly Review: Federal Reserve Bank of New York** (July 1973), p. 182.

[13]Michael W. Keran, "Selecting a Monetary Indicator - Evidence from the U.S. and Other Developed Countries," **Review: Federal Reserve Bank of St. Louis** (September 1970), pp. 14-15.

[14]William G. Dewald, p. 318.

QUESTIONS FOR REVIEW

1. Describe in brief the theory of monetary indicators and targets.
2. What do we mean by a monetary indicator? Explain the important conditions for an ideal indicator.
3. Describe different types of targets. What are the important conditions for an ideal target variable of each type?
4. Explain briefly the reasons for conducting a policy via indicators and targets.
5. Discuss points of strength and weakness of two important variables as a

candidate for an indicator.

6. Discuss the views of Keynesians and Monetarists as to the use of the money stock and interest rates as an intermediate target.

7. "Why do policymakers want to know the thrust of the policy? They know what their intentions are and what they are doing in any given period." Comment.

8. "The theory of monetary indicators and targets cannot work if reliable indicators are not available." Comment.

9. Discuss each of the following as a candidate for an operating target:
   A Federal funds rate
   B Treasury bill rate
   C Free reserves
   D RPDs

10. Evaluate the use of borrowings from Federal Reserve Banks as an indicator.

SUGGESTED FURTHER READING

1. Board of Governors of the Federal Reserve System. **Improving the Monetary Aggregates: Report of the Advisory Committee on Monetary Statistics.** Washington, D.C.: The Federal Reserve System, 1976.

2. Brunner, Karl (ed.). **Targets and Indicators of Monetary Policy.** San Francisco, California: Chandler Publishing Company, 1969.

3. Carr, Jack L. & Smith, Lawrence B. "A Suggestion for a New Monetary Indicator." **Journal of Monetary Economics.** July 1975, pp. 363-368.

4. Davis, Richard G. "Implementing Market Policy With Monetary Aggregate Objectives." **Monthly Review: Federal Reserve Bank of New York.** July 1973, pp. 170-183.

5. Duro, Lorraine E. "A Measure of Monetary Policy." **Economic Review: Federal Reserve Bank of Cleveland.** January-February 1973, pp. 19-30.

6. Federal Reserve Bank of Boston. **Controlling Aggregates II: The Implementation.** Boston, Mass.: Federal Reserve Bank of Boston, 1973.

7. Friedman, Benjamin M. "Targets, Instruments and Indicators of Monetary Policy." **Journal of Monetary Economics.** October 1975, pp. 443-473.

8. Froewiss, Kenneth C. and Judd, John P. "Optimal Control and Money Targets: Should the Fed Look at Everything?" **Economic Review: Federal Reserve Bank of San Francisco.** Fall 1979, pp. 38-49.

9. Gambs, Carl M. "Federal Reserve Intermediate Targets: Money or the Monetary Base." **Economic Review: Federal Reserve Bank of Kansas City.** January 1980, pp. 3-15.

10. Hamburger, Michael J. "Behavior of the Money Stock: Is There a

Puzzle?" **Journal of Monetary Economics.** July 1977, pp. 265-288.

11. Higgins, Bryon. "Weighting Multiple Monetary Aggregate Targets." **Economic Review: Federal Reserve Bank of Kansas City.** February 1978, pp. 3-13.

12. Holmes, Alan R. "Open Market Operations and the Monetary and Credit Aggregates - 1971." **Federal Reserve Bulletin.** April 1972, pp. 340-362.

13. Judd, John P. and Scadding, John L. "Conducting Effective Monetary Policy: The Role of Operating Instruments." **Economic Review: Federal Reserve Bank of San Francisco.** Fall 1979, pp. 23-37.

14. Keran, Michael W. "Selecting a Monetary Indicator-Evidence from the U.S. and Other Developed Countries." **Review: Federal Reserve Bank of St. Louis.** September 1970, pp. 8-18.

15. Laufenberg, D.E. "Reserve Measures as Operating Variables of Monetary Supply: An Empirical Analysis." **Journal of Finance.** June 1976, pp. 853-864.

16. Mitchell, George W. "Indicators of Monetary Policy," in **Monetary Economics: Controversies in Theory and Policy,** ed. Jonas Prager, New York: Random House, 1971, pp. 223-232.

17. Saving, Thomas R. "Monetary-Policy Targets and Indicators." **Journal of Political Economy.** August 1967, pp. 446-459.

CHAPTER X

Theory of Inflation

Inflation is a continuing rise in the general price level. It is usually measured by the consumer price index and the implicit price deflator for gross national product.

TYPES OF INFLATION

There are different types of inflation. The ones most often discussed are: true inflation, creeping inflation, suppressed inflation, hyperinflation and stagflation.

True Inflation

Keynes defines true inflation as a situation in which an increase in aggregate demand fails to increase output. This occurs when the elasticity of output with respect to aggregate demand is zero. Keynes believes that there is a point in the short run at which this can occur.

Creeping (Gradual) Inflation

Creeping inflation is a situation where the general price level is rising slowly but persistently even when aggregate demand is not rising rapidly.

Suppressed Inflation

Suppressed inflation is a situation where a rise in the price level is suppressed by government decrees such as wage and price controls.

Hyperinflation (Galloping Inflation)

Hyperinflation is a situation where prices rise to astronomical heights. It is usually the result of the aftermath of war, as was the

German experience after both world wars.

Stagflation

A rising general price level in the face of high unemployment and excess production capacity is described as stagflation.

THEORY OF INFLATION

Controversy exists between Keynesians and Monetarists as to what causes inflation, how its transmission mechanism works and how it can be controlled.

Monetarist View

All economists agree that inflation is both a short and a long term phenomenon. Monetarists, however, emphasize the latter.

Causes of inflation

Monetarists claim that although short run inflation may have many sources, long term inflation is always a monetary phenomenon. It arises when the money supply expands more rapidly than output. They reject the notion that long run inflation can be caused by non-monetary factors such as expansive fiscal actions, cost push influences, food and fuel shortages, etc. Such factors, they say, can raise prices of certain products. But, unless accompanied by an excessive increase in the money supply, the rise in the prices of those commodities will be offset eventually by declines in prices of other commodities, leaving the average price level unchanged.

Monetarists regard the quantity of money as an exogenous variable, implying that the monetary growth is an independent causal variable governing the rate of inflation. The flow of causation runs one way from money to excess demand (excess of aggregate demand over aggregate supply) to prices and not the other way around.

Stagflation, in the Monetarist's view, occurs particularly when inflationary expectations are very strong, that is, people are convinced that prices will continue to rise. In such a situation, inflationary expectations will continue to put upward pressure on prices even when aggregate demand is falling. (As will be explained in the next section, inflation is affected not only by excess demand but also by inflationary expectations resulting from a continued rise in the money supply.)

Transmission mechanism

In the Monetarist theoretical framework, the transmission mechanism of inflation works as shown in Diagram 10-1. Excessive monetary growth affects first excess demand and then current inflation. The effect also runs from past inflation and/or current information to inflationary expectations and then to current inflation. Current inflation, after an interval of one period of time, becomes past inflation.

The inflationary process works through two lags: (i) price adjustment lag and (ii) price expectation lag. Price adjustment lag refers to a lag between excess demand and inflation. This lag occurs because businessmen respond to the excess demand by increasing output and depleting inventories first and then by raising prices. When output expands, resources become increasingly scarce relative to demand. The result is that factor prices and, consequently, output prices rise.

DIAGRAM 10-1

INFLATIONARY TRANSMISSION MECHANISM AS VIEWED BY MONETARISTS

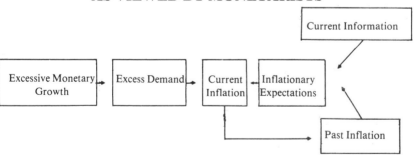

The price expectation lag refers to a lag between inflationary expectations and the current rate of inflation. The current rate of inflation is believed to be influenced by inflationary expectations of the previous period. The lag occurs because people cannot predict the future with absolute certainty. Were they able to do so, the expected rate of inflation would always be the one that actually occurs. The length of this lag depends upon how inflationary expectations are formed.

Inflationary expectations are formed on the basis of either one of two hypotheses: the adaptive expectation hypothesis and the rational expectation hypothesis. The adaptive hypothesis states that expectations about the future rate of inflation is formed from past experience. People observe the difference between expected and actual rates of past inflationary periods and then revise their expected rate by some fraction of that difference. The rational hypothesis states that people base their inflationary expectations at least as much on current information about a variety of developments such as the money-supply growth rate and imminent changes in the political administration as on past inflation rates. In other words, under the rational hypothesis people utilize all of the relevant information to form expectations about the future rate of inflation, whereas under the adaptive hypothesis they look at only a small part of the total relevant information, that is, past inflation rates.

The length of the price expectation lag depends upon how far back people go and how much weight they assign to the price experience of the distant past in formulating their expectations. The more weight that they assign to the distant past, the longer will be the lag. Since under the adaptive hypothesis more weight is assigned to past inflation rates than under the rational hypothesis, the price expectation lag under the adaptive hypothesis will be longer.

Monetarists are divided on the issue of whether expectations are formed adaptively or rationally, though the present trend is towards the acceptance of the latter (e.g., Robert E. Lucas, Thomas J. Sargent & Neil Wallace, R.J. Barro and John H. Kareken[1]).

Cure of inflation

Monetarists say that since inflation is caused by excessive monetary growth, it can be controlled by restraining monetary expansion. This prescription has a number of implications:

    i. There is no quick remedy for inflation. Because of the price adjustment and price expectation lags, it will take a long time to control inflation.

    ii. Inflation can be controlled only at the expense of a temporary recession or, at least, a marked retardation in the expansion of the economy. This is because a restrictive monetary policy reduces output and employment first and then prices.

iii. Direct controls will reduce inflation if they are accompanied by contractionary fiscal and monetary policies. The elimination of inflation requires the eradication of inflationary expectations. The only way to eradicate expectations is to create a recession. (This will cause the actual rate of inflation to fall below the expected rate and, consequently, create a downward revision of the latter.) If controls are not accompanied by contractionary fiscal and monetary policies, excess demand will be suppressed but not curtailed; people will expect prices to rise after controls are lifted.

iv. The economy may experience stagflation. This is because the restrictive policy dampens inflationary expectations only after a considerable lag. When recession occurs as a result of a contractionary policy, prices may continue to rise, at least for awhile, because inflationary expectations are not yet fully curbed.

In addition to slowing down the monetary growth, Milton Friedman, a leading Monetarist, advocates the use of indexation to control inflation. Indexation (indexing, monetary correction or escalator clause) is a plan whereby all deferred payments such as wages, salaries, rents and interest and principal payments are expressed in dollars adjusted for the rate of inflation (a 10 percent rise in the cost of living index will automatically raise wages by a like amount when wages are indexed, for example).

Proponents of indexation claim that it is not a cure for inflation but it would make it easier to terminate inflation once it gets under way. They argue that the Federal Government is the real culprit because it is usually the initial force contributing to an excessive increase in the money supply and, consequently, to inflation. The Federal Government causes an increase in the money supply when it meets the increased demand for expenditures to aid various sectors of the economy. The indexation of tax rates, interest and principal payments on Government securities, and of wages and pensions of Government workers would increase the will of the Federal Government to fight against inflation. As it stands now, the Government benefits in many ways from inflation. A rise in wages resulting from a rise in prices, for example, pushes people into higher income brackets where tax rates are higher. Consequently, people wind up paying more in real taxes than was intended by the Congress. According to Milton Friedman, because of such automatic effects of inflation, the United States Government in 1973 realized something over $25 billion in the form of tax revenues that were never legislated by the Congress.[2] The Government also benefits from the sale of its bonds because the value of money is less at maturity than when issued. Moreover, the rise in the market interest rate caused by inflation does not raise the Government's burden of interest payments.

Supporters of indexation further argue that it will reduce the side effects that effective anti-inflation measures may have on output and employment. Employers will not be stuck with high wages (or excessive wage increases) under existing union contracts. Wages will decline (or their increases will moderate) as inflation recedes. Borrowers will not be stuck with high interest rate costs. Their cost on outstanding loans will decline as inflation tapers off. When economic activity and inflation are falling off, businessmen, who would have deferred capital investment in expectation of lower prices and lower interest rates, will not do so. Therefore, with an effective anti-inflationary policy, output and employment will not decline as much as they would if there were no indexation.

Critics argue that indexation discourages the fight against inflation. If we were all protected from inflation, no one would have an incentive to do anything about it. The Government would be under no pressure to take harsh action. William Fellner says that when an inflationary process begins to develop (which he calls the first phase of the inflationary process), indexation would exacerbate inflation.[3] Under such circumstances, he reasons, the Government would more likely accommodate inflation to head off a recession than curb it in the interest of price stability. Furthermore, it is possible that the general public may interpret the adoption of indexation to mean that the Government has given up the fight against inflation and is seeking to live with it. If such an attitude develops, it would further accelerate inflation by reinforcing inflationary expectations, he concludes.

Keynesian View

Causes of inflation

Keynesians claim that inflation originates from three sources: (i)

Expansionary forces (demand pull inflation), (ii) rise in input prices (cost push inflation) and (iii) concentrated industries (profit inflation).

Expansionary forces generally result from stimulative fiscal and monetary policies. There are instances, however, where they result from the private sector, e.g., expansionary forces caused by high capital spending on plant and equipment, housing booms and heavy consumer expenditures. In some countries export booms have also, at times, contributed to expansionary forces.

The rise in input prices results from labor union pressure to raise wages to a level beyond that warranted by the level of productivity; the tendency of raw material suppliers to form a monopoly or fix prices through collusion; and commodities shortages. The rise in input prices causes a rise in output prices. Empirical studies show that most firms set prices in accordance with some version of the cost-plus principle, i.e., average cost of production plus a margin of profit based on some predetermined target rate of return on investment.[4]

Concentrated (oligopoly or monopoly oriented) industries contribute to inflation through their tendency to respond to a rise in demand by increasing prices rather than output. Oligopolists are reluctant to lower prices even when demand is declining. They are afraid that they may give their rivals a wrong signal, i.e., they are cutting prices to capture a larger share of the market.

In recent years, some Keynesian economists have pointed out a number of other factors as a source of inflation. Nordhaus regards politics as a source of inflation. He argues that the party in power attempts to blow up the economy before election to gain the support of voters and deflates it afterwards, thereby causing a certain amount of inflation over the course of a political campaign.[5] Gordon says that government itself becomes a source of inflation when it surrenders to taxpayers' resistance against tax increases made necessary by an increase in expenditures and bows to the demands of beneficiaries of government programs who resist expenditure reductions.[6] J. Charles Partee regards many institutional arrangements as a source of inflation as they are geared to inflationary solutions to income distribution problems.[7] Minimum wage laws are escalated to keep pace with inflation, social security and some other retirement benefits are indexed to the cost of living, and public employees are given comparability increases without regard to productivity or value of output. Business policies, labor contract bargaining, and government programs are all set in terms of increasing money income to maintain purchasing power, rather than attempting to achieve similar results in real terms by reducing costs and, hence, price pressures.

Keynesians agree with Monetarists that inflation cannot continue for long without monetary nourishment. Neither strong unions nor concentrated industries can put upward pressure on prices unless their actions are accommodated by an increase in the money supply.

Keynesians claim that the money supply is an endogenous variable. It is affected both by the monetary authority and by economic activity. As the economy moves upward, the demand for loans increases. New loans create new demand deposits, thereby increasing the money supply. (In statistical theory, a variable is endogenous if it is jointly determined by other variables in the system. However, many Monetarists have chosen to call a variable endogenous only if its magnitude is not under the control of policy-makers.)

Keynesians explain stagflation as a cost push phenomenon. They say that the general price level can rise during a slump in the economy because of (i) the downward rigidity in wages, (ii) the lag between changes in the cost of production and prices of output, and (iii) the ability of concentrated industries to pass on increases in production costs to consumers. Wages are flexible in the upward direction and rigid in the downward direction. Such wage behavior, Keynesians claim, puts upward pressure on the cost or production even when the demand for goods and services is declining because some unions manage to increase wages.

The lag between changes in the cost of production and prices of output contributes to stagflation because today's price rises reflect yesterday's increases in the cost of production. Due to this phenomenon, prices may continue to coast uphill for awhile even after the recession ensues. The ability of concentrated industries to pass on the increase in the cost of production to consumers even during recession also contributes to stagflation. The cost per unit rises during recession due to sub-optimal utilization of fixed-cost production facilities and institutional difficulties in making any comparable offsetting savings on wages.

Transmission mechanism

The Keynesian transmission mechanism of inflation is shown in Diagram 10-2. Inflation originates from three sources: (i) expansionary forces, (ii) rise in input prices and (iii) concentrated industries. Expansionary forces cause excess demand and, consequently, inflation. The second source of inflation is the rise in input prices, which affects costs of production and, consequently, inflation. The major factor in the cost of production is wages. When strong unions in one sector succeed in raising wages, employers in other sectors also give some sort of increases because of social forces—the need to maintain morale and efficiency of workers and/or maintain customary equalities and differentials with respect to wages. The third source of inflation is the desire of concentrated industries to maintain high profit or to increase their profit margin. Concentrated industries can raise prices more easily than others.

DIAGRAM 10-2

INFLATIONARY TRANSMISSION MECHANISM
AS VIEWED BY KEYNESIANS

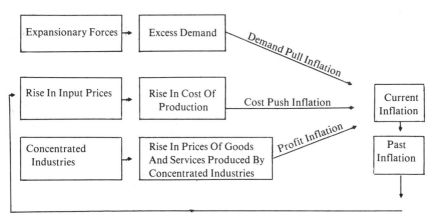

Current inflation, after a lag of one period of time, becomes past inflation. Past inflation affects current inflation via input prices. It influences wages—input prices—in two ways: One, automatically, through the operation of cost of living adjustment clauses in wage contracts. Two, through the collective bargaining process as organized workers seek to increase their real wages. James Tobin claims that the rate of inflation in the immediately preceeding period is a good predictor of the inflation rate in the following period because the trend of prices solidly builds into the economy, with a powerful and persistent momentum.

Cure of inflation

Keynesians claim that inflation can be controlled by restrictive fiscal and monetary policies, supplemented with either atomization of big business and big labor or by some sort of incomes policy (i.e., wage and price controls). An improvement in productivity can also help to curb inflation. The atomization of big unions and big business will help in the fight against inflation because they make product and labor markets more competitive, curtailing the upward pressure on costs and prices.

Keynesians further assert that restrictive fiscal and monetary policies alone may be adequate where inflation is demand related (demand pull inflation). Where inflation is cost or profit related (cost push or profit inflation), restrictive fiscal and monetary policies should be accompanied by incomes policy and/or with some measures to increase productivity. Otherwise, drastic contractionary fiscal and monetary policies will be needed to accomplish the objective, which cannot be pursued for long as they will cause too much unemployment.

Keynesians are divided as to the nature of the incomes policy that should be pursued to curb inflation. James Tobin advocates strict public control of prices and wages.[8] Arthur Okun and others advocate voluntary controls only.[9]

Recently some economists, including Arthur Okun and Henry Wallich have advocated another type of incomes policy called, Tax based Incomes Policy (TIP), to control inflation.[10] It would work something like this: Each year the government would announce a wage increase guideline as well as a TIP tax schedule for the next year. At the end of the year, firms whose wage increases went over the government's guideline would pay additional tax and those whose wage increases went below it would receive a cut in tax. Suppose the government announces a wage increase guideline of 6 percent and a tax rate of 2 percnt. This means that for each percentage point of wage increase a firm grants over (or under) 6 percent, 2 percentage points will be added to (or subtracted from) its corporate profits tax rate. If a firm grants an 8 percent wage increase (2 percentage points above the guideline), 4 percentage points will be added to its profits tax rate. If it grants a 6 percent wage increase, its profits tax rate will remain unchanged. If it grants a 4 percent wage increase (2 percentage points below the guideline), its profits tax rate will decline by 4 percentage points. Since TIP makes larger wage increases more expensive to employers, it will stiffen the employers' resistance to labor wage demands. As a result, increases in wages will slow down. Since wages are an important component in the cost of production, a slowdown in wage increases means a decline in price inflation.

Critics argue that TIP, like any other incomes policy, will be used only for a short while to hold down price increases. When it is removed, prices will shoot up even higher than they would have otherwise. This has been the experience, they claim, with wage price controls. They add that it will divert many government resources from productive use to the maintenance of a costly bureaucracy to administer a policy of this kind. Preston Miller even questions whether such a policy can temporarily hold down price increases.[11]

SUMMARY

Inflation is defined as a continuing rise in the general price level. The theory of inflation is widely debated between Monetarists and Keynesians. Monetarists claim that the excessive money supply is the real culprit of inflation. Since inflation is caused by excessive money supply it can be controlled by restraining its expansion. They further argue that although indexation is not a cure for inflation, it can make it easier to control. Regarding transmission mechanism, they believe that excessive monetary growth creates excess demand followed by a higher price level. The effect also runs from past inflation and/or current information to inflationary expectations and then to the current price level.

Keynesians, on the other hand, claim that inflation originates from three sources: (i) Expansionary forces (demand pull inflation), (ii) a rise in input prices (cost push inflation), and (iii) concentrated industries (profit inflation). Regarding transmission mechanism, they believe that expansionary forces cause excess demand and, consequently, inflation. Expansionary forces result primarily from expansionary fiscal and monetary policies. In the case of cost push inflation, a rise in input prices causes a rise in the cost of production and, consequently, inflation. Profit inflation stems mainly from attempts of concentrated industries to maintain high profit margins even when demand is slackening or just to push up profit margins. Past inflation also affects current inflation but indirectly via input prices. Keynesians believe that inflation can be controlled by restrictive fiscal and monetary policies, supplemented with either atomization of big business and big labor or by some sort of incomes policy. Measures used to increase productivity can also help to fight against inflation.

FOOTNOTES

¹Robert E. Lucas, "Econometric Testing of the Natural Rate Hypothesis," in **The Econometrics of Price Determination,** ed. Otto Eckstein (Washington, D.C.: The Board of Governors of the Federal Reserve System, 1972), p. 54; Thomas J. Sargent & Neil Wallace, "Rational Expectations, the Optimal Monetary Instrument, and the Optimal Money Supply Rule," **Journal of Political Economy** (April 1975), p. 254; Robert J. Barro, "Rational Expectations and the Role of Monetary Policy," **Journal of Monetary Economics** (January 1976), pp. 1-32; and John H. Kareken, "Inflation: An Extreme View," **Quarterly Review: Federal Reserve Bank of Minneapolis** (Winter 1978), p. 11.

²Eileen Shanahan, Moderator, **Indexing and Inflation** (Washington, D.C.: American Enterprise Institute for Public Policy Research, 1974), p. 2.

³**Ibid.**, p. 6.

⁴Yvonne Levy, "The Outlook for Inflation Based on Cost-Push & Capacity Factors," **Economic Review: Federal Reserve Bank of San Francisco** (Spring 1977), p. 22.

⁵William D. Nordhaus, "The Political Business Cycle," **Review of Economic Studies** (April 1975), p. 187.

⁶Robert J. Gordon, "The Demand and Supply of Inflation," **Journal of Law and Economics** (December 1975), p. 808.

⁷J. Charles Partee, "Some Economic Policy Issues," **Voice: Federal Reserve Bank of Dallas** (May 1978), p. 3.

⁸James Tobin, "Inflation and Unemployment," **American Economic Review** (March 1972), p. 14.

⁹Arthur M. Okun, Henry H. Fowler and Milton Gilbert, **Inflation: The Problems, Its Causes and the Policies It Requires** (New York: New York University Press, 1970), p. 27.

¹⁰Henry C. Wallich, "Stabilization Goals: Balancing Inflation and Unemployment," **American Economic Review** (May 1978), pp. 28-30; and Arthur M. Okun, "The Great Stagflation Swamp," **The Brookings Bulletin** (Fall 1977), pp. 1-7.

¹¹Preston Miller, "TIP: The Wrong Way to Fight Inflation," **Quarterly Review: Federal Reserve Bank of Minneapolis** (Spring 1978), p. 12.

QUESTIONS FOR REVIEW

1. Describe in brief the following:
    i. True Inflation
    ii. Creeping Inflation
    iii. Suppressed Inflation
    iv. Hyperinflation
2. What is stagflation? What causes it?
3. Evaluate critically the use of indexation as a tool for controlling inflation.
4. Describe the transmission mechanism of inflation as viewed by Keynesians.
5. Define inflation. How is inflation caused in the Keynesians theoretical framework?
6. Describe the differences between Keynesians and Monetarists as to the cause of inflation.
7. Explain rational and adaptive hypotheses as they pertain to inflationary expectations.
8. Explain price adjustment and expectation lags. What role do they play in the Monetarist transmission process?
9. Discuss the important policy implications that may arise by following the Monetarist prescription for curing inflation.
10. What do we mean by endogenous and exogenous variables? Would you treat the money supply as an endogenous or exogenous variable? Why?

SUGGESTED FURTHER READING

1. Berman, Peter I. "The Basic Cause of Inflation." **Across the Board.** May 1978, pp. 67-70.
2. Cloos, George W. "Indexation and Inflation." **Economic Perspective: Federal Reserve Bank of Chicago.** May/June 1978, pp. 3-9.
3. Dobson, Steven W. "Inflation-The Role of Market Structure." **Review: Federal Reserve Bank of Dallas.** June 1977, pp. 1-9.
4. Eastburn, David P. "Voluntary Inflationary Restraint and Corporate Social Responsibility." **Business Review: Federal Reserve Bank of Philadelphia.** January/February 1979, pp. 3-4.
5. Eckstein, Otto (Ed.). **The Econometric of Price Determination.** Washington, D.C.: Board of Governors of the Federal Reserve System and Social Science Research Council, June 1972.
6. Friedman, Milton. **Monetary Correction: A Proposal for Escalator Clauses to Reduce the Costs of Ending Inflation.** Westminister, England: The Institute of Economic Affairs, 1974.
7. Friedman, Milton and Samuelson, Paul A. "The President's New Economic Program: Domestic Wage-Price Controls." Testimony before

the Joint Economic Committee, in **Readings in Macro-economics: Current Policy Issues,** ed. William E. Mitchell, John H. Hand and Ingo Walter. New York: McGraw-Hill Book Company, 1974.

8. Gennaro, Vincent. "Indexing Inflation." **Business Review: Federal Reserve Bank of Philadelphia.** March 1975, pp. 3-13.

9. Gordon, Robert J. "Recent Developments in the Theory of Inflation and Unemployment." **Journal of Monetary Economics.** January 1976, pp. 185-219.

10. Gramm, Philip W. "Inflation: Its Causes and Cure." **Review: Federal Reserve Bank of St. Louis.** February 1975, pp. 2-7.

11. Haberler, Gottfried. "Depression and Inflation on Spaceship Earth." **Economic Notes.** January-April 1975, pp. 7-24.

12. Humphrey, Thomas M. "Some Current Controversies in the Theory of Inflation." **Ecomonic Review: Federal Reserve Bank of Richmond.** July/August 1976, pp. 8-18.

13. Humphrey, Thomas M. "The Persistence of Inflation." in **1975 Annual Report.** Richmond, Virginia: Federal Reserve Bank of Richmond, 1976, pp. 4-16.

14. Johnson, Harry G. **Inflation and the Monetarist Controversary.** Amsterdam: North-Holland Publishing Company, 1972.

15. Laidler, David and Parkin, Michael. "Inflation: A Survey." **Economic Journal.** December 1975, pp. 741-809.

16. Laidler, David. "The 1974 Report of the President's Council of Economic Advisers: The Control of Inflation and the Future of the International Monetary System." **American Economic Review.** September 1974, pp. 535-543.

17. Miller, Preston. "TIP: The Wrong Way to Fight Inflation." **Quarterly Review: Federal Reserve Bank of Minneapolis.** Spring 1978, pp. 9-15.

18. Karekan, John H. "Inflation: An Extreme View." **Quarterly Review: Federal Reserve Bank of Minneapolis.** Winter 1978, pp. 7-13.

19. Modigliani, Franco. "The Monetarist Controversy or Should We Foresake Stabilization Policies?" **American Economic Review.** March 1977, pp. 1-19.

20. Okun, Arthur M. "Inflation: Its Mechanics and Welfare Costs." **Brookings Papers On Economic Activity: 2.** 1975, pp. 351-390.

21. Okun, Arthur M. Fowler, Henry H., and Gilbert, Milton. **Inflation: The Problems, Its Causes and the Policies It Requires.** New York: New York University Press, 1970.

22. Perlman, Richard. **Inflation: Demand-Pull or Cost Push.** Boston, Massachusetts: D.C. Heath and Company, 1965.

23. Seldon, Richard. "Monetary Growth and the Long-Run Rate of Inflation." **American Economic Review.** May 1975, pp. 125-128.

24. Shanahan, Eileen (Moderator). **Indexing and Inflation.** Washington, D.C.: American Enterprise Institute for Public Policy Research, 1974.
25. Sommers, Albert T. (Ed.). **Answers to Inflation and Recession: Economic Policies for a Modern Society.** New York: The Conference Board, 1975.
26. Stein, Jerome L. "Unemployment, Inflation and Monetarism." **American Economic Review.** December, 1974, pp. 867-887.
27. Tucker, F. James & Weber, Warren E. "Indexation as a Response to Inflation: An Experimentation." **Economic Review: Federal Reserve Bank of Richmond.** November/December, 1974, pp. 17-21.
28. Wiegand, G.C. (Ed.). **Inflation and Monetary Crisis.** Washington, D.C.: Public Affairs Press, 1975.

CHAPTER XI

Keynesian vs. Monetarist Doctrine: Policy Issues

Keynesians and Monetarists disagree on many policy issues, the most important among them are:

A. Rules vs. Discretion
B. Monetary vs. Fiscal Policy
C. Monetary Aggregates vs. Money Market Conditions as a Policy Guide
D. Fixed vs. Flexible Exchange Rates
E. Rational Expectations
F. Trade-off vs. No Trade-off
G. Structural Model vs. Single Equation (Reduced Form) Approach.

RULES VS. DISCRETION

Should monetary policy be conducted by fixed rules or by discretion of the authority? Keynesians favor discretion. Monetarists favor rules. Keynesians support their position on the ground that the economy is inherently unstable. Discretionary action helps to stabilize it. There is no self-corrective mechanism in the economy. Nor is there any assurance that self corrective tendencies will prevail if policymakers stick to fixed rules. If the economy wanders off its ideal path, discretionary action is needed to put it back on course. Moreover, long run relationships between policy instruments and economic activity are not precisely known and thus proper rules cannot be determined. But the short run impact of policy instruments is known with some degree of certainty, making it possible to improve expected outcomes with discretionary actions. Furthermore, Keynesians argue, such actions have worked well in the past in the

United States as well as in other industrialized nations.

Monetarists, proponents of rules, argue that we do not have adequate knowledge about the economy and thus the authority with discretionary power is likely to do more harm than good. According to Milton Friedman, the monetary authority occasionally has moved in the wrong direction.[1] More frequently, it moved in the right direction but erred by moving either too late or too far. Monetarists claim that the authority would do better if it follows predetermined rules. But rules are not looked upon as so rigid that they cannot be broken. They consider rules as a temporary solution because the possibility always exists that, one day, better ones may be found. Milton Friedman says that, in case of major disturbances, the authority may be allowed to depart from rules. Monetarists do not view rules as a means to achieve the best result, but rather a procedure that will, on the average, provide a reasonably satisfactory result.

The rule often advocated by Monetarists is a steady rate of money growth. They believe that such a rule would provide a stable monetary framework for economic growth without itself being a source of instability and disturbance. According to them, major inflations and deflations of the past were caused by excessive variations in the money supply.

Keynesians argue against the rule of a steady rate of money growth on the ground that the economy is inherently unstable. The money supply needs to be increased well above the rate suggested by the rule when the aggregate demand for goods and services is unusually weak or when the demand for liquidity is unusually high. If the economy is experiencing severe cost push inflation, monetary growth which is higher than the fixed rate may have to be tolerated for some time because at that time the attempt to curtail the money supply to meet the fixed rule may cause adverse effects on the economy. Furthermore, the monetary authority has a number of other responsibilities such as the maintenance of favorable credit conditions, which may at times require a change in the money supply well beyond the rate suggested by the rule. Arthur Okun argues that the rule of a steady rate of monetary growth would not help much because it would be a rare coincidence for the same rate to be appropriate two years in a row.[2] Franco Modigliani, another Keynesian, claims that a stable money growth does not guarantee a stable economy. In the post World War II era, there were two periods (one, beginning of 1953 through the first half of 1957 and the other, 1971 through 1974) when the money supply increased at a fairly steady rate. But, during both periods, the economy experienced wild fluctuations in output and prices.[3]

FISCAL VS. MONETARY POLICY

Controversy exists between Keynesians and Monetarists as to the strength of fiscal and monetary policies. Keynesians claim that both are potent weapons: how much each affects the economy depends upon circumstances. They add that fiscal policy works faster than monetary policy. Monetarists, on the other hand, claim that the effect of fiscal policy is weak and of monetary policy, strong. They further assert that monetary policy works faster.

Keynesians say that the effect of pure fiscal policy depends upon the size of shift of IS and slopes of both IS and LM. (A pure fiscal policy exists when a change in expenditure or taxes affects income but leaves the money supply unaffected.) Suppose the fiscal authority pursues an expansionary policy by increasing government spending and uses bonds to finance it. An increase in government spending will shift IS to the right. As shown in Figure 11-1, such a policy will be most effective if IS intersects LM in the liquidity trap range (where LM is perfectly elastic); somewhat effective if it occurs in the intermediate range (where LM is somewhat elastic); and completely ineffective if it occurs in the classical range (where LM is vertical or perfectly inelastic). In the liquidity trap range, such an action will be most effective because the shift of IS (from IS_1 to $IS_{(1+g)}$) does not increase the interest rate, thereby causing no adverse effect on private investment. However, in the classical range, similar action causes such an increase in the interest rate that private investment equal to the increase in government spending is crowded out. In the figure, when the shift occurs from IS_3 to $IS_{(3+g)}$ the interest rate rises from i_3 to $\bar{i}_3$. But income stays at the same level, i.e., Y_3. The interest rate rises because the increase in government spending causes an increase in its borrowing from the market. In the case of the intermediate range, similar action is somewhat effective because only a portion of its effect is offset by a reduction in private investment. In Figure 11-1, when shift occurs from IS_2 to $IS_{(2+g)}$, the interest rate rises from i_2 to $\bar{i}_2$ and income, from Y_2 to $\bar{Y}_2$. Thus, the effect of fiscal action depends, among other things, upon the slope of the LM curve. The steeper the LM curve, the less will be its effect. Keynesians claim that there is overwhelming evidence that the short run LM is not vertical: the demand for money is negatively related to the interest rate.

FIGURE 11-1

EFFECT OF FISCAL POLICY ON INCOME

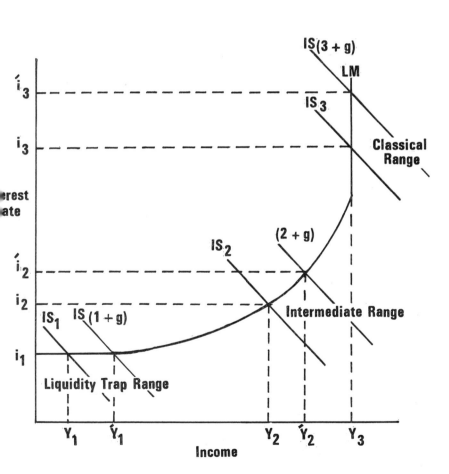

Regarding monetary policy, Keynesians claim that it is completely ineffective when LM is in the liquidity trap range, partially effective when it is in the intermediate range, and most effective when it is in the classical range (Figure 11-2). Suppose the monetary authority increases the money supply to stimulate the economy. It will shift LM to the right, from LM_1 to $LM (1+m)$. If LM is in the liquidity trap range, an increase in the money supply will be fully absorbed by an increase in the demand for money (demand for idle cash balances). As a result, the interest rate will remain unchanged. If the interest rate does not decline, neither investment nor income will rise. Income will remain at Y_1 level.

FIGURE 11-2

EFFECT OF MONETARY POLICY ON INCOME

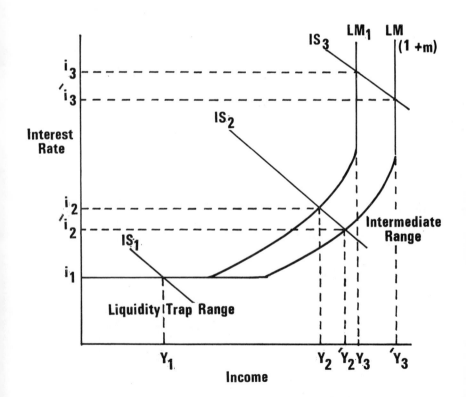

If the money supply is increased when LM is in the intermediate range, the interest rate will fall from i_2 to i_2'. As a result, investment and, consequently, income will rise. Income will rise from Y_2 to Y_2'. The interest rate falls because the increase in the money supply is only partially absorbed by the increase in the demand for idle cash balances.

Monetary policy will be most effective if the money supply is increased when LM is in the classical range. Since here the demand for money is perfectly interest inelastic, an increase in the money supply will cause a significant reduction in the interest rate. This will, in turn, produce a large stimulative effect on investment. Consequently, income will rise. In Figure 11-2, when LM shifts from LM_1 to $LM_{(1 + m)}$, the interest rate falls from i_3 to i_3' and income rises from Y_3 to Y_3'.

Monetarists maintain that pure fiscal policy has a weak impact on the economy. If government increases its expenditure to stimulate the economy and expenditure is financed by borrowing from the public, its effect will be weak because it will crowd out private expenditure by increasing the interest rate. (In the IS and LM framework, this will happen when LM is relatively interest inelastic.) The effect will also be weak, if the increased expenditure is financed by taxes because it will leave taxpayers less to spend. Monetarists recognize that fiscal policy has a re-allocative effect on long run output. If an expenditure program re-allocates resources from consumption to investment (say, it cuts down low income subsidies and increases expenditure on education), long run output will rise. Output will also rise if a tax program is designed to encourage private investment. But they argue that such effects are minor and take a long time before they appear. Monetary policy, on the other hand, produces a strong impact (stronger than fiscal policy) because it does not cause any crowding out effect.

As explained earlier, fiscal policy is completely ineffective if LM is vertical (demand for money is perfectly interest inelastic). Friedman says that though LM is not vertical, it is steeper than what Keynesians think.[4] Furthermore, he asserts that there is a much broader category of interest sensitive private expenditures than Keynesians think, which reduce the size of shift of IS caused by a fiscal action. (Hamm says that the size of shift of IS is reduced significantly, if consumption expenditure is highly sensitive to the interest rate because the interest sensitivity of business expenditure is already taken into account in the slope.⁵) Thus, a small shift in IS combined with a steeply sloped LM produces a weak impact on income. The St. Louis model (a major Monetarist model) shows that the effect of pure fiscal policy on income is not only minor but also short lived. At the end of five quarters the effect completely disappears. However, the MPS model (a major Keynesian model) shows that the same policy exerts a significant effect lasting for several years.

Both groups agree that fiscal policy has a longer policy lag (time required to implement a change in policy after its need is recognized) than monetary policy, because most of the changes in fiscal policy have to be approved by the Congress and speed has never been one of the Congress' strong points. Monetary policy can be changed within a short time because the Federal Reserve has complete authority in such matters.

Keynesians and Monetarists differ, though, about the outside lag (time required for the economy to respond to a change in policy after it is implemented). Keynesians claim that fiscal policy has a shorter outside lag than monetary policy. Monetarists claim just the opposite. Keynesians argue their position on the ground that most fiscal actions, such as government expenditure and changes in personal income tax, affect the economy almost immediately. But this is not the case with monetary actions. It takes time for an action of the Federal Reserve to affect the money supply; for a change in the money supply to affect the interest rate; and for a change in the interest rate to affect the economy. Monetarists disagree. They support their position with empirical evidence such as the study of Andersen and Jordan, which concludes that monetary actions affect the economy faster than fiscal ones.⁶

MONETARY AGGREGATES VS. MONEY MARKET CONDITIONS AS A POLICY GUIDE

Whether monetary policy should be guided by monetary aggregates or money market conditions is also debated between Keynesians and Monetarists. Monetary aggregates include such things as the money supply and total reserves. Money market conditions are generally expressed on the basis of short-term interest rates, free reserves and bank borrowings from the Federal Reserve.

Monetarists favor monetary aggregates as a policy guide, i.e., indicators and operating and intermediate targets should be expressed in these terms. Keynesians advocate the use of both monetary aggregates and money market conditions. Monetarists claim that since the money supply (an important monetary aggregate) is the main source of disturbance, the economy will be better regulated if monetary aggregates are used. Keynesians, however, disagree. They say that the exclusive emphasis on monetary aggregates means that money market conditions don't count. But there are times when the monetary authority has to pay close attention to them. For example, it has to pay close attention to interest rates when they seriously affect the capacity of thrift institutions to perform their intermediary role between savers and the mortgage market.

As indicated in Chapter IX, an ideal indicator is that which is responsive to policy instruments and exhibits a response within a short interval. Moreover, it is not influenced by nonpolicy variables but associated with economic activity in a somewhat predictable fashion. Monetarists claim that the money stock (a monetary aggregate) is a better indicator of monetary policy than any other variable. The study of Andersen and Jordan shows that changes in the money stock reflect mainly discretionary actions of the Federal Reserve.[7] Studies of Friedman and Meiselman, and Keran conclude that the money stock is highly associated with economic activity, implying that the latter can be predicted from changes in the former.[8] Keynesians disagree. They say that the money stock is very much affected by nonpolicy variables such as bank lending and the public asset preferences, and it responds to policy instruments after a long lag. Keynesians further argue that, because of the reverse causation effect, the high degree of association, which Monetarists find between the money stock and economic activity, does not necessarily suggest that the latter can be reliably predicted from the former.

Keynesians say that, though monetary aggregates and measures of money market conditions are important indicators, more attention should be given to interest rates (money market conditions) because the economy is affected through them. Moreover, data on interest rates are readily available. They recognize, however, that interest rates, like monetary aggregates, are affected by nonpolicy variables. Monetarists disapprove the use of interest rates as an indicator. They argue that interest rates, at times, give a misleading signal. For example, at the time of recovery, rising interest rates reflect a growing demand for credit. If at that time interest rates are used as an indicator, policy will be wrongly interpreted as restrictive. Moreover, Monetarists claim that changes in ultimate targets cannot be reliably predicted from interest rates.

Whether one argues for monetary aggregates or for money market conditions, it is difficult to find a variable that is completely independent of nonpolicy influences. In recent years attempts have been made to develop an index of the money stock by adjusting it for nonpolicy influences.[9] Though such efforts have not been successful, they point toward the possible development of a good indicator.

Keynesians and Monetarists also argue about the selection of operating and intermediate target variables. An ideal operating target variable is that which can be precisely measured, is achievable by the monetary authority within a short period of time, provides a visible signal to financial market participants about the intent of policy, and is related to intermediate targets in a somewhat predictable fashion. Monetarists claim that reserve aggregates (monetary base, bank reserves, nonborrowed reserves, RPDs, etc.) will be better than interest rates as operating targets when the money stock is used as an intermediate target. However, they differ among themselves as to the specific reserve aggregate to be used. Meltzer suggests that the monetary base should be used as an operating target.[10] Ruebling favors RPDs (reserves available to support private nonbank deposits) over other reserve aggregates.[11]

In recent years economists with a Keynesian bent have narrowed the choice of operating targets from a host of reserve aggregates, on the one hand, and money market conditions, on the other, to a choice between nonborrowed reserves (total reserves minus borrowing from Federal Reserve Banks) and the Federal funds rate. Studies of both Davis and Meek show that if the money stock is accepted as an intermediate target both measures—nonborrowed reserves and Federal funds rate—would be equally effective as an operating target. Each measure has advantages and disadvantages but neither one has a clear overall superiority over the other.[12] (For advantages and disadvantages of these two measures as an operating target, see Chapter IX.) Keynesians further add that if money market conditions are selected as an intermediate target, Federal funds rate would have a definite edge over nonborrowed reserves.

Regarding the intermediate target, Monetarists claim that the money stock is the most appropriate candidate. It can be easily controlled by operating targets and is related to the economic activity in a somewhat known fashion. Keynesians advocate that both these sets of variables—monetary aggregates and measures of money market conditions—should be used as intermediate targets. Money is important and so are interest rates. If monetary aggregates are chosen as the only target variables, they would cause fluctuations in interest rates. They add that the monetary authority should achieve targets of monetary aggregates over a long time horizon and of interest rates over a short time horizon. By doing this, it would maintain stability in interest rates at least over short periods. Keynesians believe that, over short periods, it is neither feasible to hit targets of monetary aggregates with accuracy nor is it costly in terms of ultimate objectives for failing to hit them. Davis claims that a minimum of six months is needed to hit the average target of money growth. Simulations of Davis and Corrigan suggest that even sizeable deviations from the old M_1 target, lasting up to six months, do not create any problems provided they are subsequently adjusted.[13] Monetarists disagree with Keynesians that targets of monetary aggregates cannot be achieved over shorter periods. They claim that they can be achieved provided the authority tries hard enough and uses reserve aggregates as operating targets.

Poole (a prominent Keynesian) evaluates the choice between the money stock target and the interest rate target in the LM and IS framework. He concludes that the target of money stock is superior to that of interest rate in a world where LM is stable and IS is not.[14] The opposite is true where IS is stable and LM is not. Suppose LM is stable and IS is unstable, and IS varies between IS_1 and IS_2 as shown in Figure 11-3. Under these conditions, if the target of money stock is used (i.e., its amount is fixed at a certain level), the position of LM_1 will be fixed and known, and income will vary between Y_1 and Y_2. But if the target of interest rate is used and is set at, say, i_0, income will vary between $\acute{Y}_1$ and $\acute{Y}_2$. The range of income variation will be wider than the previous case. Hence, the target of money stock is better where LM is stable and IS is not.

Suppose now IS is stable and known, and LM varies between LM_1 and LM_2 as shown in Figure 11-4. With a money stock target, income will vary between Y_1 and Y_2. But, with an interest rate target, LM will be fixed at LM_3 so that it intersects IS at a point that provides the desired level of income (Y_3). Unexpected shifts in LM will not be per-

FIGURE 11-3

EFFECT OF MONEY STOCK AND INTEREST RATE TARGETS ON INCOME WHERE "LM" IS STABLE AND "IS" IS NOT

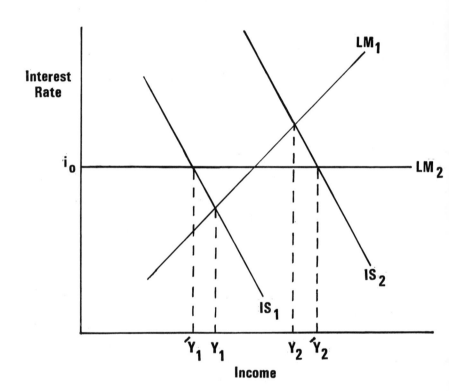

mitted to affect the interest rate. The authority will adjust the money stock in response to a shift in LM in order to keep the interest rate on target. Hence, the target of interest rate will prove better where IS is stable and LM is not.

No matter what Keynesians think about monetary aggregates as a

FIGURE 11-4

EFFECT OF MONEY STOCK AND INTEREST RATE TARGETS ON INCOME WHERE "IS" IS STABLE AND "LM" IS NOT

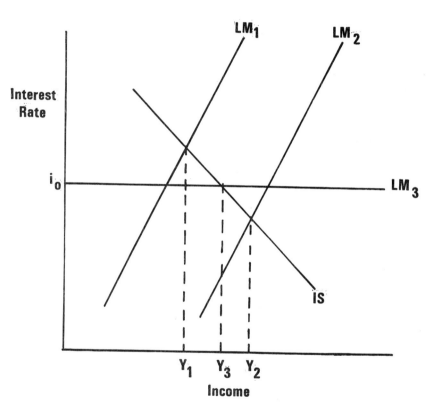

guide to monetary policy, the Federal Reserve in recent years has started to place greater emphasis on them. Prior to 1970, the Federal Open Market Committee (FOMC) emphasized money market conditions. Since that year, it has made greater use of money stock measures to define its policy objectives and to guide open market operations between FOMC meetings.

FIXED VS. FLEXIBLE EXCHANGE RATES

Though the issue of fixed and flexible exchange rates is also debated among Keynesians and Monetarists, their differences are not as sharp and distinct as they are on other issues. Keynesians favor a system ranging from almost completely fixed exchange rates to very limited flexible exchange rates. Very limited flexible exchange rates refer to systems such as crawling peg and band proposal. Under the crawling peg, the parity of a given day is determined by an average of past rates established in the market. Under the band system, exchange rates are permitted to fluctuate within a specified range, any deviation from it is corrected by direct intervention. Monetarists favor a system ranging from almost completely to a somewhat limited flexible exchange rates. Keynesians who favor a system of almost completely fixed exchange rates are Robert V. Roosa, Robert Triffin and Charles P. Kindleberger. Those who belong to the Keynesian camp, but who would allow a limited flexibility in exchange rates, are Paul Samuelson, William Poole and Gotfried Haberler. Monetarists who advocate almost completely flexible exchange rates are Milton Friedman and Harry Johnson. Monetarists such as George McKenzie accept a system that imposes a minor limitation on their flexibility.

Keynesians make their case for fixed exchange rates on the ground that it promotes international commerce since it enables merchants, investors and bankers to do business at determinable rates. Further, under this system, the balance of payments often reveals, in outlines if not in detail, mistakes and achievements of the economy. When a country's external accounts are continuously and seriously out of balance, the implication is that wage increases have exceeded productivity, investment demands have outrun resources, production of export items has been restricted, or government requirements (including overseas spending) have added undue strain on total capacity. Proponents of fixed exchange rates also claim that such a system has served the world quite well. Since the end of World War II, economic expansion has proceeded at rates never previously achieved. At least, some of this progress can be attributed to the improvement in international commerce which was made possible by fixed exchange rates.

Monetarists favor flexible exchange rates. They claim that they provide an automatic mechanism for restoring equilibrium in the balance of payments. If a country experiences a deficit in the balance of payments, the value of its currency will depreciate. Currency depreciation helps to restore equilibrium by increasing exports and decreasing imports. Moreover, with flexible exchange rates, monetary and fiscal policies can be directed toward pursuing internal stability without being hamstrung by the balance of payments. Monetarists further argue that fixed exchange rates cause more uncertainty than flexible ones. If exchange rates are fixed and difficulty occurs in external balances, action is delayed until it reaches crisis proportions. Action is delayed because the authority has to take unpleasant measures such as imposing restrictions on imports, exports and capital movements, and deflating the economy to control wages and prices. The inaction causes a great uncertainty. However, with flexible exchange rates, uncertainty manifests itself in exchange rates promptly but gradually and does so in a way people can adjust to without any difficulty.

Keynesians do not trust the automatic mechanism of the flexible-exchange rate system in restoring equilibrium. They claim that deliberate policy actions are needed to manage the balance of payments. Further, the problem of automatically floating rates would be compounded under a less automatic system, the one which is realistically conceivable. Under a less automatic system, central banks do not abstain permanently from market intervention. Such a system creates a number of problems: First, interventions by different central banks will most probably work at cross purposes. There is only one dollar-sterling exchange rate, not two. Who will manage it? The Bank of England or the Federal Reserve System or both? Triffin, a Keynesian, says that it is just like a public bath house where each of them is equipped with a faucet that regulates the heat of the water for all of them. Bathers would come out and fight. Second, it would exhibit a strong devaluation bias since deficit countries would let their rates go down as much as necessary, while surplus countries would not allow their rates to go up as much as the free market permits. Third, it would cause global inflation. Countries whose currencies are depreciating would experience a rise in domestic prices due to a rise in exports. But countries whose currencies are appreciating would experience either no or a little decline in domestic prices because prices move up more easily than they move down. Thus, flexible exchange rates cause world wide inflation by pushing up prices of certain countries without pushing them down anywhere else, argue Keynesians.

RATIONAL EXPECTATIONS

Rational expectations are an assumption about people's behavior which state that people make economic decisions in a way that takes into account all the available information and makes it difficult to repeat their past mistakes. Information includes such things as the current and expected policy of the government. The idea of rational expectations first appeared in 1961 in an article by J.F. Muth. Recently, a number of economists, such as Thomas J. Sargent, Neil Wallace and Robert E. Lucas, used it to explain certain aspects of macroeconomics. This idea supports many of the views of Monetarists and challenges those of Keynesians.

Rationalists (proponents of rational expectations idea) claim that discretionary policy (fiscal and monetary stimulus in times of recession and restraint in times of boom) does not work because it is based upon assumptions that do not hold true in the real world. It assumes that people do not act rationally, i.e., they behave contrary to their best interest, repeatedly neglect important information they have or can have about any systematically applied policy. Or, policy action surprises people.

Rationalists explain why discretionary action is ineffective when people act rationally as follows: Suppose policymakers pursue an expansionary policy. Expansionary policy generally causes a rise in output prices. Policy will work if output prices rise and wages (a major input cost) do not because then and only then business profits will rise, thereby causing investment, and consequently production, to go up. A rise in output prices reduces real wages. If workers behaved rationally, they would guard their real wages against price increases. They would not only fully anticipate price increases, but also manage to incorporate them into their wage bargains. If workers did that, business profits would not rise and neither investment nor output would increase. Expansionary policy would cause inflation only.

They also explain the ineffectiveness of an expansionary action via interest rates. Expansion in the money stock ultimately raises the general price level. Foreseeing that outcome, lenders add an inflation premium to interest rates. If long-term interest rates relevant for business capital expansion go up by the full amount of expected inflation, as Rationalists argue happens with any foreseen inflation, exploitable opportunities for businessmen would not occur. As a result, neither investment nor production would rise.

Expansionary action that surprises people increases output and employment by creating exploitable opportunities for businessmen. When workers do not expect expansionary action, they do not take action to protect real wages against the resulting inflation. Similarly, when lenders do not anticipate inflation, they do not add an inflation premium to interest rates. As output prices rise and production costs remain stable, exploitable opportunities for businessmen increase. Consequently, output and employment increase. Rationalists believe that policymakers can surprise people once or twice but not all the time because, after awhile, they develop an awareness of what policymakers are likely to do in any given situation. Some Rationalists go even further and state that discretionary policy will not work even if policymakers, with their ingenuity and resources, succeed in creating a surprise every time. Frequent surprises, they claim, will cause great uncertainty in people's expectations about future prices, wages and interest rates, making it difficult to predict their response to a given action. If policymakers cannot predict the nature of that response, they cannot use discretionary actions to achieve a desired outcome.

Rationalists conclude that since neither expected changes nor surprise changes in the money supply can smooth cyclical fluctuations, credibility of a policy is paramount. The only way to make any policy credible is to announce it, implement it faithfully, and avoid shifting it abruptly. Such a procedure, according to them, will create long term, steady economic growth and high employment. They add that a steady growth in the money supply, as advocated by Monetarists, will not have a detrimental effect on employment levels.

Critics argue that Rationalists expect too much wisdom and perception from the public. But supporters say that the validity of rational expectations does not require that every person or businessman be the complete seer of future prices and other economic events. In the case of the labor sector, only union leaders, not each and every rank-and-file member, need to have an informed view about what government policy is and what its consequences for future prices are likely to be because they are the ones who participate in bargaining. In the case of the financial sector, only large borrowers and suppliers of funds are expected to have such wisdom. Small borrowers and investors can learn what the experts are expecting from various published sources such as newspapers and newsletters.

TRADE-OFF VS. NO TRADE-OFF

Keynesians and Monetarists also differ on the issue of inflation-unemployment trade off (Phillips curve). Keynesians claim that there is a trade-off, meaning that unemployment can be lowered by accepting inflation. The Phillips curve, shown in Figure 11-5, shows that the inflation rate is P_1 at U_1 unemployment rate. If we want to lower the unemployment rate to U_2, we must be willing to accept a higher inflation rate, i.e., P_2, and so on. Monetarists, on the other hand, assert that there is no permanent trade-off, that it may exist in the short run only. In the long run, there is no trade-off and the Phillips curve is completely vertical.

FIGURE 11-5

PHILLIPS CURVE

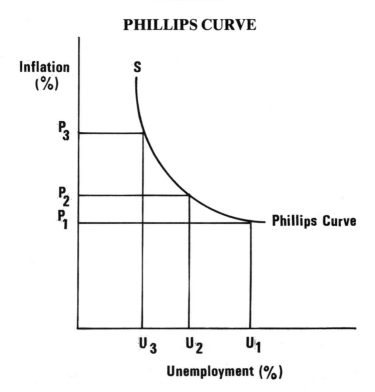

Monetarists explain the absence of a permanent trade-off this way: Suppose that there is price stability and the economy is operating at the natural rate of unemployment. (The natural rate of unemployment is the rate at which, given the frictions and structural characteristics of the economy, both labor and product markets are at equilibrium, and expected inflation equals actual inflation.) The authorities take an expansionary action to stimulate the economy. This bids up both output prices and wages. Since output prices rise more rapidly than wages, real wages decline. When real wages decline, business profits rise. The rise in business profits causes a rise in investment and, consequently, in production and employment. At this point, the trade-off exists because the inflationary stimulus causes a decline in unemployment. But this will not last long. At first, workers are fooled because they failed to recognize that inflation was eroding their real wages. But, over time, they become wiser. They realize that inflation is hurting them. They learn not only how to fully anticipate inflation but also how to incorporate it in wage bargains. When money wages catch up with price increases, real wages return to the pre-inflation level. The rise in real wages cause a cutback in production and employment, thereby increasing unemployment to the natural level. When this happens, the trade-off ceases to exist. Whatever is gained in the beginning in the way of reduction in unemployment is lost in the end.

Policy implications of the Monetarist view are as follows:

1. The attempt to hold unemployment below the natural rate only accelerates inflation. Maintenance of unemployment below the natural rate requires that real wage rates be kept low enough to induce businessmen to expand investment. This can be achieved only by increasing inflation at a rate higher than what workers expect. Alternately stated, actual inflation must be kept running continuously ahead of the expected inflation that workers incorporate into their wage demands. Since expected inflation always rises in an attempt to catch up with actual inflation, the latter must be continuously accelerated. Hence, the attempt to hold unemployment below the natural level only accelerates inflation further.

2. Since unemployment cannot be kept below the natural rate for long and the natural rate is consistent with any rate of steady inflation, the best thing for policymakers to do is to strive for a zero rate of inflation. The natural rate is consistent with any

rate of inflation because at that rate the Phillips curve is vertical (see Figure 11-6).

FIGURE 11-6

SHORT AND LONG RUN PHILLIPS CURVES

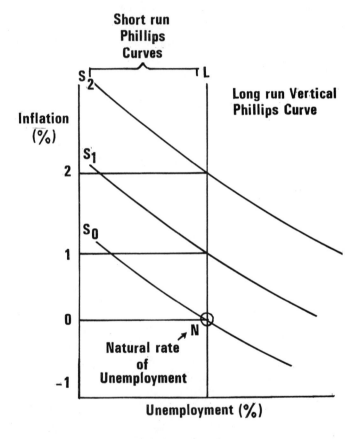

3. To hit a lower inflation rate target, policymakers have a choice between a low unemployment rate for a long period of time or a high unemployment rate for a short period of time. To achieve such a target, slack (excess supply) has to be created in the economy. Slack curbs inflationary expectations (an im-

portant source of inflation) by causing the actual rate to fall below the expected rate, resulting in a downward revision of the latter. If policymakers wish to achieve a lower inflation rate fast, a large amount of slack has to be created. The economy will experience a high unemployment rate but only for a short period of time because a large amount of slack is required for faster reduction in inflationary expectations. The high unemployment rate will last for a short duration because the fast decline in inflationary expectations will cause a fast decline in the factor prices which, in turn, help to reduce unemployment. Conversely, if policymakers want to achieve a lower inflation rate gradually, a small amount of slack is needed. This produces a relatively low level of unemployment for a long period of time.

Rationalists go one step further and claim that the trade-off does not exist even in the short run. As explained earlier, trade-off results if people cannot accurately anticipate inflation or do not act on it, or both. If people act rationally neither of them will occur. Except for a very short period, when unavoidable surprise is caused by a purely random shock, price expectations will always be correct and the economy will always be at its long run equilibrium (natural level). In such an economic environment, no exploitable trade-off exists. Stabilization policy has no effect on real variables.

Keynesians reject the inflation-employment trade-off views of both Monetarists and Rationalists. (As explained earlier, Monetarists claim that the trade-off exists only in the short run. Rationalists claim that it does not exist at all.) Keynesians point out that a number of studies show that the trade-off exists not only in the short run but also in the long run.[15] They add that the long-run Phillips curve is steeper but not vertical. Keynesians concede that it is possible that over a very long period, e.g., several decades, steady inflation might cause the curve to become vertical. But this does not mean that stabilization policy has no role to play. Policy can be effectively used even if trade-offs occur only during short periods.

Keynesians argue that the views of the Rationalists are based on assumptions that are highly implausible. Rationalists assume that information used to form expectations can be obtained and processed without any cost. But nothing is free in this world. If individuals have to pay for acquiring and processing information, many of them might not use it in forming their expectations, and thus expectations in many cases might not be formed rationally. Secondly, Rationalists assume that private forecasters possess as much information about the inflationary process and the resources to process it as do the policymakers. But this is not true. Thirdly, Rationalists assume that prices respond fully and immediately to anticipated changes in monetary growth and other events. By making this assumption, Rationalists deny that prices are sticky and costly to adjust. Department stores, for example, may not immediately increase prices of their merchandise when they anticipate an increase in them because of the cost of changing the price tag of each and every item and for other reasons. If these assumptions are not valid, the conclusion based on them—the Phillips curve is vertical both in short and long run—will not be valid either.

Some Keynesians argue that if workers accept a reduction in ,real wages because of a rise in prices, it does not mean that their behavior is irrational. They say that workers care more about relative wages than about absolute wages. Since inflation hits all workers alike, their relative wage relationships are not affected.

STRUCTURAL MODEL VS. SINGLE EQUATION (REDUCED FORM) APPROACH

Keynesians and Monetarists also argue about how the effect of a monetary or fiscal action on economic activity should be measured. Keynesians advocate the structural model approach whereas Monetarists advocate the single equation (reduced form) approach. The structural model approach involves three stages: In the first stage the structure of the model is specified, which is basically a description of relationships believed to exist among economic variables (or a postulation of the transmission mechanism). These relationships are written in the form of general mathematical equations. In the second stage specific numerical values for certain coefficients that appear in structural equations are estimated. For example, one structural equation is based on the relationship between capital investment on the one hand and stock market yield and the industrial bond rate on the other. There will be as many equations as there are endogenous aggregate variables. Since economists do not yet know the statistical relationships between stock market yield and capital investment, and industrial bond rate and capital investment, they must estimate. In the second stage economists, based upon the most recent data, estimate the average values of relationships expressed in all structural equations. The last stage is to solve the model, which, in the context of policy, is to forecast the effect of a policy action on economic activity, using the most efficient methods. In doing this, all necessary input data and input assumptions will be plugged into the model. Input assumptions, for the most part, are the values that policy variables will assume in the period to be forecasted. In the single equation approach, the effect of a policy action is measured by direct estimation of a single equation. Some measure of economic activity is regressed directly against the policy variable without specifying the transmission mechanism (or structural relationships).

Keynesians support the structural model approach on the grounds that it allows one to distinguish between direct and indirect influences of a policy action and to see how subsectors of the economy are affected, which is not possible with the single equation approach. They add that the single equation approach assumes that policy variables are completely exogenous, but they are not. If policy variables are not completely exogenous (or somewhat endogenous), it will be difficult to estimate their effect on the economy because the effect runs not only from policy variables to the economy but also the other way around.

Monetarists say that the economy is too complex to understand. How different economic variables are related to each other are not known with certainty. Under these conditions, they claim, the best way to measure the effect of a policy is to use the single equation approach because it does so directly and without constraining itself to imperfect notions of how the economy operates.

SUMMARY

Keynesians and Monetarists debate policy issues. Keynesians favor discretion over rules, while Monetarists favor rules over discretion. Keynesians claim that while both fiscal and monetary policies are potent, their effectiveness varies with circumstances. They add that fiscal policy, after it is executed, works faster than monetary policy. Monetarists assert that monetary policy is more powerful and works faster than fiscal policy. Keynesians believe that, though both monetary aggregates and money market conditions are important as a guide to monetary policy, more attention should be given to the latter. Monetarists advocate that monetary policy should be guided by monetary aggregates alone. Regarding exchange rates, Keynesians recommend a system ranging from almost completely fixed exchange rates to very limited flexible exchange rates. Monetarists, on the other hand, recommend a system ranging from almost completely to somewhat limited flexible exchange rates. Keynesians and Monetarists also differ on the issue of trade-off. Keynesians claim that an exploitable trade-off exists. Monetarists assert that there is no permanent trade-off, and thus stabilization policy is irrelevant. Concerning the measurement of the effect of a policy action, Keynesians advocate the use of the structural model approach and Monetarists, the single equation approach.

FOOTNOTES

[1] Milton Friedman, "The Role of Monetary Policy," **American Economic Review** (March 1968), p. 15.

[2] Arthur M. Okun, "Fiscal-Monetary Activism: Some Analytical Issues," **Brookings Paper on Economic Activity: 1** (1972), p. 157.

[3] Franco Modigliani, "The Monetarist Controversy Or Should We Forsake Stabilization Policies?" **American Economic Review** (March 1977), p. 11

[4] Milton Friedman, "Comments on the Critics," **Journal of Political Economy** (September/October 1972), p. 916.

[5] Bobby L. Hamm, **Theoretical Controversy and Macroeconomic Policies: 1960's and 1970's** (Ruston, Louisiana: Louisiana Tech University, 1974), p. 19.

[6] Leonall C. Andersen and Jerry L. Jordan, "Monetary and Fiscal Actions: A Test of Their Relative Importance in Economic Stabilization," **Review: Federal Reserve Bank of St. Louis** (November 1968), p. 22.

[7] **Ibid.**

[8] Milton Friedman and David Meiselman, "The Relative Stability of Monetary Velocity and the Investment Multiplier in the United States, 1897-1958," in **Monetary Economics: Controversies in Theory and Policy**, ed. Jonas Prager (New York, Random House, 1971), p. 215 & Michael W. Keran, "Monetary and Fiscal Influences of Economic Activity," **Review: Federal Reserve Bank of St. Louis** (November 1969), p. 23.

[9] Patrick H. Hendershott, **The Neutralized Money Stock: An Unbiased Measure of Federal Reserve Policy Actions** (Homewood, Illinois: Richard D. Irwin, Inc., 1968), p. 1 & Lorraine E. Dure, "A Measure of Monetary Policy," **Economic Review: Federal Reserve Bank of Cleveland** (January-February 1973), p. 22.

[10] Allan H. Meltzer, "Controlling Money," **Reviews: Federal Reserve Bank of St. Louis** (May 1969), pp. 18-20.

¹¹Charlotte E. Ruebling, "RPDs and Other Reserve Operating Targets," **Review: Federal Reserve Bank of St. Louis** (August 1972), pp. 6-7.

¹²Richard G. Davis, "Implementing Open Market Policy With Monetary Aggregate Objectives," **Monthly Review: Federal Reserve Bank of New York** (July 1973), p. 182 & Paul Meek, "Nonborrowed Reserves or the Federal Funds Rate as Desk Target—Is There Difference?" **New England Economic Review** (March/April 1975), p. 46.

¹³Ibid., pp. 175-176 & Gerald Corrigan, "Income Stabilization and Short-run Variability in Money," **Monthly Review: Federal Reserve Bank of New York** (April 1973), p. 98.

¹⁴William Poole, "Rules-of-Thumb for Guiding Monetary Policy," in **Open Market Policies and Operating Procedures—Staff Studies** (Washington, D.C.: Board of Governors of the Federal Reserve System, 1971), pp. 139-140.

¹⁵O. Eckstein and R. Brinner, **The Inflation Process in the United States**, 92nd Congress, 2nd Session (Washington, D.C.: U.S. Government Printing Office, 1972); Robert J. Gordon, "Inflation in Recession and Recovery," **Brookings Papers on Economic Activity: 1** (1971), pp. 136-140; Robert J. Gordon, "Wage-Price Controls on the Shifting Phillips Curve," **Brookings Papers on Economic Activity: 2** (1972), pp. 413-416; and G.L. Perry, **Unemployment, Money Wage Rates and Inflation** (Cambridge, Mass.: MIT Press, 1966).

QUESTIONS FOR REVIEW

1. Evaluate critically the views of Keynesians and Monetarists regarding the effectiveness of fiscal and monetary policies.

2. Explain how Keynesians argue against the use of "rules" in conducting stabilization policies.

3. How does William Poole evaluate the choice between the money stock and the interest rate as a monetary target? Explain.

4. Evaluate the issue of fixed vs. flexible exchange rates in the light of current experience.

5. What do we mean by "rational expectations"? What are their policy implications?

6. Is there a trade-off between inflation and unemployment? Evaluate.

7. What is the difference between a structural model and a single equation model? Explain their pros and cons with respect to policymaking.

8. Describe in brief the major policy issues that divide economists into two groups, Keynesians and Monetarists.

9. Some economists argue, "if workers accept a reduction in real wages because of a rise in prices, it does not mean that their behavior is irrational." Evaluate this statement.

10. Discuss the policy implications of a hypothesis that a permanent trade-off between unemployment and inflation does not exist.

SUGGESTED FURTHER READING

1. Andersen, Leonall C. "A Monetarists View of Demand Management: The United States Experience." **Review: Federal Reserve Bank of St. Louis.** September 1971, pp. 3-11.

2. _____ "Monetary and Fiscal Actions: A Test of Their Relative Importance in Economic Stabilization." **Review: Federal Reserve Bank of St. Louis.** November 1968, pp. 11-24.

3. Artus, Jacques R. & Crockett, Andrew D. "Floating Exchange Rates - Some Policy Issues." **Finance & Development.** December 1977, pp. 26-30.

4. Baron, David P. "Flexible Exchange Rates, Forward Markets, and the Level of Trade." **American Economic Review.** June 1976, pp. 253-266.

5. Barro, Robert J. "Rational Expectations and the Role of Monetary Policy." **Journal of Monetary Economics.** April 1976, pp. 1-32.

6. _____ and Fischer, S. "Recent Development in Monetary Theory." **Journal of Monetary Economics.** April 1976, pp. 133-167.

7. Berkman, Neil G. "A Rational View of Rational Expectations." **New England Economic Review.** January/February 1980, pp. 18-29.

8. Blinder, Alan S. & Solow, Robert M. "Does Fiscal Policy Still Matter?" **Journal of Monetary Economics.** November 1976, pp. 501-510.

9. Cacy, J.A. "Is the Federal Reserve Hitting Its Money Supply Targets?" **Monthly Review: Federal Reserve Bank of Kansas City.** February 1976, pp. 3-10.

10. _____ "The Choice of a Monetary Policy Instrument." **Economic Review: Federal Reserve Bank of Kansas City.** May 1978, pp. 17-35.

11. Carlson, Keith M. "Does the St. Louis Equation Now Believe in Fiscal Policy?" **Review: Federal Reserve Bank of St. Louis.** February 1978, pp. 13-19.

12. Christ, Carl F. "Monetary and Fiscal Influences on U.S. Money Income, 1891-1970." **Journal of Money, Credit and Banking.** February 1973, pp. 279-300.

13. Eastburn, David P. "Preserving Discretion in Economic Policy." **Business Review: Federal Reserve Bank of Philadelphia.** May/June 1979, pp. 3-4.

14. Federal Reserve Bank of Boston. **After the Phillips Curve: Persistence of High Inflation and High Unemployment.** Boston, Massachusetts, Federal Reserve Bank of Boston, 1978.

15. Federal Reserve Bank of Minneapolis. "Eliminating Policy Surprises: An Inexpensive Way to Beat Inflation," in **1979 Annual Report.** Minneapolis, Minnesota: Federal Reserve Bank of Minneapolis, 1978, pp. 1-7.

16. Federal Reserve Bank of Minneapolis, "Rational Expectations-Fresh

Ideas That Challenge Some Established Views of Policy Making," in **Annual Report 1977**. Minneapolis, Minnesota, Federal Reserve Bank of Minneapolis, 1977, pp. 1-13.

17. Friedman, Benjamin. "Even the St. Louis Model Now Believes in Fiscal Policy." **Journal of Money, Credit and Banking.** May 1977, pp. 365-367.

18. Friedman, Milton. **How Well Are Fluctuating Exchange Rates Working?** Washington, D.C.: American Enterprise Institute, 1973.

19. _____ **The Counter-Revolution in Monetary Theory.** England: The Wincott Foundation, 1970.

20. _____ "The Role of Monetary Policy." **American Economic Review.** March 1968, pp. 1-17.

21. Gramlich, Edward M. "The Usefulness of Monetary Policy as Discretionary Stabilization Tools." **Journal of Money, Credit and Banking.** May 1961, pp. 506-532.

22. Hansen, Bent. "On the Effects of Fiscal and Monetary Policy: A Taxonomic Discussion." **American Economic Review.** September 1973, pp. 546-571.

23. Higgins, Bryon. "Monetary Growth and Business Cycles." **Economic Review: Federal Reserve Bank of Kansas City.** April 1979, pp. 3-11.

24. Humphrey, Thomas M. "Changing Views of the Phillips Curve." **Economic Review: Federal Reserve Bank of Richmond.** July 1973, pp. 2-13.

25. _____ "Some Recent Developments in Phillips Curve Analysis." **Economic Review: Federal Reserve Bank of Richmond.** January/ February 1978, pp. 15-23.

26. Kemp, Donald S. "A Monetary View of the Balance of Payments." **Review: Federal Reserve Bank of St. Louis.** April 1975, pp. 14-22.

27. Kohn, Donald. "Interdependence, Exchange Rate Flexibility, and National Economics." **Monthly Review: Federal Reserve Bank of Kansas City.** April 1975, pp. 3-10.

28. Krause, Lawrence B. "Fixed, Flexible and Gliding Exchange Rates." **Journal of Money, Credit and Banking.** May 1971, pp. 321-338.

29. Kydland, Finn E. & Prescott, Edward C. "Rules Rather Than Discretion: The Inconsistency of Optimal Plans." **Journal of Political Economy.** June 1977, pp. 473-491.

30. Laporte, Anne Marie. "Monetary Aggregates Compared." **Business Conditions: Federal Reserve Bank of Chicago.** June 1976, pp. 11-15.

31. "Letter from Chairman Burns to Senator Proxmire." **Monthly Review: Federal Reserve Bank of New York.** November 1973, pp. 266-272.

32. Lucia, Joseph L. "Money Market Strategy or Money Aggregates: An Analysis of Recent Federal Reserve Policy." **Economic and Social Review.** October 1973, pp. 31-45.

33. Lucas Jr., Robert E. & Sargent, Thomas J. "After Keynesian Macro-

economists." **Quarterly Review: Federal Reserve Bank of Minneapolis.** Spring 1979, pp. 1-16.

34. McDonough, William R. "Effectiveness of Alternative Approaches to Monetary Control." **Business Review: Federal Reserve Bank of Dallas.** August 1976, pp. 1-7.

35. McNees, Stephen K. "The Phillips Curve: Forward-Or Backward-Or Backward-Looking?" **New England Economic Review.** July/August 1979, pp. 46-54.

36. Meek, Paul. "Nonborrowed Reserves or Federal Funds Rate as Desk Targets—Is There Difference?" **New England Economic Review.** March/April 1975, pp. 31-47.

37. Miller, Preston and Kaatz, Ronald. **Introduction to the Use of Econometric Models in Economic Policy Making.** Minneapolis, Minnesota; Federal Reserve Bank of Minneapolis, 1974.

38. Modigliani, Franco. "The Monetarist Controversy or Should We Forsake Stabilization Policies?" **American Economic Review.** March 1977, pp. 1-19.

39. Okun, Arthur M. "Fiscal-Monetary Activism: Some Analytical Issues." **Brookings Papers on Economic Activity: 1.** 1972, pp. 123-163.

40. Order, Robert Van. "Unemployment, Inflation, and Monetarism: A Further Analysis." **American Economic Review.** September 1977, pp. 741-746.

41. Poole, William. "Rule-of-Thumb for Guiding Monetary Policy," in **Open Market Policies and Operating Procedures: Staff Studies.** Washington, D.C.: Board of Governors of the Federal Reserve System, 1971, pp. 135-189.

42. Rache, Robert H. "A Comparative Static Analysis of Some Monetarist Propositions." **Review: Federal Reserve Bank of St. Louis.** December 1973, pp. 15-23.

43. Santomero, Anthony M. & Seater, John J. **The Inflation-Unemployment Trade-Off: A Critique of the Literature.** Philadelphia, Pennsylvania: Federal Reserve Bank of Philadelphia, 1977.

44. Sargent, Thomas J. & Wallace, Neil. **Rational Expectations and the Theory of Economic Policy.** Minneapolis, Minnesota: Federal Reserve Bank of Minneapolis, 1978.

45. Shiller, Robert J. "Rational Expectations and the Dynamic Structure of Macroeconomic Models: A Critical View." **Journal of Monetary Economics.** January 1978, pp. 1-44.

46. Stein, Jerome L. (Ed.). **Monetarism.** Amsterdam: North-Holland Publishing Company, 1976.

47. Tobin, James. "Inflation and Unemployment." **American Economic Review.** March 1972, pp. 1-18.

48. Vernon, Jack. "Money Demand Interest Elasticity and Monetary Policy Effectiveness." **Journal of Monetary Economics.** April 1977, pp. 179-190.

49. Westerfield, Janice M. "Would Fixed Exchange Rates Control Inflation?" **Business Review: Federal Reserve Bank of Philadelphia.** July/August 1976, pp. 3-10.

50. Whitman, Marina V.N. "Global Monetarism and the Monetary Approach to the Balance of Payments." **Brookings Papers on Economic Activity: 3.** 1975, pp. 491-536.

PART II

MONETARY POLICY

CHAPTER XII
Goals of Monetary Policy

Nations seek to achieve social goals through economic policy. Social goals are many and varied. Some are directly related to economic policy while others are indirectly related. In either case, a nation's welfare is affected by the success or failure of economic policy.

Economic goals that are believed to have the greatest impact on a nation's welfare are:

A. Full Employment
B. Price Stability
C. Economic Growth
D. Balance-of-Payments Equilibrium

Since policies pursued by the monetary authority impact those goals, monetary policy must be geared to their achievement.

The U.S. Congress wrestled with the problem of determining national goals in the Employment Act of 1946. It called for maximum employment, maximum production and maximum purchasing power. Maximum employment implies full employment. Maximum production implies rapid economic growth. Maximum purchasing power is rather obscure but, apparently, is related to price stability.

The Humphrey-Hawkins Full Employment and Balanced Growth Act was passed in 1978. This act strengthens the Employment Act in five essential respects: (1) It emphasizes the increasing role of the private sector to promote full employment, growth in productivity and price stability. (2) It stresses a goal of balanced Federal budgets. (3) It calls upon policymakers to improve the trade balance of the United States, while promoting fair and free trade and a stable international monetary system. (4) It establishes procedures for developing and reviewing economic policies. (For example, the act requires the

Administration to set annual numerical goals for key indicators such as employment and unemployment, production, real income, productivity and prices over a five year period. Goals for the first two years of a five year period are considered short term goals and for the final three years, medium term goals.) (5) It requires the President, once a year, and the Board of Governors, twice a year, to delineate to the Congress their targets and outline their plans on how they intend to reach them. In addition, the Board is required to comment on the relation between its plans for monetary policy and the short-term economic goals established by the President. These requirements were included in an effort to improve coordination between fiscal and monetary policies.

FULL EMPLOYMENT

Full employment means that every person who is willing and able to work has a job. For practical purposes, it is an impossible goal to achieve because there are certain types of unemployment that cannot be eliminated. The most important among them are technological, seasonal, voluntary and frictional unemployment. Technological unemployment arises from the development of new products and techniques. Since economic progress rests heavily on technological development, it is difficult to eliminate this type of unemployment. However, with the improvement of labor market information, accelerated programs of job training and increased mobility of labor, its impact can be reduced.

Seasonal unemployment arises from seasonal businesses such as construction and farming. To provide gainful employment to everyone who is laid off temporarily due to seasonal factors is not an easy task in a democratic society.

Voluntary unemployment is another type of unemployment that cannot be wiped out in a free society. There are always some workers who quit their jobs for personal reasons: they do not like the nature of their work, their boss or management policies. There are people who work for one month and then need a vacation of six months. On the other hand, there are some workers who are fired for one reason or another. The only way to eliminate this type of unemployment is by denying a worker the right to quit and the employer to fire him. But such a solution is unacceptable in a free society.

Frictional unemployment represents time spent looking for jobs by new entrants into the labor market and by others in search of suitable jobs. Some economists regard short term unemployment represented by the number of individuals unemployed for less than five weeks as an indicator of the amount of frictional unemployment.

If zero unemployment is unattainable in a free economy, what maximum unemployment can we tolerate? It is difficult to answer this question. However, for several years, a four percent unemployment rate has been considered an appropriate target of unemployment in the United States. The Full Employment and Balanced Growth Act stipulates that the President should aim at targets of four percent for workers aged 16 and over and three percent for workers aged 20 and over for 1983—the first fifth year under the act.[1]

PRICE STABILITY

Price stability is another important economic goal. Wild fluctuations in prices are harmful to any economy. Declining prices are harmful because they cause a recession. Generally speaking, when prices fall profits fall. A decline in prices causes a cutback in investment. When investment falls the economy starts sagging.

Rising prices (inflation) also create problems. A large flow of savings is important to economic progress. But rising prices discourage savings. They play havoc with people who live on fixed incomes. They worsen the balance of payments of a nation if its prices rise faster than the rest of the world. Rising prices result in distortion in the allocation of resources. They weaken the incentive of businessmen to improve efficiency. Above all, rising prices tend to feed on themselves. If they are left unchecked, they become more and more severe, eventually leading the economy to a complete collapse.

Price stability does not mean constant prices. Generally, a three percent annual increase in prices is considered consistent with the goal of price stability.

Price behavior is generally measured by the consumer price index, the wholesale price index and the GNP-implicit price deflator. The consumer price index measures the average change in prices of all types of goods and services purchased by urban wage earners and clerical workers. This is also called the cost of living index. The wholesale price index is designed to measure changes in prices of commodities (raw materials and semi-finished and finished goods) sold in primary markets. The GNP-implicit price deflator considers prices of all final goods consisting of consumer and capital goods and of government purchases. Among these three ways of measuring price variations, the consumer price index is most widely used. The Full Employment and Balanced Growth Act stipulates that the President should aim at bringing down the rate of increase in the consumer price index to a 3 percent level in 1983.[2]

ECONOMIC GROWTH

Economic growth generally signifies improvement in the well being of people. It can be measured by a year-to-year change in (1) real national income, (2) per capita income and (3) output per man hour. The measure of real national income captures changes in national income adjusted for inflation. But an increase in it does not necessarily mean improvement in the well being of people because it can be swallowed by an increase in population. This problem can be overcome if growth is measured on the basis of per capita income. If people work fewer hours they can be better off even with the same per capita income. But this type of measurement does not reflect it. This weakness can be corrected if growth is measured by output per man hour. Though all these methods are discussed in economic literature, economic growth is generally measured by a change in real national income.

Economic growth has both benefits and costs. It improves the standard of living of people. It makes inequity in the distribution of income more tolerable. Above all, it provides challenges and a sense of achievement that distinguishes a vibrant from a stagnant economy. Growth also has many costs. It calls for people to sacrifice their consumption in order to provide the necessary funds for expanding productive facilities. It causes air and water pollution and spoils natural resources. It overcrowds cities.

Economists debate over the target of growth rate. Some economists even believe that no specific rate of growth be set as a target. For example, Milton Friedman says, "There is no way in a free society to say in advance that one or another numerical rate of change is needed or desirable, or that a higher rate of change is better than a lower (one)...Whatever rate of change in the statistical aggregate results from the efforts of free men to promote their own aspirations is the right rate.''[3] Other economists such as Stanley H. Ruttenberg believe that there should be a specific target. Sheldon Stahl claims if the U.S. economy has to be maintained close to full employment, given the historical rate of increase in productivity in the labor force, its real national income must expand at a rate of between 4 and 5 percent a year.[4]

BALANCE-OF-PAYMENTS EQUILIBRIUM

The balance-of-payments equilibrium is a new goal that has been recently added to the list. Balance of payments refers to a summary statement of a country's total receipts from other nations against its total payment obligations. Things such as the export and import of goods and services, inflow and outflow of capital, gifts and foreign aid, all determine the size of receipts and payment obligations of a nation. Balance of payments are in equilibrium when total receipts become equal to total payment obligations.

The goal of balance-of-payments equilibrium was not recognized in the United States until recently when large deficits in her balance of payments began to present serious problems. For several years after World War II, the United States had large surpluses in her balance of payments. The situation, however, changed in 1950 when the Western European nations recovered from the ruins of war and became competitive in international markets. In 1958, things took a turn for the worse when large deficits began to persist in U.S. balance of payments. In 1971, for the first time since 1893, the United States experienced an adverse balance of trade, importing more goods from abroad than it was able to export.

Continuous deficits in balance of payments create many problems. They deplete gold stock. They shake the confidence of foreigners in a nation's currency. Above all, persistent deficits in balance of payments point up underlying weaknesses inherent in an economy.

There are many other possible goals of economic policy. These include freedom and opportunity for every individual, equitable distribution of income, conservation of natural resources, providing greater aid to less developed nations, etc. Some of these would be accepted as desirable goals. Others would be rejected as undesirable by many economists. Some of these goals are broad and full of ambiguities. For example, what do we mean by freedom for every individual? Every person may have a different idea about it. Moreover, certain goals such as conservation of natural resources, providing greater aid to underdeveloped countries, etc. do not lie strictly within the scope of fiscal and monetary policies.

CONFLICTS AMONG GOALS

The problem with these goals is that, in many cases, they conflict with one another. If we want to accomplish one goal we may have to sacrifice another. Major goals, discussed earlier, conflict with each other as follows:

1. Full employment vs. price stability
2. Price stability vs. economic growth
3. Full employment (or economic growth) vs. balance-of-payments equilibrium

Full Employment Vs. Price Stability

Goals of full employment and price stability are difficult to achieve together because when policymakers try to reduce unemployment, inflation tends to rise. Normally, when the economy moves toward full employment, two things happen: One, the cost of production shoots up because of the scarcity of factors of production. Two, the aggregate demand increases. Both put upward pressure on prices.

Economists usually use the Phillips curve to discuss the trade-off between unemployment and inflation. A number of studies have been made to show how much inflation must be tolerated to achieve a certain amount of unemployment or how much unemployment the society has to live with in order to hold down inflation to a certain level (Samuelson and Solow, 1960;[5] Klein and Bodkin, 1964[6] Hymans, 1970;[7] and Gordon, 1971[8]).

As explained in the previous chapter, the Phillips curve has come under attack. Monetarists claim that there is no permanent trade-off. A trade-off may exist in the short run but not in the long run. Rationalists go even further and state that trade-offs do not exist at all. Keynesians disagree. They assert that trade-offs exist and policymakers can successfully exploit them for stabilization purposes. They support their position with a number of studies done in this area in recent years. (For more detail, see Chapter XI, section, Trade-off Vs. No Trade-off.)

Price Stability Vs. Economic Growth

Some economists claim that price stability is incompatible with economic growth, and therefore goals of price stability and economic growth cannot be achieved together. They add that inflation helps growth. When prices rise business profits rise. A rise in business profits stimulates economic growth. However, many economists disagree. They argue that it is inflation, not price stability, that is incompatible with economic growth. Inflation encourages wasteful and speculative activities, frees inefficient firms from the fear of bankruptcy and reduces savings necessary for investment. It makes a nation's goods noncompetitive in international markets. Above all, if inflation is left unchecked, it would eventually lead the economy to a complete disaster.

Based upon the study of 16 underdeveloped countries, the Federal Reserve Bank of New York concludes that stable prices tend to promote orderly and rapid growth. The study showed that where prices advanced moderately or not at all during 1950-57, the rate of growth was, by and large, steady and clustered around the average of 6 percent annually.[9] In contrast, where there was sustained inflationary pressure during this period the growth was somewhat sporadic, the average ranging from less than 1 percent to more than 7 percent with an overall average of 4 percent.

Using evidence from many countries over a wide range of periods, the Commission on Money and Credit, on the other hand, concludes that with price changes from zero to 6 percent a year there is no appreciable association between price changes and economic growth.[10] However, beyond these limits there exists a relationship between them. Countries with declining prices or with price increases greater than 6 percent appear to have lower growth rates than those operating within these limits.

Economic Growth (Or Full Employment) Vs. Balance-Of-Payments Equilibrium

Another conflict of goals is between economic growth (or full employment) and balance-of-payments equilibrium. Rapid economic growth or a high level of employment can create problems in balance of payments by raising domestic prices, thereby causing imports to rise and exports to fall. But this adverse effect can be offset by an increase in the inflow of foreign capital. Rapid growth helps to attract foreign capital by raising business profits at home. However, if growth contributes to high costs, even domestic businessmen may be forced to invest abroad. Economic growth also causes interest rates to rise. High interest rates attract foreign funds.

In the end, it can be said that even though some goals are mutually consistent and others, to a certain extent, conflict with each other, all of them can be achieved simultaneously provided we do not expect to attain each goal one hundred percent and are willing to compromise.

SUMMARY

Major goals are: full employment (everyone who is willing and able to work has a job), price stability (elimination of wild fluctuations in prices), economic growth (continuous increase in the real national income) and balance-of-payments equilibrium.

It would be easier to achieve these goals if they were compatible. But they are not. The goal of full employment conflicts with price stability because as we move closer toward full employment prices tend to rise. Price stability conflicts with economic growth because rapid growth is generally accompanied by a moderate rise in prices. Rapid growth (or high level of employment) can bring disequilibrium in the balance of payments. It does so by causing domestic prices to rise, thereby making our goods noncompetitive in foreign markets.

Besides four major goals discussed earlier, there are many other goals such as freedom and opportunity for every individual, equitable distribution of income, conservation of natural resources, providing cleaner air, etc. But goals like freedom for everyone cannot be achieved to the satisfaction of every individual. Certain goals like conservation of natural resources, providing cleaner air, etc., are not quite within the reach of fiscal and monetary authorities.

FOOTNOTES

[1]Council of Economic Advisers, **Economic Report of the President: January 1979** (Washington, D.C.: U.S. Government Printing Office, 1979), p. 108.

[2]**Ibid.**

[3]United States Joint Economic Committee, **Employment, Growth, and Price Levels,** Hearings, Part 9A, 86th Congress, 1st Session (Washington D.C.: U.S. Government

Printing Office, 1959), pp. 3019-3020.

⁴Sheldon W. Stahl, "On Economic Growth," **Monthly Review: Federal Reserve Bank of Kansas City** (February 1975), pp. 7-8.

⁵Paul A. Samuleson and Robert T. Solow, "Problems of Achieving and Maintaining a Stable Price Level: Analytical Aspects of Anti-Inflation Policy," **American Economic Review** (May 1960), p. 192.

⁶Commission on Money and Credit, **Inflation, Growth, and Employment** (Englewood Cliffs, N.J.: Prentice-Hall, Inc., 1964), p. 393.

⁷Saul H. Hymans, "The Inflation-Unemployment Trade-off: Theory and Experience," in **Readings in Money, National Income and Stabilization Policy**, ed. Warren L. Smith & Ronald L. Teigen (Homewood, Illinois: Richard D. Irwin, Inc., 1970), p. 157.

⁸Robert J. Gordon, "Inflation in Recession and Recovery," **Brookings Papers on Economic Activity: 1** (1971), p. 144.

⁹Federal Reserve Bank of New York, "Inflation and Economic Development," **Monthly Review: Federal Reserve Bank of New York** (August 1959), p. 126.

¹⁰Commission on Money and Credit, **Money and Credit, Their Influence on Jobs, Prices and Growth** (Englewood Cliffs, N.J.: Prentice-Hall, Inc., 1961), p. 44.

QUESTIONS FOR REVIEW

1. Describe the four main economic goals. To what extent are they attainable?
2. What is "full employment?" Is a zero rate of unemployment attainable? Explain.
3. What are the different ways of measuring price behavior? Which one do policymakers often use to determine whether or not the goal of "price stability" is being met? Why?
4. How does the Humphrey-Hawkins Full Employment and Balanced Growth Act strengthen the Employment Act? Explain.
5. What is technological unemployment? What can we do to reduce it?
6. What is meant by "economic growth?" What are the different ways of measuring it? In your opinion, should planners set a specific target for rate of growth?
7. What is the "balance-of-payments equilibrium?" What kinds of problems does a continuous deficit in balance of payments create?
8. Do you see any conflict between "full employment" and "price stability?"
9. Can "price stability" and "economic growth" be achieved simultaneously? Explain.
10. How do "rapid economic growth" and "high employment" generate disequilibrium in the balance of payments?

SUGGESTED FURTHER READING

1. Christian, James W. "A Further Analysis of the Objectives of American

Monetary Policy." **Journal of Finance.** June 1958, pp. 465-477.

2. Friedman, Milton. "Noble Lecture: Inflation and Unemployment." **Journal of Political Economy.** June 1977, pp. 451-472.

3. Humphrey, Thomas M. "Changing Views of the Phillips Curve." **Monthly Review: Federal Reserve Bank of Richmond.** July 1973, pp. 2-13.

4. "Some Recent Development in Phillips Curve Analysis." **Economic Review: Federal Reserve Bank of Richmond.** January/February 1978, p. 15-23.

5. McMillan, Robert A. "A Re-examination of the Full Employment Goal." **Economic Review: Federal Reserve Bank of Cleveland.** March/April 1973, pp. 3-18.

6. Santomero, Anthony M. & Seater, John M. **The Inflation-Unemployment Trade-Off: A Critique of the Literature.** Philadelphia, Pennsylvania: Federal Reserve Bank of Philadelphia, 1977.

7. Smith, Sharon P. "An Examination of Employment and Unemployment Rates." **Quarterly Review: Federal Reserve Bank of New York.** Autumn 1977, pp. 14-18.

8. Stahl, Sheldon W. "On Economic Growth." **Monthly Review: Federal Reserve Bank of Kansas City.** February, 1975, pp. 3-9.

CHAPTER XIII

Organization Of The Federal Reserve System

The responsibility for setting and carrying out a nation's monetary policy rests with its central bank. The Federal Reserve System is the central bank of the United States. It was established by the Federal Reserve Act of 1913.

UNDERLYING PRINCIPLES IN THE COMPOSITION OF THE FEDERAL RESERVE STRUCTURE

The structure of the Federal Reserve System is built primarily on two major principles: (1) It should be an independent agency, accountable but not subservient to the Congress. (2) It should have regional banks with central supervision and coordination. It was feared that if the Federal Reserve was made subservient to the Congress or to the President, it would become subject to political expedience and thus fail to serve the national interest. The Federal Reserve structure incorporated regional banks because it was felt that without them the System could not totally comprehend the interests of different regions nor could it administer them effectively. Moreover, some feared that without regional banks, the System might succumb to the influence of the Eastern financial centers.

THE FEDERAL RESERVE SYSTEM

The organizational structure of the Federal Reserve System can be understood in terms of the following:
1. Board of Governors
2. District Banks
3. Member Banks

4. Federal Open Market Committee
5. Federal Advisory Council

Board of Governors

The Board of Governors of the Federal Reserve System consists of seven members appointed by the President of the United States and confirmed by the Senate. Their appointments are for a term of fourteen years, with terms so arranged that one expires every two years. The President designates one of the members as Chairman and one as Vice Chairman for a period of four years. In the interest of geographical representation, no two members can come from the same Federal Reserve District.

The Board of Governors is primarily responsible for formulating monetary policy and supervising its execution. It has full authority over changes in reserve requirements. It reviews and determines discount rates established by directors of Reserve Banks; constitutes a majority in the Federal Open Market Committee, which sets policy for open market operations; regulates stock market credit; and establishes the maximum rates of interest that member banks may pay on time deposits.

District Banks

The Federal Reserve System divides the nation into twelve districts, each with a Federal Reserve Bank of its own. The name and District number of each Federal Reserve Bank are as follows:

NAME	DISTRICT
Federal Reserve Bank of Boston	1
Federal Reserve Bank of New York	2
Federal Reserve Bank of Philadelphia	3
Federal Reserve Bank of Cleveland	4
Federal Reserve Bank of Richmond	5
Federal Reserve Bank of Atlanta	6
Federal Reserve Bank of Chicago	7
Federal Reserve Bank of St. Louis	8
Federal Reserve Bank of Minneapolis	9
Federal Reserve Bank of Kansas City	10
Federal Reserve Bank of Dallas	11
Federal Reserve Bank of San Francisco	12

Boundaries of Federal Reserve Districts and their branch territories are illustrated in Diagram 13-1. The central administrative agency, the Federal Reserve System, which has the responsibility of coordinating and directing policy, is located in Washington, D.C. Each Federal Reserve Bank is a federally chartered corporation with stockholders, directors and a president. Stockholders of a Federal Reserve Bank are member banks located in its district. Each member bank is required to purchase stock of its Federal Reserve Bank in an amount equal to 6 percent of its own capital and surplus—3 percent in cash and 3 percent on demand. When profits are made, member banks receive a dividend, which is limited by law to a maximum return of 6 percent on their investment.

Each Federal Reserve Bank has nine directors—three each of Class A, Class B and Class C. Class A and B directors are elected by member banks. Banks are divided into three groups: (i) small banks, (ii) medium banks and (iii) large banks. Each group elects one director for Class A and another for Class B.

Class A directors may or may not be bankers but class B and C directors must be nonbankers. Class C directors are appointed by the Board of Governors. The Board of Governors designates one of the Class C directors as chairman and one as deputy chairman of the board of directors of each Federal Reserve Bank. The chairman of the board of directors, in addition to regular duties at the Federal Reserve Bank, serves as a Federal Reserve Agent, which requires him to make regular reports to the Board of Governors in Washington.

The board of directors appoints the president of the bank for a term of five years, subject to the approval of the Board of Governors.

Each Federal Reserve District Bank issues and supplies Federal Reserve notes, offers check clearing services, stores coins, handles government debt issues, provides banking services to the Treasury and other Federal Government agencies, establishes its own discount rates subject to review and determination by the Board of Governors, advises the Board of Governors on business conditions and public attitudes in its area as well as on general policy matters, and examines and supervises state-chartered member banks.

Member Banks

All national banks (banks chartered by the Comptroller of the

DIAGRAM 13-1

BOUNDARIES OF FEDERAL RESERVE DISTRICTS AND THEIR BRANCH TERRITORIES

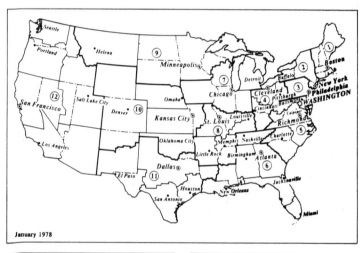

January 1978

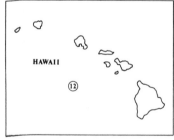

LEGEND

▬▬ **Boundaries of Federal Reserve Districts**	◉ **Federal Reserve Bank Cities**
▬▬ **Boundaries of Federal Reserve Branch Territories**	• **Federal Reserve Bank Cities**
✪ **Board of Governors of the Federal Reserve System**	· **Federal Reserve Bank Facility**

Source: i. **Federal Reserve Bulletin** (May 1979), p. A78.

Currency) are required by law to become members of the Federal Reserve. State-chartered commercial banks may choose to join the Federal Reserve by meeting the membership requirements.

Commercial banks that are members of the Federal Reserve have certain obligations and privileges. The major obligations of a member bank are as follows:

i. It must maintain required reserves set by the Federal Reserve
ii. It must remit, at par, checks cleared through the Federal Reserve
iii. It must comply with various Federal laws, regulations and conditions of membership regarding the adequacy of capital, mergers with other banking institutions, establishment of branches, relations with bank holding companies, and loan and investment limitations

The major privileges of a member bank, on the other hand, are as follows:

i. It can borrow at the discount window to meet a temporary need for funds
ii. It can use the facilities for clearing checks
iii. It can obtain various kinds of services, such as advisory service dealing with accounting and record systems

Federal Open Market Committee

The Federal Open Market Committee (FOMC) is the principle policy making body in the Federal Reserve System. Seven members of the Board of Governors and the presidents of five Federal Reserve Banks comprise the Committee. Since open market operations are performed in New York City, the president of the Federal Reserve Bank of New York is a permanent member. The other four positions are rotated among the 11 remaining presidents of District Banks. By statute the Committee determines its own organization, and by tradition it elects the Chairman of the Board of Governors to serve as its Chairman and the President of the Federal Reserve Bank of New York as its Vice Chairman.

The FOMC determines the posture of monetary policy which is implemented through the purchase and sale of U.S. Government and Federal agency securities, bankers' acceptances and foreign exchange. The responsibility for executing the policy rests with the Manager of the System Open Market Account.

Federal Advisory Council

To establish ongoing communication between the Board of Governors and the community of business and banking, the Federal Reserve Act provides for the Federal Advisory Council consisting of 12 members, one from each district. The board of directors of each District Bank annually selects the Council member of its district. The Council usually meets four times a year in Washington. It confers with the Board of Governors and makes recommendations on matters pertaining to business conditions, operations of District Banks and questions on policy. Since the Council has no power to act or set policy, the Board is free to accept or reject its recommendations.

RELATIONSHIP BETWEEN THE FEDERAL RESERVE AND OTHER INSTITUTIONS

The ability of the Federal Reserve to make decisions independently of other Government and private institutions rests on its statutory relationship to the Congress, the Treasury, the Administration and financial institutions.

The Federal Resrve and the Congress

The constitution of the United States gives the Congress the right to govern the nation's monetary system. In order to free monetary decisions from political and private pressures, the Congress created the Federal Reserve System as an independent government agency to which it delegated its monetary power. To provide a maximum amount of independence, the Congress gave the Federal Reserve the right to control its own budget and do its own auditing.

Although the Federal Reserve is an independent agency, it is not completely free from the influence of the Congress. At least twice a year, the Board is required to report to the Congress on the course of monetary policy and expected ranges of growth in the major monetary and credit aggregates for the year ahead. This provides members of the Congress the opportunity to express their views on the appropriateness of Federal Reserve action. The Congress expresses such views by conducting hearings on a specific action or policy of the Federal Reserve, informal meetings between one or more members of the Congress and one or more members of the Board, or by written communications to the Board pertaining to a certain issue. When a majority of the members of both Houses are at odds with the Board, a resolution is adopted expressing the "sense" of the Congress. Congressional views, regardless of the form in which they are expressed, have no legal standing—the Federal Reserve may ignore them. However, Congressional views do influence policy, especially when expressed by certain members or committees. Moreover, the Federal Reserve recognizes that it is the Congress that gave it the monetary power and that it is the Congress that can alter it. The need for Congressional support on future legislation pertaining to the monetary system also serves as leverage. The freedom that the Federal Reserve acquired from the Treasury through the Accord of 1951 was due, in large measure, to the backing it received from the Congress, for example.

The Federal Reserve And The Treasury

Ever since the Federal Reserve negotiated the "Accord," it has acquired a great deal of independence from the Treasury in conducting monetary policy. Previously, the Federal Reserve was required to provide price support to Government securities at the time of Treasury financing so that the Treasury could raise funds at a fixed pattern of rates, which ranged from ⅜ of 1% on ninety-day Treasury bills to 2½% for 20- to 25-year Government bonds (excluding Savings Bonds).[1] In so doing, the Federal Reserve, at times, took an action contrary to its own objectives. If interest rates went above the fixed rates at the time of Treasury financing, the Federal Reserve took an expansionary action to lower them, even when the objective was to curb inflation.

Although the Federal Reserve is not now required to maintain interest rates at certain levels when the Treasury is in the market, it recognizes that the Government has a huge task of financing. With this understanding, it follows the policy of "even keel" whenever it feels necessary. During the period of even keel, the Federal Reserve does not undertake any action to change the thrust of monetary policy. In most circumstances, it changes neither discount rates nor reserve requirements. Open market operations are conducted in a manner that suggests no policy change to the market. An even keel period usually begins a few days before the announcement of a Treasury financing and continues until a few days after payment and delivery of securities. The Federal Reserve adopts the policy of even keel because it does not want to become a source of instability in the securities market at the time of Treasury financing.

Direct Treasury borrowing from the Federal Reserve is dangerous as it is potentially inflationary. The Federal Reserve can be pressured into making such loans, particularly at the time of a large Government deficit. But the law protects it by restricting the size (maximum of $5 billion) and duration (maximum of 6 months) of each loan. In the past, most Federal Reserve loans to the Treasury have been for less than $500 million and for a period of less than 10 days. The largest loan ever given was $2.6 billion that was over the weekend of March 31, 1979, and the longest period was 28 days in 1943.[2]

The Federal Reserve needs independence as well as cooperation from the Treasury. Without cooperation, the action of the Federal Reserve may, at times, be neutralized by a Treasury action. But cooperation exists. A luncheon meeting with senior staff of the Treasury is generally held each week. These luncheons are sometimes attended by the Chairman of the Board of Governors or perhaps another member of the Board and by the Under Secretary of the Treasury for Monetary Affairs. To avoid the disruptive effect of the transfer of funds from Tax and Loan accounts to the Treasury account at the Federal Reserve, the Fiscal Assistant Secretary of the Treasury consults the Manager of the Federal Open Market Committee or his deputy each day to determine how much money should be transferred on that day and from which banks.

To help the Treasury in refinancing, the Federal Resrve allows almost all, or a large portion, of its holdings of maturing Treasury issues to roll over (continue in effect beyond the maturity date). Some economists claim that it cannot afford to do otherwise. The redemption of maturing issues will complicate its task of managing bank reserves, because once they are disturbed, they cannot be restored to an original level without affecting the money market. Besides roll over, the Federal Reserve provides certain services to the Treasury such as handling of its securities and conducting transactions in the market for its various accounts.

The Federal Reserve And The Administration

There is a very close relationship between the Federal Reserve and the Administration. The Chairman of the Board frequently meets with the President. In addition, he participates in discussions concerning the evaluation of economic conditions, objectives, and possible courses of action with the Secretary of the Treasury, the Chairman of the Council of Economic Advisers, and the Director of the Office of Management and Budget. From time to time, the Chairman of the Board has been called upon by the President to serve on a number of policy making bodies such as the Committee on Interest and Dividends, the Cost of Living Council and the Emergency Loan Guarantee Board. Other Board members also frequently meet people responsible for economic policy in the Administration. At scheduled intervals, the Board as a whole meets with the Council of Economic Advisers. Hence, when the Federal Reserve takes any action, it does so with full knowledge of the plans and objectives of the Administration.

Since there is no clear cut mandate on the legal authority of the Federal Reserve regarding its independence from the Administraiton, some people doubt that the Federal Reserve can act independently in case of a difference of opinion. One way to determine its legal authority is to analyze its power on the basis of: (1) The Federal Reserve Act, (2) Judicial decisions, and (3) The Humphrey-Hawkins Full Employment and Balanced Growth Act.

Federal Reserve Act

A study of the Federal Reserve Act of 1913 reveals that the Congress did not originally conceive the idea of the Federal Reserve as a completely autonomous agency, though it wanted to keep it out of politics. The Federal Reserve was created as a bureau of the Treasury. The Secretary of the Treasury was required to serve as an exofficio Chairman of the Federal Reserve Board. This status of the Secretary of the Treasury was terminated in 1935. Mariner S. Eccles was the first Chairman of the Board of Governors. He considered the Board a nonpolitical agency, yet a part of the Administration. Eccles interpreted the term "nonpolitical" to mean that the Board would not participate in party politics. This relationship was altered by President Harry S. Truman in 1946. Eccles was told that in any appearance before the Congress he must make it clear that he was speaking for the

Federal Reserve and not for the Administration.[3]

To keep the Federal Reserve out of politics, the Congress encouraged the President to restrict Board membership to people with competence in the field and not to use membership as a reward for political activities. Moreover, the long term (fourteen years) of the office for Board members and the fact that a member, after serving a full term, is not eligible for reappointment frees the Board from the pressures of the Administration.

Although the Congress has played an important role in strengthening the autonomy of the Federal Reserve, there is no evidence, either in the Federal Reserve Act or in subsequent amendments, to suggest that the Congress intended to preclude the possibility of Presidential influence or control in matters involving the national welfare. M.J. Rossant says that it does not matter what kind of power the Federal Reserve has and what it says in the open, in practice it works with the Administraiton, knowing that any overt attempt to defy the Executive or the Congress might pose a threat to its power.[4] The Eisenhower and Kennedy Administrations were always able to get whatever they wanted from the Federal Reserve. However, there have been times when the Federal Reserve acted contrary to the wishes of the Administration. For example, in December 1965, the Federal Reserve, contrary to the wishes of President Johnson, approved the increase in the discount rate from 4 to $4\frac{1}{2}\%$ in an effort to curb inflation.[5]

Judicial decisions

The issue of whether the Federal Reserve is completely independent of the President has never been put to a court test. However, there are two decisions of the Supreme Court that are frequently cited to support the independence of the Federal Reserve. One is the 1935 decision, Humphrey's Executor vs. United States (295 U.S. 602), which involves the Federal Trade Commission. In this case, the Supreme Court ruled that the power of the President to remove a member of the Commission is restricted where its members are an "independent, nonpartisan body of experts charged with duties neither political nor executive, but predominantly quasi-judicial and quasi-legislative..." The relevance of this ruling to the issue of Federal Reserve autonomy is questioned by some who say that it is doubtful that the Federal Reserve can be assumed to be quasi-judicial and quasi-legislative as the court held in the FTC case. On the contrary, there is strong presumptive evidence that the Congress intended the Federal Reserve to be a part of the Executive Branch, they claim.

The second is the 1838 decision, Kendall vs. United States (12 Peters 210), which involves the Postmaster General. In this case, the Supreme Court ruled that the branch of the Government is not the essential consideration in establishing the nature and extent of the independence of a Federal Government official but the statutory mandate of his office. This has been interpreted to mean that the President has no power under the constitution to interfere with, set aside, correct or revise any decision of the Federal Reserve in any matter because such power has been delegated to the Board's exclusive jurisdiction by the Congress.

Humphrey-Hawkins Full Employment & Balanced Growth Act

The Humphrey-Hawkins Full Employment and Balanced Growth Act of 1978 suggests that the Federal Reserve Board is independent of the Administration as it places the responsibility of coordination between fiscal and monetary policies not on the President but on the Congress. The act requires the President (once a year) and the Board (twice a year) to appear before the Congress. The President is expected to report on economic goals he has established and how he plans to achieve them. The Board is required to report on its objectives and plans with respect to monetary policy and to comment on the relationship between its plans and short-term economic goals established by the President. All these imply that, although the Board is expected to work with the Administration, in case of a difference of opinion and the difference can be adequately justified, the Board can go its own way.

THE FEDERAL RESERVE AND FINANCIAL INSTITUTIONS

Among financial institutions, the one which is most directly related to the Federal Reserve is commercial banking. The relationship between the Federal Reserve and member commercial banks is of an agency and a client (the Federal Reserve provides various services to member banks such as lending money for temporary needs, clearing checks, etc.), of a regulator and a regulatee (the Federal Reserve has a general regulatory and supervisory responsibility for operations of all member banks), of stockholders and management (member banks by law are required to purchase capital stock of District Banks), and of electorate and government (two thirds of the board of directors of each District Bank are elected by member banks). It should be noted that though national banks are member banks and abide by all of the rules and regulations of the Federal Reserve, they are supervised by the Comptroller of the Currency and not by the Federal Reserve.

It is often alleged that the Federal Resrve is unduly influenced by member banks. The allegation is based upon the idea that member banks being stockholders and electorate have the power to influence the policy of the Federal Reserve. Officials of the Federal Reserve deny it, however. They say that even though member banks subscribe to the capital stock of Federal Reserve Banks, their stocks do not carry the usual rights of stock ownership. Stockholders have no power to change the management. The principal power for making decisions is vested in the Board of Governors, whose members are not elected but appointed by the President, subject to the approval of the Senate. Elected directors cannot do much for their constituents as they have very little to say in the formulation of monetary policy and most of the functions their District Banks perform are administered under rules and regulations set by the Board. The Board has the final say regarding the selection of the president and first vice president of each District Bank. As an ultimate safeguard against undue private influence, the Board has the authority to suspend or remove any officer or director of a District Bank.

SUMMARY

The Federal Reserve System is the central banking system of the United States, built on principles of independence of the agency and of regional banks with central supervision and coordination. Its organizational structure includes the Board of Governors, District Banks, the Federal Open Market Committee, and the Federal Advisory Council. The analysis of the Federal Reserve's relationship with other institutions shows that it has a fair amount of independence from the Congress, the Treasury, the Administration and financial institutions.

FOOTNOTES

[1]Allan Sproud, "The Accord - A Landmark in the First Fifty Years of the Federal Reserve System," **Monthly Review: Federal Reserve Bank of New York** (November 1964), p. 228.

[2]Federal Reserve Bank of New York, **Special Treasury Borrowings From the Fed,** Fedpoints No. 23 (New York: Federal Reserve Bank of New York, May 1979), pp. 1-2.

[3]Leo Fishman, "The White House and the Fed," **Challenge** (July/August 1966), pp. 22.

[4]M.J. Rossant, "Mr. Martin and the Winds of Change," **Challenge** (February 1964), p. 13.

[5]Fishman, p. 21.

QUESTIONS FOR REVIEW

1. Discuss in detail the nature of the relationship that exists between the Federal Reserve and the Congress.
2. What do we mean by the "even-keel" policy? Why does the Federal Reserve follow such a policy at the time of Treasury financings?
3. Analyze the independence of the Federal Reserve from the Administration on the basis of:
   a. The Federal Reserve Act
   b. Judicial decisions
   c. The Employment Act
   d. The Humphrey-Hawkins Act.
4. "The Federal Reserve is unduly influenced by member banks." Comment.
5. Explain in brief the organizational set up of the Federal Open Market Committee.
6. Describe in brief the following:
   a. Roll over
   b. Obligations of a member bank
   c. Privileges of a member bank
   d. Functions of a District Bank
7. Explain the major principles on which the structure of the Federal Reserve is built.
8. Explain the relationship between the Treasury and the Federal Reserve in the light of the Federal Reserve Act.
9. Explain how the Treasury Accord of 1951 frees the Federal Reserve from the Treasury?
10. Describe in brief the following:
    a. Board of Governors
    b. District Banks
    c. Member Banks

d. Federal Advisory Council

SUGGESTED FURTHER READING

1. Baughman, Ernest T. "The Federal Reserve and the Economy." **Voice: Federal Reserve Bank of Dallas.** March 1978, pp. 1-4.
2. Board of Governors of the Federal Reserve System. **The Federal Reserve System: Purposes and Functions.** Washington, D.C.: Board of Governors, 1974.
3. Burns, Arthur F. **Reflections of an Economic Policy Maker.** Washington, D.C.: American Enterprise Institute for Public Policy Research, 1978, pp. 379-385.
4. "Characteristics of Federal Reserve Bank Directors." **Federal Reserve Bulletin.** June 1972, pp. 550-559.
5. Clifford, A. Jerome. **The Independence of the Federal Reserve System.** Philadelphia, Penn.: University of Pennsylvania Press, 1965.
6. Federal Reserve Bank of Chicago. "The Fed in Perspective: 1776-1976," in **1976 Annual Report.** Chicago, Illinois: Federal Reserve Bank of Chicago, 1977.
7. Federal Reserve Bank of Minneapolis. "Perspectives on Federal Reserve Independence: A Changing Structure for Changing Times," in **Annual Report 1976.** Minneapolis, Minnesota: Federal Reserve Bank of Minneapolis, 1977.
8. Fishman, Lee. "The White House and the Fed." **Challenge.** July/August 1966, pp. 21-23 & 41.
9. Gustus, Warren J. "Monetary Policy, Debt Management, and Even Keel." **Business Review: Federal Reserve Bank of Philadelphia.** January 1969, pp. 3-10.
10. Kane, Edward J. "How Much Do New Congressional Restraints Lessen Federal Reserve Independence?" **Challenge.** November/December 1975, pp. 37-44.
11. Maisel, Sherman L. **Managing the Dollar.** New York: W.W. Norton & Company, 1973, pp. 132-166.
12. Sproul, Allan. "The 'Accord' - A Landmark in the First Fifty Years of the Federal Reserve System." **Monthly Review: Federal Reserve Bank of New York.** November 1964, pp. 227-237.
13. Yohe, William P. & Gasper, Louis C. "The Even Keel Decisions of the Federal Open Market Committee." **Financial Analyst Journal.** November/December 1970, pp. 105-115.

CHAPTER XIV

General Instruments Of Monetary Control

Various monetary instruments are available to the Federal Reserve for regulating the general availability of money and credit. They are:

  A. General Instruments of Control
      1. Discount rate
      2. Open market operations
      3. Reserve requirements
  B. Selective Controls
      1. Interest rate ceilings
      2. Margin requirements
      3. Consumer credit
      4. Real estate credit
  C. Moral Suasion
      1. Informal requests to member banks
      2. Publicity
      3. Direct contacts

The general instruments of control are discussed in this chapter. The next chapter deals with the other instruments. General instruments of control are used individually as well as in conjunction with each other. Of the three instruments, the one that plays the most important role in the U.S. monetary policy is open market operations.

DISCOUNT RATE

Discount rate policy refers to rates Federal Reserve Banks charge on loans made to banks and other qualified depository institutions and conditions of eligibility of paper for discount and advances. The term "discount" refers to the sale of eligible paper; and "advance," to a loan. The Depository Institutions Deregulation and Monetary Act of 1980 extends access to discount window of all depository institutions that hold transactions accounts or nonpersonal time deposits.

Types of Credit

Depository institutions are eligible for three types of credit: adjustment, seasonal and emergency.

Adjustment credit

Adjustment credit is very short term borrowing—usually no more than for a few days—to make temporary adjustments in reserves. It cannot be used for the following purposes:

i.   To finance speculative loans and investments
ii. To substitute credit for bank capital
iii. To finance lending in the Federal funds market
iv. To secure securities or other money market paper at a profit
v.   To refinance existing indebtedness to private lenders at a lower discount rate

Federal Reserve Banks seldom deny a request for a loan. They do, however, discourage overly frequent borrowing under some circumstances. Adjustment credit is more often used by large than by small banks for the following reasons:[1]

i.   People who deposit at large banks are more sensitive to changes in the interest rates than are those who deposit at small banks and, therefore, are inclined to shift their funds to sources that yield the highest return. This type of depositor behavior, at times, forces large banks to seek funds at the discount window.

ii. Large banks are more subject to sudden changes in loan demand, particularly from businessmen. Many businessmen raise funds either by drawing on their lines of credit at banks or by issuing commercial paper, depending upon which is less expensive. As the relative cost of borrowing from banks and issuance of commercial paper changes, banks experience a sudden and substantial shift in demand for business loans.

iii. Small banks are generally conservative and thus prefer to sell some liquid assets to cover shortages in reserves. In addition, they view the practice of borrowing from Reserve Banks as an indication of poor management.

Seasonal credit

Seasonal credit refers to borrowing from a Reserve Bank to meet a seasonal need. At present, the seasonal borrowing privilege is based upon the following conditons:

   i. The bank lacks reasonable reliable access to the national money market

   ii. The seasonal need arises from recurring movements in a bank's deposits and loans

   iii. Seasonal need persists for at least four consecutive weeks

   iv. Seasonal need exceeds five percent of the bank's average total deposits in the preceding year

   v. Bank has deposits of $100 million or less

Banks that profit from seasonal borrowing privileges are small because they normally qualify for the privilege. Seasonal privilege enables banks to make arrangements in advance and draw funds as needed without a detailed review by Federal Reserve officials at the time of each borrowing as is customary with adjustment credit. It also provides them an assured source of funds for longer periods and in larger amounts than would be considered appropriate under adjustment credit guidelines.

Under the law, the Federal Reserve Bank can extend credit for up to 90 days only. In the event that a seasonal need persists beyond such a period, a Reserve Bank may consider an extension under the seasonal credit program.

Emergency Credit

Emergency credit is extended only where immediate failure of the borrower can be expected to have a severe adverse effect on the economy. Franklin National Bank, which in 1974 obtained this type of credit from a Reserve Bank, is an example. The objective of this type of credit is not to bail out a troubled depository institution, but to protect the public from the side effects of its failure.

Collateral For Borrowing

Every loan requires collateral, which must be held by Federal Reserve Banks unless prior arrangements have been made to permit another approved commercial bank to hold the securities under a custody receipt arrangement. Institutions have an option of borrowing or of discounting eligible paper. However, at present, virtually all funds are obtained from the Federal Reserve by means of borrowing.

The law identifies three types of collateral for securing a loan from the Federal Reserve:

   i. U.S. Government or Federal agency obligations (or other debt fully guaranteed by the U.S. Government or a Federal Agency).

   ii. Eligible and acceptable paper: Eligible paper generally consists of notes, drafts and bills of exchange that have been issued or drawn for a commercial, agricultural or industrial purpose. Acceptability depends upon the Reserve Bank's determination of the credit worthiness of the issuing company. For a paper to be eligible, it must fulfill the following conditions:

     a. Its proceeds have been or are to be used in producing, purchasing or marketing goods or services; to meet current operating expenses of a commercial, agricultural or industrial business; or to purchase, carry or trade in direct obligations of the United States. A paper is not eligible if its proceeds have been or are to be used for the purpose of investment, speculation, or carrying or trading in bonds, except those that are direct obligations of the United States. Borrowing to finance a bank's own investment is considered contrary to the spirit of the Federal Reserve Act because it is not a short-term, temporary need that the bank management cannot reasonably anticipate. Borrowing for speculative purposes is regarded inappropriate because such loans frequently lead banks to financial difficulties.

     b. It has a period remaining to maturity of not more than 90 days, except in the case of agricultural paper where the remaining period of maturity can be as long as 9 months.

   iii. Other paper: Paper that does not meet the eligibility criteria is termed "other." It can be used as collateral provided it is acceptable to a Reserve Bank.

Though all three types of collateral described above can be used, the major part of all borrowing is backed by U.S. Government obligations. The reason for this is convenience. Many member banks hold their U.S. Government securities at Reserve Banks for safekeeping, which makes it easier for them to borrow at the discount window. Paper, whether eligible or not, cannot be used easily because it has to be thoroughly examined by the officials of a Reserve Bank as to the credit worthiness of the issuing company or government entity before it is accepted. This sometimes causes a delay in obtaining a loan.

Federal Reserve Interest Rates

There are four different types of Federal Reserve interest rates. Two rates are charged on adjustment and seasonal borrowings. Which of them is charged depends on the type of collateral used. The basic discount rate is charged when the loan is collateralized by U.S. Government securities, Federal Agency obligations or eligible paper. When other paper (paper other than eligible ones) are used as collateral, a rate at least one half of one percent higher than the basic rate is charged. The other two rates apply to emergency credit. One rate is for emergency credit to depository institutions that hold transactions accounts or nonpersonal time deposits and the other for the same type of credit when given to other institutions. Typically, the rate charged for emergency credit to qualified depository institutions is set 1 to 2 percentage points above the basic discount rate. Reserve Banks have some discretion to classify a given credit as emregency credit. Generally speaking, credit is classified emergency when it is given for a period of more than eight weeks and exceeds, on average, the borrowing institution's required reserves. The rate charged for emergency credit to other institutions is generally set 3 percentage points above the basic rate.

All these rates are reviewed every 14 days by the board of directors of each Reserve Bank. Any change in the rates must be approved by the Board of Governors. If the discount rate changes while a bank has an outstanding loan, the interest rate on this loan is adjusted from the effective date of change.

Discount Rate As A Stabilization Tool

As described earlier, the discount rate policy refers to the rate that the Federal Reserve charges on loans to banks and other qualified depository institutions and conditions as to the eligibility of paper for discount and advances. If the objective of the Federal Reserve is to stimulate the economy, it can lower the discount rate and liberalize the eligibility conditions, and vice versa.

A change in the discount rate affects the money market—availability of funds for loans and investment and the cost of borrowing—in three ways:

One, by changing the cost of borrowing at the discount window. An increase in the discount rate raises the cost of borrowing and thus discourages banks from borrowing. A reduction in the discount rate tends to do the opposite.

Two, by altering the whole structure of market rates. There is a close relationship between the discount rate and short term rates (Treasury bill rate, Federal funds rate, etc.) because Reserve Banks and the money market are alternative sources of adjusting cash and reserve positions. If the discount rate is above the short term rates, there will be an incentive for banks to liquidate short term assets instead of borrowing at the discount window. This will tend to push short term rates up. (Prices of securities are inversely related to interest rates. The liquidation of short term maturities will lower their prices and raise their rates.) A rise in short term rates makes short term maturities more attractive relative to intermediate and long term maturities. As investment funds are diverted into shorter maturities, intermediate and long term rates rise.

Three, by giving a signal to the market as to the intention of the Federal Reserve. For example, a rise in the discount rate is interpreted as a move by the Federal Reserve toward tighter credit and higher interest rates. This may induce banks to restrict loans to their customers in anticipation of higher interest rates.

The use of the discount rate as a stabilization tool has points of strength and of weakness.

Points of Strength

The four major points of strength of the discount policy that have been identified are:

  i. It provides a temporary means of adjustment to reserve deficiencies that occur at times of pressure on reserves. Such a feature enables the Manager of open market operations to move vigorously when an excessively stringent action is needed since he knows that, if his action causes a reserve problem for some banks, a remedy is available at the discount window. The use of this safety valve does not, by any means, offer an escape from monetary restraint because the adjustment credit is usually for not more than a few days. Banks must resort to other action for a permanent solution.

ii. It has an announcement effect. When the rate is changed, headlines appear, giving a signal to both banks and the public as to the direction of Federal Reserve policy. However, at times, the signal may be misinterpreted. The Federal Reserve keeps the discount rate in line with other short term rates. If it is raised simply to align with other rates, it may falsely signal the market that the Federal Reserve is trying to tighten the money market. (The Federal Reserve attempts to keep the discount rate in line with other short term rates, which are an alternative source of borrowed funds for banks. If a bank borrows from the market, the banking system uses old reserves intensively. If it borrows from the Federal Reserve, the banking system gains new reserves. To a bank, old and new reserves are indistinguishable. But, from the point of view of monetary policy, it makes a difference whether the bank chooses to borrow from the Federal Reserve or from the market. The choice is influenced by the spread between the discount rate and other rates.) The adverse effect can be, to some extent, overcome if the change in the discount rate is accompanied by a statement, explaining the reason underlying the action. Warren Smith says this is ineffective.[2] A change in the discount rate requires action by a large number of people—the boards of directors of all Federal Reserve Banks and the Board of Governors of the Federal Reserve. They, themselves, may not be in general agreement as to the reason for a given change.

iii. It serves as a guide to the Manager for conducting open market operations.[3] When the objective is to ease the money market, the Federal Reserve not only lowers the discount rate, but also tries to keep the Federal funds rate somewhat below it. If the Federal funds rate is maintained below the discount rate and bank borrowing from the Federal Reserve falls to a bare minimum, the Manager can be sure that open market operations are working effectively in achieving the objective. They are supplying reserves more rapidly than the banking system is using them and thus keeping pressure on banks to expand loans and investment. On the other hand, when the objective is to tighten the money market, open market operations will be considered working effectively if the Federal funds rate is maintained above the discount rate and bank borrowing is rising.

iv. It keeps monetary decision makers' option open. The discount mechanism is available if and when open market operations become unworkable. It is true that the discount mechanism, at the present time, is not vital to the system. However, in the case of an emergency situation, when securities have lost their market, it might become the only practical way of providing (or absorbing) reserves.

Points of Weakness

The three major points of weakness of the discount policy that have been identified are:

i. It cannot force businessmen and consumers to borrow. Nor can it force banks to borrow from the Federal Reserve. If businessmen and consumers are pessimistic about the future, they have no desire to borrow from banks, despite lower interest rates. If banks have excess reserves, they have no incentive to borrow at the discount window even when the discount rate is reduced.

ii. It may create a problem in the balance of payments when the rate is lowered. As mentioned earlier, a reduction in the discount rate tends to lower market rates. Lower market rates may encourage capital to flow to foreign markets where rates are higher.

iii. Lending guidelines (conditions and terms of loan other than interest rate) can also be used as a counter-cyclical measure— making it easier to borrow during periods of recession and difficult during periods of inflation. Because of administrative problems, they are not used.

OPEN MARKET OPERATIONS

Open market operations involve the buying and selling of securities by the Federal Reserve for the purpose of regulating bank reserves and, consequently, the money market. When the Federal Reserve buys securities, banks' reserves expand. When it sells, reserves contract. Open market operations are conducted mainly in U.S. Government securities. Federal agency securities and banker's acceptances are also used but their volume of transaction is very small. (A banker's acceptance is a time draft, essentially an "order to pay" a specified sum of money at a specified date, drawn on individuals, business firms or financial institutions and "accepted" by a bank. By accepting the draft, a bank assumes the responsibility to make payment at maturity of the draft. The Federal Reserve in the open market deals only with those banker's acceptances that are eligible for discount.)

Types of Transactions

Open market transactions are conducted in one of three ways: (i) outright purchases and sales, (ii) repurchase agreements and (iii) sales purchase transactions.

Outright Purchases and Sales

Outright purchases and sales are those transactions in which neither the buyer nor the seller commits himself to resell or rebuy. These transactions are usually made through an auction process in which all government dealers (currently 36 in all) are requested to submit bids to buy or offers to sell securities that the Manager of the System Open Market Account has elected to sell or buy that day. Once dealer tenders have been received, they are arranged according to price. The Manager accepts them in sequence from low to high in the case of offers and high to low in the case of bids until his need is fulfilled.

Not all outright transactions are made through the dealer market. If, on any day, the Federal Reserve has an order from a customer for whom it serves as an agent (U.S. Treasury and foreign central banks) and the order matches the Manager's need, the Manager may fulfill it directly through the Federal Reserve account.

Outright purchases may be for cash or for regular delivery. If for cash, delivery payments are made on the same day; if for regular delivery, they are made on the following day. The advantage of cash transactions is that the Federal Reserve can inject or withdraw funds on the same day.

Repurchase Agreements

Repurchase agreements are an arrangement in which the Manager buys securities from dealers with a stipulation that they will buy back after a specified time. The Manager enters into such agreements when a temporary expansion in bank reserves is needed.

Repurchase agreements are dated to terminate within one to 15 business days, though less than 7 days is the period frequently used. Such agreements are offered only to nonbank dealers and are made by auction. Bank dealers are not invited to enter into repurchase agreements because they have access to the Federal funds market and, under certain circumstances, to the discount window.

Sale Purchase Transactions

Sale purchase transactions are just the opposite of repurchase agreements. Here, the Manager sells securities with a stipulation to buy them back after a specified period—usually in a day or so. Such transactions are initiated only when a temporary absorption of bank reserves is needed. All dealers—bank and nonbank—are permitted to enter into such transactions. The Manager offers to dealers immediate delivery of a given type of security at a stated price. At the same time, he asks for offerings in the form of an auction, indicating the amounts and prices at which they are prepared to sell back after a specified period. When all the offerings are in, the Manager selects the best to meet his need.

Manager's Operating Procedure

The directive issued by the Open Market Committee gives the stance of the policy and targets to be achieved over a period of time. Targets are expressed in terms of monetary aggregates, money market conditions or both. But the Committee does not give a precise plan as to how many and which securities should be bought or sold each day or each week to hit targets. Nor does it indicate the types of transactions to be arranged. Therefore, the Manager of the System Open Market Account, who maintains an office in New York City, must map out such a plan. The Manager takes the following steps to arrive at a decision for each day's operations:

Step 1. Absorbs all information that comes to the office as a matter of routine, as well as that solicited by the staff by telephone and other methods of communication. The Manager studies seven basic pieces of information each morning:

i. The reserve positions and Federal funds transactions, as of the close of business on the previous day, of 8 major New York banks and 38 other major banks scattered throughout the country. These banks also furnish information about the amount of money they lent to government dealers on the previous day.

ii. Amount of money loaned by the Federal Reserve to banks and other depository institutions on the previous day.

iii. Government dealers' holding of securities and the volume of trading of the previous day. Information from nonbank dealers regarding the volume of funds they need to replace loans maturing that day and to finance securities for which payments have to be made on the same day. This enables the Manager to determine the dealers' needs for loans on that day. To get dealers' views about the securities market and factors influencing the availability of money, two dealers are asked to confer in person each business day on a rotating basis with officials directly responsible for the conduct of open market operations.

iv. Developments in the securities markets in Europe and expectations regarding buy or sell orders from foreign central banks.

v. Quotations on securities and Federal funds. Bid and offer quotations of securities are obtained shortly after 10 a.m. each morning by telephone calls to securities dealers.

vi. Projection of bank reserves as prepared by the research staffs in New York and Washington. The projection covers daily estimates of float, currency in circulation, banks' vault cash, gold and foreign operations, the Treasury balance and required reserves, together with weekly reserves averages for the next four weeks. The research department of the Federal Reserve Bank of New York also furnishes projections of the money supply and bank credit and how they compare with long range targets established by the Committee.

vii. The amount of funds to be transferred from the Tax and Loan accounts at commercial banks to the Treasury account at the Federal Reserve. This is decided together on the phone by the Fiscal Assistant Secretary of the Treasury and the Manager of the System Open Market Account (or his deputy).

Step 2. Based upon the above information, the targets and stance of the policy outlined in the Committee's directives, the Manager prepares a tentative plan for the day, outlining the number and types of securities to buy or sell, and the form of transaction to be arranged that day. Generally speaking, when there is a need to supply (or withdraw) reserves to the banking system and the situation is expected to persist for more than the current bank statement week, the decision will be to buy (or sell) securities on an outright basis for prompt delivery. If the need is to contract reserves, the Manager will allow maturing securities to run off without replacement and also sell securities. When the situation calls for a temporary provision of reserves, repurchase agreements with dealers will be made; when it is for a temporary withdrawal, matched-sale purchase transactions will be arranged.

Step 3. Discuss the plan in a three-way telephone hookup with the staff of the Board of Governors in Washington and the president of the Reserve Bank who is then serving on the Committee. Those who participate in New York are the Manager, officers of the securities department and, at times, the president of the Federal Reserve Bank of New York. (Since open market operations are conducted in New York, the president of the New York District Bank has a permanent position on the Committee, although he may skip some daily meetings.) The participants express their views as to the appropriateness of the proposed action. The conversation is usually completed by 11:30 a.m.

Step 4. Review any other information that becomes available and finalize the decision. This is normally done shortly before noon. The Manager gives the decision to the Trading Desk, where buying and selling of securities is carried on. Within 30 minutes the decision is executed. At about 1 p.m. the Manager again assesses the situation. If he finds that the decision has not brought about the desired change in the money market, he may do more buying or selling of securities. Here is an example: The Manager, in an effort to ease up the money market, buys $300 million worth of Treasury bills. After the first round, the market is not eased as much as expected or has become tighter because of other developments. He decides to purchase an additional $200 million worth of securities to accomplish his objective.

Open Market Operations As A Stabilization Tool

Open market operations are the major tool used by the Federal Reserve to regulate the money market and, consequently, the economy. The Federal Reserve buys securities when the economy needs to be stimulated; sells them when inflation has to be curbed.

Open market operations affect the money market via bank reserves and interest rates. When the Federal Reserve follows an expansionary policy to stimulate the economy, it buys securities, causing bank reserves and, consequently, the availability of funds for loans and investment, to rise. The purchase of securities by the Federal Reserve bids up their prices and lowers the yield. Since Treasury obligations represent the major segment of the securities market, a lower yield on them tends to spread to private securities, resulting in a general rise in security prices and a decline in yields (or interest rates). Moreover, purchasing of securities by the Federal Reserve causes excess reserves. Banks, in an effort to dispose of excess reserves via loans, may reduce interest rates. When the Federal Reserve follows a policy of constraint, it sells securities to siphon off bank reserves. This leads to lower securities prices, higher yields and tighter loan policies.

Open market operations may be defensive or dynamic. The purchase or sale of securities is said to be "defensive" when either is used to offset day-to-day fluctuations in bank reserves resulting from factors outside the control of the Federal Reserve, such as changes in Federal Reserve float, currency in circulation, and Treasury and foreign deposits at the Federal Reserve. In the absence of such operations, these factors can be expected to cause abrupt changes in bank reserves and, consequently, in the supply and cost of credit even over short periods. Operations are considered dynamic when they are used to affect reserves in order to pursue long-run stabilization goals. To Bryan and Heins, defensive operations offset short-run "unwanted" changes; and dynamic operations promote long-run "wanted" changes.[4] Though the Federal Reserve uses both, the bulk of its operations are defensive in nature.

Like other tools, open market operations have points of strength and weakness, though points of strength far exceed the others, particularly in the case of the United States where the Government securities market is well developed.

Points of Strength

Open market operations have five points of strength. They are:

i. It is the most flexible tool available to the Federal Reserve. The amount of money that can be injected into or siphoned out of the system is under the complete control of the Manager as is the timing of the transactions.

ii. The Federal Reserve has greater control over open market operations than on the discount rate policy because changes in the former occur at the initiative of the Federal Reserve. While it is true that the Federal Reserve has the same control over the discount rate, the decision to borrow is in the hands of banks. If they decide not to borrow funds at the discount window at the lower rate, the discount rate policy fails.

iii. Open market operations can be used to support the discount rate policy. When banks have excess reserves, for example, the contractionary discount rate policy alone is ineffective. Banks will continue easy, low-cost loan policies because the excess reserves eliminates the need for borrowing from the discount window to meet loan demand from their customers. The Manager can absorb those reserves by selling securities, thus forcing banks to borrow from the Federal Reserve at the higher discount rate. The higher rate, coupled with the fact that borrowing from the Federal Reserve is usually for short periods, usually forces banks to adopt more cautious lending and investment policies, thus making a contractionary discount rate policy more effective.

iv. Open market operations can be used to supplement reserve requirements. If a change in reserve requirements causes an adjustment problem, offsetting open market operations can be used to make the adjustment process smoother and easier. Sometimes changes in reserve requirements are made for structural purposes (such as to make reserve requirements of different size banks more equitable) and not for stabilization purposes. In these cases, their effect on bank reserves will be "unwanted." Open market operations can be used to offset such an "unwanted" effect.

v. Open market operations can be used to affect different interest rates differently. The objective of increasing short term rates in order to discourage the outflow of capital and decreasing long term rates in order to encourage private investment can be achieved by the sale of short term and the purchase of long term securities by the Federal Reserve.

Points of Weakness

The two points of weakness of open market operations that have been identified are:

i. Open market operations lack announcement effect because they, unlike the discount rate and reserve requirements, are conducted every day. In addition, the public cannot distinguish between dynamic and defensive operations. The stance of the policy can be determined only from dynamic operations.

ii. The initial impact of open market operations is concentrated in money market centers because this is where the government dealers are. It takes time for their impact to filter through smaller and more remotely located areas. Many economists disagree, however. They claim that though these transactions take place in large financial centers, their effects quickly spread to other parts of the country. They argue that a large portion of these transactions is directly or indirectly for the account of banks, financial institutions and business corporations located in other parts of the country. Bank reserve positions are tied together by the network of correspondent relations. If a bank loses reserves because of open market operations, it can replenish them by borrowing from its correspondent banks. With an electronic transfer system, funds can be transferred from one part of the country to another in no time. The existence of the Federal funds market further speeds up the process of spreading the effects of open market operations. If banks in financial centers lose reserves, they can borrow from banks located in other parts of the country in a matter of hours through this market.

RESERVE REQUIREMENTS

Reserve requirements can be broadly classified into three types: (1) Basic reserve requirements (covered in Regulation D), (2) marginal reserve requirements (also covered in Regulation D), and (3) reserve requirements governing foreign activities of U.S. banks (covered partly in Regulation A and partly in Regulation M). The Monetary Act of 1980 extends the reserve requirements of the Federal Reserve to all depository institutions having transactions accounts or nonpersonal time deposits.

Basic reserve requirements are traditional requirements against savings and demand deposits. Marginal reserve requirements are requirements against certificates of deposit (CDs), particularly large ones (CDs to the denomination of $100,000 and more) and bank-related commercial paper. Bank-related commercial paper is that issued by bank holding companies or affiliates and their proceeds are used to purchase loans from banks. Reserve requirements governing foreign activities deal with: (1) Net balances due from domestic banks (net of borrowing and lending) to their foreign branches, and lending by foreign branches of domestic banks to U.S. residents (covered in Regulation M) and (2) U.S. bank borrowings from foreign offices of other banks (covered in Regulation D).

Reserve Requirements As A Stabilization Tool

Basic reserve requirements refer to the amount required to support demand and regular saving deposit liabilities. Reserve requirements are reduced to stimulate the economy and increased to contract it. They affect the money market via excess reserves and via banks' policy toward loans and investment. When reserve requirements are reduced, excess reserves and, consequently, the availability of funds rise. The availability of funds will further rise if banks are reduced by this action to adopt a more liberal policy toward lending and investment. Normally, at such times, banks liberalize their policy because they regard the funds generated from this source as more permanent than those from other sources.

Marginal reserve requirements are used to influence either the availability of funds to banks or their liquidity, or both. To tighten the money market, the Federal Reserve can raise reserve requirements against CDs and bank-related commercial paper, which would reduce the availability of funds to banks for loans and investment. In June 1973, for example, when banks were issuing great quantities of large CDs and their holding companies and affiliates were issuing commercial paper to meet the growing demand for business loans, the Federal Reserve dampened their growth by placing an 8-percent reserve requirement on increases in such issues at banks that had on hand more than $10 million worth.[5] This was raised to 11 percent in September of that year. When business demand for loans moderated in December, the reserve requirement was cut back to 8 percent.

Marginal reserve requirements can also be used to influence banks' liquidity pressure. Lowering the liquidity pressure of banks tends to ease the money market, and vice versa. The Federal Reserve can lower the liquidity pressure by encouraging banks to issue long term CDs, which can be accomplished by reducing reserve requirements against them. Long term CDs lower the liquidity pressure because they do not mature fast. In September, 1974, for example, the Federal Reserve eased somewhat the liquidity problem of banks by reducing the reserve requirement to 5 percent against large CDs with initial maturity of four months or more.[6]

The Federal Reserve can also affect the money market by changing reserve requirements against foreign activities such as borrowing from abroad (the Eurodollar market). The money market is eased when domestic banks borrow from abroad and when foreign branches/banks lend directly to U.S. residents. Though this type of reserve requirement can be used as a stabilization tool, it has not, so far, been used as such. The Federal Reserve used it simply to plug loopholes. For example, in the past, shortages of funds forced domestic banks to borrow from abroad. The Federal Reserve stopped the practice by imposing a reserve requirement.

Reserve requirements as a stabilization tool has points of strength and weakness:

Points of Strength

The three major points of strength of the reserve requirement as a stabilization tool that have been identified are:

    i. It is the most powerful tool available to the Federal Reserve. A small change in reserve requirements causes a great change in the availability of reserves to banks for loans and investment. It is estimated a change as small as one-quarter of one percentage point supplies or withdraws such reserves in the amount of $257 million in one operation.[7] For this reason, this tool is considered most appropriate for correcting long run redundancies or deficiencies of reserves.

    ii. It affects all banks and does so directly and immediately. In contrast, open market operations do not affect all banks— only those whose customers either bought or sold government securities. Their effect is gradual because the initial impact is mainly in money market centers. The discount rate also does not affect every bank—only those that need funds and can meet the Federal Reserve requirement for loans.

    iii. Changes in reserve requirements are made infrequently. When they are changed, they send a signal to the market regarding the intention of the Federal Reserve. The action normally leaves an impression in the minds of bankers that expansion or contraction in the availability of reserves is somewhat permanent and that something has to be done by them. For example, if excess reserves increase from the action, banks are likely to expand long term assets by purchasing mortgages and making customer commitments extending longer into the future.

Points of Weakness:

The reserve requirement tool has two main points of weakness. They are:

    i. The Federal Reserve cannot pursue an overly aggressive contractionary policy because such action may intensify the already existing problem of declining membership in the Federal Reserve System. State laws governing reserve requirements offer banks a better deal. Their major attraction is the form in which the required reserves can be held. The

Federal Reserve requires that required reserves be maintained in vault cash and in deposits with the Federal Reserve. State requirements are satisfied by keeping deposits in other banks and, in some cases, by holding interest-bearing Federal and State securities. However, the Monetary Act of 1980 solves this problem by extending the reserve requirements of the Federal Reserve to all depository institutions having transactions accounts or nonpersonal time deposits.

ii. Some claim that the structure of reserve requirements as it stands now hampers monetary control over short periods. This view is usually stated in terms of a money supply model in which the money supply, M, is a product of the monetary multiplier, m, and the monetary base, B, —(M = m•B). The monetary base is composed of currency in circulation and member bank reserves. The Federal Reserve can affect the base via open market operations. The quantity of money that can be supported by a given base depends upon the monetary multiplier (m). The monetary multiplier, as explained in Chapter IV, depends upon various factors including "r" (ratio of total reserves to total deposits). The argument that reserve requirements disrupt the monetary control is based upon the instability in the monetary multiplier, making it difficult to control the money supply by controlling the monetary base. The instability in "r" contributes instability to the monetary multiplier. The instability in "r" arises from different reserve requirements for different size banks (higher for large banks and lower for small banks), for demand and time deposits (higher for demand deposits and lower for time deposits), etc. The "r" changes every time funds shift from one category of bank to another. For example, when funds shift from large banks to small banks, "r" declines.

SUMMARY

The major instruments of monetary control are: discount rate, open market operations and reserve requirements. Discount rate refers to the rate that Federal Reserve Banks charge on their loans to qualified depository institutions and conditions as to the eligibility of paper for discount and advances. When the objective is to stimulate the economy, the Federal Reserve lowers the discount rate and liberalizes eligibility conditions, and vice versa. It has some good and some bad points when used as a stabilization tool. Its good points are: (i) serves as a safety valve—provides a temporary means of adjustment to reserve deficiencies resulting from open market operations and from a change in reserve requirements. (ii) It has an announcement effect. (iii) The relation between the discount rate and Federal funds rate, and bank borrowing from the Federal Reserve can be used as a guide for conducting open market operations. (iv) It keeps the option of the Federal Reserve open, i.e., it can be used if and when open market operations become unworkable. Points against the discount rate are: (i) It cannot force banks to borrow. (ii) It may create a problem in the balance of payments when the rate is lowered.

Open market operations refer to the buying and selling of securities by the Federal Reserve. If the objective is to stimulate the economy, the Federal Reserve buys securities, and vice versa. Points of strength of open market operations as a stabilization tool are: (i) It is very flexible. (ii) The Federal Reserve has greater control over it than over any other tool. (iii) It can be used to support both discount rate and reserve requirement tools. (iv) It can affect different interest rates differently. Points against open market operations are: (i) It lacks announcement effect. (ii) Its initial effect is concentrated in money market centers.

Reserve requirements refer to the amount required to support time and demand deposit liabilities. They are reduced when the economy needs to be stimulated, and vice versa. Like any other tool, it has both good and bad points. In its favor: (i) It is a very powerful tool—a small change in reserve requirements causes a great change in the availability of funds for loans and investment. (ii) It affects all banks directly and immediately. Against it are: (i) It cannot be used vigorously to pursue a contractionary policy because such action might induce banks to withdraw from Federal Reserve membership. However, the Monetary Act of 1980 will discourage such a withdrawal. (ii) Some claim that the structure of reserve requirements as it exists now—different requirements for different size banks, different requirements for time and demand deposits, etc.—make it difficult for the Federal Reserve to control the money supply over short periods.

FOOTNOTES

¹Clifford L. Fry, "Discount Window—Member Borrowing Soared in Eleventh District Last Year," **Business Review: Federal Reserve Bank of Dallas** (July 1974), pp. 3-4.

²Warren Smith, "The Instruments of General Monetary Control," **National Banking Review** (September 1963), pp. 60-61.

³Paul Meek, **Fundamental Reappraisal of the Discount Mechanism** (Washington, D.C.: The Board of Governors of the Federal Reserve System 1968), p. 3.

⁴William R. Bryan and James Heins, "Defensive Open Market Operations, Proximate Objectives, and Monetary Instability: A Comment," **Journal of Money, Credit and Banking** (February 1972), p. 99.

⁵Clifford L. Fry and Edward E. Veazey, "Certificates of Deposits: Changes in Reserve Requirements Influence Volume and Maturity," **Business Review: Federal Reserve Bank of Dallas** (August 1975), p. 2.

⁶**Ibid.**, pp. 2-3.

⁷David P. Eastburn, **The Federal Reserve on Record: Readings on Current Issues from Statements by Federal Reserve Officials** (Philadelphia: Federal Reserve Bank of Philadelphia, 1965), p. 132.

QUESTIONS FOR REVIEW

1. Explain the different types of Federal Reserve credit. Under what circumstances is each one available to a bank?
2. "Larger banks make more use of adjustment credit than smaller banks." Explain.
3. What are the conditions for qualifying for seasonal credit? Which banks—smaller or larger—normally profit from this type of credit? Why?
4. Explain in detail the types of collateral that can be used to obtain a loan from the Federal Reserve. Which are used more often than others? Why?
5. Describe the pros and cons of the discount rate as a tool of economic stabilization.
6. Why does the Federal Reserve enter repurchase agreements only with non-bank dealers?
7. Outline the procedure used by the Manager of the System Open Market Account to arrive at a decision for each day's operation.
8. Explain the pros and cons of open market operations as a monetary tool of stabilization.
9. What do we mean by marginal requirements? How can they be used as an instrument of monetary control?
10. Explain the pros and cons of reserve requirements as a tool of monetary control.

SUGGESTED FURTHER READING

1. Board of Governors of the Federal Reserve System. **The Federal Reserve System: Purposes and Functions.** Washington, D.C.: Board of Governors of the Federal Reserve System, 1974, pp. 49-89.
2. Brewer, Elijah. "Some Insights on Member Bank Borrowing." **Economic Perspectives: Federal Reserve Bank of Chicago.** November/December 1978, pp. 16-21.
3. Bryan, William R. & Heins, James. "Defensive Open-Market Operations, Proximate Objectives, and Monetary Instability, A Comment." **Journal of Money, Credit and Banking.** February 1972, pp. 98-107.
4. Cacy, J.A., "Reserve Requirements and Monetary Control." **Monthly Review: Federal Reserve Bank of Kansas City.** May 1976, pp. 3-13.
5. Carson, Deane. "Should Reserve Requirements be Abolished?" **The Bankers Magazine.** Winter 1973, pp. 12-17.
6. Cox III, William N. "The Discount Rate: Problems and Remedies." **Monthly Review: Federal Reserve Bank of Atlanta.** June 1972, pp. 94-98.
7. Eastburn, David P. **The Federal Reserve on Record: Readings on Current Issues from Statements by Federal Reserve Officials.** Philadelphia: 1965.
8. Federal Reserve Bank of Minneapolis. **Proceedings: Federal Reserve Bank of Minneapolis: 1969 Money and Banking Workshop.** Minneapolis, Minnesota: Federal Resrve Bank of Minneapolis, 1969.
9. Frost, A. Peter & Sargent, Thomas J. "Money-Market Rates, the Discount Rate and Borrowing from the Federal Reserve." **Journal of Money, Credit and Banking.** February 1970, pp. 56-82.
10. Fry, Clifford L., "Discount Window Member Bank Borrowing Soared in Eleventh District Last Year." **Business Review: Federal Reserve Bank of Dallas.** July 1974, pp. 1-8.
11. Gilbert, Alton R. "Benefits of Borrowing from the Federal Reserve When the Discount Rate is Below Market Interest Rates." **Review: Federal Reserve Bank of St. Louis.** March 1979, pp. 25-32.
12. Gravy, George. "Reserve Requirements Abroad." **Monthly Review: Federal Reserve Bank of New York.** October 1973, pp. 256-262.
13. Guttentag, Jack M. "Defensive and Dynamic Open Market Operations, Discounting and the Federal Reserve System's Crisis—Prevention Responsibilities." **Journal of Finance.** May 1969, pp. 249-263.
14. Hackley, Howard H. **Lending Functions of the Federal Reserve Banks: A History.** Washington, D.C.: Board of Governors of the Federal Reserve System, 1973.
15. Holmes, Alan R. "A Day at the Trading Desk." **Monthly Review: Federal Reserve Bank of New York.** October 1970, pp. 234-238.
16. Madeley, Carol C. "Through the Window at the Fed." **Voice: Federal**

Reserve Bank of Dallas.** November 1978, pp. 16-18.

17. Meek, Paul. **Fundamental Reappraisal of the Discount Mechanism: Discount Policy and Open Market Operations.** Washington, D.C.: Board of Governors of the Federal Reserve System, 1968.

18. Meek, Paul. **Open Market Operations.** New York: Federal Reserve Bank of New York, 1973.

19. Organization for Economic Co-operation and Development. **Monetary Policy in the United States.** Paris, France: Organization for Economic Co-operation and Development, 1974.

20. Poole, William and Lieberman, Charles. "Improving Monetary Control." **Brookings Papers on Economic Activity: 2.** 1972, pp. 293-335.

21. Smith, Warren L. "The Instruments of General Monetary Control." **The National Banking Review.** September 1963, pp. 47-76.

22. Veazey, Edward E. "Reserve Requirements: Structure and Impediment to Monetary Control?" **Business Review: Federal Reserve Bank of Dallas.** December 1976, pp. 9-18.

23. Young, Ralph A. Instruments of Monetary Policy in the United States: **The Role of the Federal Reserve System.** Washington, D.C.: International Monetary Fund, 1973.

CHAPTER XV
Selective Controls & Moral Suasion

Selective controls are used to affect the availability of credit in specific sectors. Moral suasion is used to influence the availability of general credit as well as of credit in specific sectors. Measures used to implement it are not mandatory as is the case with general and selective controls.

SELECTIVE CONTROLS

The major selective controls that are currently used or have been used in the past are:
1. Interest rate ceilings
2. Margin requirements
3. Consumer credit
4. Real estate credit

Interest Rate Ceilings

Interest rate ceilings are the maximum rates banks are allowed to pay for savings and other time deposits. Since the Federal Reserve covers interest rate ceilings in Regulation "Q", they are sometimes referred to by the name of this regulation. Both member and non-member banks adhere to interest rate ceilings. The Federal Reserve establishes such ceilings for member banks. The Federal Deposit Insurance Corporation, through its own regulation, sets the same ceilings for nonmember banks. Interest rate ceilings for nonbank thrift institutions (mutual savings banks and savings and loan associations) are regulated by the Federal Deposit Insurance Corporation or the Federal Home Loan Bank Board, depending upon the agency insuring their deposits. The Federal Reserve is required to consult the Federal Deposit Insurance Corporation and the Federal Home Loan Bank Board to change these ceilings.

Interest Rate Ceilings As A Stabilization Tool

Regulation "Q" was not initially intended as a stabilization tool, although it has been used as such. In the beginning, interest rate ceilings were intended to curb rate competition among banks. Competition for time deposits, it was believed, had weakened the soundness of the banking system. The high interest rates paid to depositors forced banks to invest funds in high risk assets to earn more.

As a stabilization tool, interest rate ceilings can be raised when the objective is to stimulate the housing industry, and vice versa. A rise in interest rate ceilings stimulates this industry because it increases the funds available to nonbank thrift institutions that specialize in home mortgages.

Some economists claim that a change in interest rate ceilings affects not only the housing industry but also the economy as a whole by influencing: (i) the amount of funds channeled through banks and other intermediaries, (ii) other interest rates and (iii) the availability of total credit.

They say that when interest rate ceilings are raised, time deposits become a more attractive investment than open market securities, causing funds to move from those securities to time deposits and creating excess funds in banks. (This process is known as intermediation.) Since banks are more efficient than other intermediaries in distributing funds, an increase in the amount of money channeled through them stimulates the economy. (Banks are considered more efficient than other intermediaries because they make funds available to the public faster and at a lower cost.[1]) A reduction in ceilings has the opposite effect.

A change in interest rate ceilings affects other interest rates in the following manner: An increase in ceilings creates an excess supply of short term claims such as Treasury bills and commercial paper, and an excess demand for long term claims such as mortgages. An excess supply of short term claims occurs because time deposits become more attractive. An excess demand for long term claims develops because institutions that acquire additional funds as a result of expansion in time deposits are in the market to buy long term claims. An excess supply of short term claims lowers their prices and raises their rates, while an excess demand for long term claims raises their prices and lowers their rates. Since expenditures on consumer durables, machine and equipment, and construction of state and local governments is related to long term rates, a decline in these rates stimulates the economy by increasing expenditures in those areas.

A change in interest rate ceilings affects the availability of total credit. The amount of available credit depends upon the extent to which funds are shifted from cash balances, demand deposits and open market securities to time deposits, according to Adrian Throop.[?] A shift of this nature increases the availability of total credit and a shift in the opposite direction decreases it. The degree of impact on the availability of total credit depends upon whether the public shifts funds from cash balances, from demand deposits or from interest bearing securities. Their effect will be more expansionary if transfer is from cash balances to time deposits than if it is from demand deposits to time deposits because the public cannot create money with cash balances but the banking system can. Shifting of funds from demand to time deposits is a shift within the banking system and thus expansion in the money supply (or total credit) is caused only by the difference in their reserve requirements. Some economists, however, believe that transfers in either direction have little effect on total credit. As a stabilization tool, interest rate ceilings have points of both strength and weakness.

Points of Strength

    i. It is a good instrument for affecting the availability of credit in the housing sector.

    ii. Some believe that since interest rate ceilings influence bank credit primarily, they can be used to exert a direct influence on business spending. If ceilings are not raised when money is tight, investors shift funds from time deposits to higher-yielding open market securities. This reduces the volume of credit available from the banking system but not total credit available from the market. Since businessmen are the main users of bank credit and use it primarily for inventories and plant and equipment, a decline in the supply of bank credit reduces such expenditures. In the past, such business expenditures have been a dominant factor in business cycles. Critics however, view it differently. They claim that such an action will not change the expenditure on inventories, plant and equipment. The effect of interest rate ceilings is neutralized by the ingenuity of banks to invent new access routes to the money market. In the past, there has been a cat and mouse game between the Federal Reserve and banks. As the Federal Reserve plugged one loophole, banks created another. During periods of tight money, banks invented new sources of funds such as Eurodollars and bank-related commercial paper. During the early part of 1969, for example, banks borrowed a large sum of money from the Eurodollar market to meet their needs. To restrict this practice, the Federal Reserve imposed a reserve requirement on this type of borrowing. This led to a wider issuance of commercial paper by bank holding companies or affiliates, proceeds of which were used to purchase loans from banks. To counteract this, the Federal Reserve imposed a reserve requirement against funds obtained by banks from such sources. Critics add that businessmen neutralize the effect of interest rate ceilings by selling their own commercial paper to the public. In this way, critics contend, funds fall into the hands of those whose credit usage the authority is seeking to curb.

Points of Weakness

i. Interest rate ceilings are discriminatory and cause waste. They discriminate against small savers, small firms and small banks. Small savers have limited alternatives and thus keep their funds in time deposits irrespective of interest rates. Large savers, on the other hand, invest their funds in other assets when banks and other depository institutions do not offer high interest rates. Large firms, unlike small ones, have access to other sources of funds, such as their own commercial paper. Small banks are discriminated against because they do not have the talent and other sources that help large banks to develop innovative ways to counteract the effects of interest rate ceilings. Waste occurs when banks squander their money and resources to find loopholes. This, in turn, forces the authority to waste its scarce legal and regulatory talent in plugging loopholes.

ii. Interest rate ceilings make it difficult to interpret monetary aggregates because, over time, they destroy the homogeneity of recorded statistics and, consequently, the stability of the relations between these aggregates and other economic magnitudes. For example, some of the indirect ways of paying interest on demand deposits change the meaning of demand deposits over time. When market rates rise above the mandated ceilings, funds shift from time deposits to open market securities and then to demand deposits. Demand deposits acquired in this way earn interest, though indirectly, and thus are not the same as demand deposits at other times. Milton Friedman says when market rates rise above the ceilings, they overstate the growth of the homogenous magnitude of old M_1 and understate that of M_2.[3]

iii. With interest rate ceilings, a restrictive policy hits the housing industry the hardest as high interest rates divert funds away from time deposits. However, in 1978-1980, the Federal Reserve succeeded in not letting housing bear the brunt of high interest rates by allowing banks to pay an interest rate up to the most recently issued 6-month U.S. Treasury bill rate on a nonnegotiable certificate of deposit, issued in the denomination of $10,000 and over, for a period of 26 weeks. (Thrift institutions could pay ¼ percentage point more on the same type of deposit. But later, this differential was permitted only when the 6-month Treasury bill rate was 8¾ percent or less.) This measure kept mortgage money flowing despite high interest rates.

A number of economists, including Milton Friedman and James Tobin, are against interest rate ceilings. Two recent government studies of U.S. financial markets—the Hunt Commission of 1971 and the FINE study of 1975—recommend the removal of these ceilings.

Margin Requirements

Margin requirements fix the maximum amount of a loan that can be extended for purchasing or carrying securities as a percentage of the value of the underlying securities. If the margin requirement is 65%, for example, the holder of the security must pay 65% in cash and may borrow the balance. If the price of a security declines after the loan is extended, the law does not require the borrower either to put up the additional collateral or reduce his indebtedness. But the lender, on his own, may require additional collateral and usually does.

Regulatory limitations apply only to: (i) margin stocks (all corporate stocks registered on national exchanges plus selected over-the-counter stocks—the Board periodically puts out a list of over-the-counter stocks to be considered as margin stocks), (ii) convertible bonds (bonds which can be converted into margin stocks) and (iii) short sales (sales of margin stocks that a seller does not own but promises to furnish if required. Short sales are made by investors who believe the price of the security will decline. If it does, the investor profits by buying the security at the lower price, thus "covering" his short position.) The burden of adhering to margin requirements has been placed both on lenders and borrowers. Regulations "T", "U" and "G" control security credit provided by brokers and dealers, banks, and other domestic lenders, respectively. Other domestic lenders include partnerships, associations and business trusts. Borrowers of such credit, whether obtained from domestic sources or from abroad, are regulated by Regulation "X." Brokers and dealers are permitted to extend credit only against regulated securities. Banks, however, can extend credit against both regulated and unregulated securities. In the case of unregulated securities, banks are not subject to securities credit controls. Banks are not affected by these controls even when they extend a loan for a purpose other than purchasing or carrying of securities but collateralized by any security or when they give an unsecured loan for purchasing or carrying of regulated securities as is the case with a credit worthy borrower.

The main reason for regulating security credit is to reduce fluctuations in stock prices because it is believed that unregulated credit of this kind contributes to such fluctuations.

Other arguments, though weak and less frequently mentioned, in favor of regulating security credit are to maintain stability in the banking system and to increase the flow of funds from unproductive to productive uses. Those who argue for security credit on the ground of maintaining stability in the banking system believe that such credit is financed largely through the banking system either through direct loans to customers or indirectly via loans extended to brokers and dealers. Banks treat most security credit as short term loans such as call loans. If and when they need reserves they can call them back on short notice. However, in the event of a serious decline in stock prices, this may not be possible. As a result, the solvency of banks may be jeopardized. This argument may have had some merit in the past. But, banks now hold large amounts of U.S. Government securities that can be readily converted into cash. In addition, they have access to many other sources of funds such as Federal funds, Eurodollars and bank-related paper markets. These sources of funds have obviated the use of call loans as an important secondary reserve for banks.

Those who argue for controlling security credit to increase the flow of funds to productive uses believe that such loans are unproductive as they finance only speculative activities. They add that when funds are made available to finance securities, less is available for productive uses. This argument is very weak. Security credit facilitates the exchange of securities from one party to another. It does not represent a claim on real resources and, hence, does not reduce the overall availability of funds for other uses.[4] Proceeds from a security loan must end up as a source of finance for business, consumer or government expenditure.

Margin Requirements As A Tool of Stabilization

Margin requirements can be used to control stock price fluctuations in particular and fluctuations in the whole economy in general. Margin requirements are lowered when the objective is to curb a downward trend in stock prices and to stimulate the overall economy, and raised when the opposite effect is desired. A reduction in margin requirements increases prices of stocks via credit and announcement effects. A reduction in margin requirements causes an increase in stock market credit. An increase in stock market credit expands the demand for stocks and, consequently, their prices. The announcement effect further puts an upward pressure on stock prices. The reduction in margin requirements gives a signal to the public that the Federal Reserve is serious in causing a buoying effect on the economy in general and stock prices in particular.

A reduction in margin requirements stimulates the economy in four ways:[5] (i) By increasing business expenditure. A decline in margin requirements, as described above, tends to increase stock prices. Rising stock prices encourage floatation of new stocks. The use of funds obtained by this source increases business expenditure. (ii) By increasing the supply of money. As described earlier, a reduction in margin requirements tends to expand stock market credit. A large part of this credit is directly or indirectly financed by banks. When banks' credit expands, the money supply rises. (iii) By increasing consumption expenditure. Rising stock prices result in capital gains and expectations of further rises and gains. Capital gains, whether realized or not, increase consumption expenditure. (iv) By activating idle balances. Rising stock prices foster optimism in the economy. Optimism encourages people to activate idle balances by investing them in stocks or in other assets such as machine and equipment. An increase in such investments directly or indirectly stimulates the economy.

As a stabilization tool, it has points of both strength and weakness.

Points of Strength

    i. Margin requirements offer selectivity, enabling the authority to restrict stock market credit even when the overall policy calls for easy availability of credit. Critics argue that margin policy affects the stock market but its effect is so modest that it can be hardly regarded as more than trivial.[6]

   ii. It is an effective tool in dampening the stock market when high interest rates fail to discourage speculative borrowing to finance stock purchases in a rising market.

Points of Weakness

    i. This tool is ineffective for controlling either the stock market or overall fluctuations in countries where a stock market is not well developed.

   ii. There are many gaps in margin requirements as they currently exist in the United States. To begin with, they do not apply to unsecured loans, which constitute a significant portion of the total. During June 1972 and May 1973, such loans constituted about 42% of the total bank loans extended for purchasing stocks. Borrowers can easily evade margin rules by telling banks that loans will be used for purposes other than purchasing stocks. (As discussed earlier, loans extended for purposes other than buying stocks are not subject to margin rules.) Furthermore, many unregulated stock market loans have a tendency to destabilize stock prices but they are free from margin rules.

Consumer Credit

Consumer credit control refers to the regulation of credit for the purpose of purchasing consumer durables. It is used by regulating the down payment (minimum amount to be paid in cash to buy a product) and the period of repayment (maximum period to be allowed for repaying a loan). Consumer credit control has a checkered history in the United States. It was instituted in 1941 under executive order of the President and remained in effect until 1947. The Federal Reserve administered it under Regulation "W." In 1948, it was reinstated by a special authorization from the Congress and terminated in the following year. Consumer credit controls were restored once again in 1950 under the Defense Production Act and suspended in 1952. The Credit Control Act of December 23, 1969 gives stand-by power to the President to institute such controls during peacetime.[7] Whenever the President determines that such action is necessary for the purpose of controlling inflation caused by excessive consumer credit, he can authorize the Board of Governors to regulate any or all extension of such credit. Under the terms of this act, President Carter in 1980 authorized the Federal Reserve to exercise special restraint on the growth of certain kinds of credit in order to curb inflation.

Consumer Credit As A Stabilization Tool

Consumer credit can be used to control expenditures for consumer durables. If the objective is to stimulate it, decrease the down payment and increase the period of repayment, and vice versa. Terms of installment credit are viewed as an important determinant of the demand for high-priced consumer durables.

Some claim that a change in consumer credit affects not only consumer durable producing industries but also the economy as a whole and does it in four different ways: (i) Since consumption expenditure is a component of total expenditures (GNP = consumption expenditure + investment expenditure + government expenditure + excess of exports over imports), an increase in it will increase the national income. (ii) An expansion in consumer credit causes an increase in bank credit and, consequently, in the money supply. An increase in the money supply stimulates the economy. According to William Mc-Chesney Martin, a substantial portion of the consumer credit outstanding is financed either directly or indirectly by bank loans.[8] (iii) An expansion in expenditure for consumer durables increases the income of industries related to these products. The economy is stimulated when their incomes are spent.

Points of strength and weakness of consumer credit as a stabilization tool are as follows:

Points of Strength:

i. It is an effective tool for controlling fluctuations caused by excessive extension of credit for purchasing consumer durables.

ii. It has a special significance in periods of short supply and of limited production as is the case during a war. At such times, the authority can use the tool to effectively curb the inflationary pressure arising from consumer expenditures for durables. In the absence of such a tool, very stringent measures for restraining general credit may have to be used to accomplish the same objective.

iii. Some claim that it is effective during a slack period because at such times it is unlikely for an increase in the availability of consumer credit to cause a decrease in the availability of credit to other sectors. However, when the economy is booming such a tool may merely alter the composition of credit.

Points of Weakness

i. It is difficult to administer. There are a large number of firms that have to be watched for compliance. In 1941, about 200,000 firms were registered for granting this type of credit. Furthermore, this control can be easily evaded. It can be evaded by overstating both the price of an article and the value of a trade in. It can also be evaded by showing the sale of component parts rather than of assembled, ready to use units. (In the United States, whenever such a control was used component parts were kept free from this regulation.)

ii. It discriminates against the lower and middle classes because it is they who normally buy consumer durables on credit.

Real Estate Credit

Real estate credit control refers to the regulation of credit extended to finance real estate purchases. As is the case with consumer credit control, it is used by regulating the down payment and the period of repayment. Among all selective controls, this had the shortest life in the United States. It was imposed in 1950 and suspended in 1952. The Federal Reserve administered it under Regulation "X."

Real Estate Credit As A Stabilization Tool

Real estate credit can be used to regulate real estate expenditures. If the objective is to stimulate it, lower the down payment and increase the period of repayment, and vice versa. Since real estate expenditures depend very much on credit, they are markedly affected by the terms on which a loan is offered.

An increase in real estate credit affects the economy in two important ways: (i) By increasing real estate expenditures. (ii) By increasing the general availability of credit. Real estate expenditures, particularly those for new homes and business structures, stimulate the economy because they are seldom complete in themselves. Factory, store and office buildings need machinery, equipment, fixtures and furnishing of a wide variety before they are ready for use. New houses and apartments are normally furnished with new durables. Residential construction in new areas opens up new stores, theaters, schools, hospitals and other community services. All these developments provide impetus to the economy. An increase in real estate credit also stimulates the economy by increasing the general availability of credit. Other things remaining constant, a rise in credit in a given sector gives rise to the general availability of credit.

Points of strength and weakness of real estate credit control as a stabilization tool are as follows:

Points of Strength

    i. Where instability in real estate expenditures is the main cause of general instability, it can be effectively controlled by regulating real estate credit. At times, real estate expenditures have contributed to general instability.

   ii. Restrictive real estate credit can help to conserve building materials in a period of intensified defense activity. The production and distribution of such materials, according to

William McChesney Martin, are difficult to regulate with other controls.[9]

iii. It is relatively easy to administer. A significant portion of real estate credit is extended by major financial institutions (commercial banks, mutual savings banks, savings and loan associations and life insurance companies) from whom a workable degree of cooperation can be expected for administering this regulation since they are under the direct supervision of either a Federal or state agency, or both.

Point of Weakness

i. Broad economic and social considerations impose limits on the use of real estate credit restraint as an anti-inflationary device. Many believe that since shelter is one of the basic necessities of life, a restrictive real estate credit policy must be viewed in the light of adequacy of existing housing in relation to the basic shelter needs of the population rather than as a tool of monetary policy.

SELECTIVE CONTROLS: AN OVERVIEW

Selective controls are effective where credit in specific sectors needs to be affected. There are occasions when such an action is needed. It is needed when priority sectors are not getting a sufficient amount of credit or credit in certain sectors is to be dampened. It is also needed when certain sectors have to be protected from the undesired impact of countercyclical policy. Nevertheless, selective controls create a number of problems. They are discriminatory and lead to inefficiency. They replace individual choice with bureaucratic decisions. Above all, they are difficult to administer.

Whether selective controls affect the general credit is debated among economists. Some claim that the effect of credit stringency or ease generated in a particular sector eventually spreads to other sectors. As a result, total credit is affected. It is just like throwing a pebble in a pond. No matter where it is thrown, ripples, if unchecked, eventually reach all corners. Those who claim that selective controls do not affect general credit argue that such controls only cause substitution of one type of credit for another with no impact on the total.

MORAL SUASION

Moral suasion (sometimes called "jawboning" or "open mouth" policy) can be used to regulate general credit as well as credit in a specific sector. Credit is regulated by voluntary means. The most important tools of moral suasion are:

1. Informal requests to member banks
2. Publicity
3. Direct contacts

Informal Requests To Member Banks

Since Federal Reserve Banks have a very close relation with their member banks, they, to some degree, can influence bank credit through informal requests. The representative of a Federal Reserve Bank meets regularly with officials of a bank in the process of examination and visitation. Examination is done to see whether or not a bank is adhering to the rules and regulations established by the Federal Reserve. Visitation is arranged to help a bank with a specific problem and/or to acquire information on economic activity in the bank's area. In the course of a meeting, the representative of a Federal Reserve Bank can make informal requests to the bank about what it should or should not do. If the Federal Reserve is pursuing a restrictive policy and a given bank is making too many loans for speculative purposes, the representative of the Federal Reserve may request the bank not to do so. On the other hand, if the Federal Reserve is following an expansionary policy and a given bank is very timid in making loans, the representative may tell the bank that it is not meeting the legitimate needs of its community.

Publicity

Publicity is another tool by which the Federal Reserve can influence the credit extended by banks and other financial institutions without resorting to regulatory methods. It is done through such means as press releases, periodicals put out by District Banks, speeches, and Congressional testimony by members of the Board of Governors, including the Chairman. The objective of this type of publicity is to advise the public as to the problem and what needs to be done to overcome it. It is hoped that the more the public understands the problem, the more it can lend support to the policy used to rectify it.

Direct Contacts

Direct contacts involve informal meetings about credit problems with member banks and leaders of other financial institutions. The purpose of such meetings is to impress upon these institutions the importance of sound credit conditions for national stability and cultivate a sense of participation in the solution to the problem. The Federal Reserve has on some occasions used this approach to regulate credit.

Like any other tool, moral suasion has points of both strength and weakness.

Point of Strength

i. It is considered effective when backed by a threat that more positive action will be taken if the central bank's advice is not heeded; when accompanied by a vigorous use of other instruments; and in an emergency situation such as during a war when support from the public in favor of the policy can be easily obtained.

Points of Weakness

i. It can be a cumbersome tool in dealing with a large number of banks—about 14,500 in the United States. It can be effective in England where the central bank has to deal only with a few banks.
ii. It works inequitably between those who are patriotic, sensitive to public opinion and hold a conspicuous position in the community and those who care nothing except for their own benefit.
iii. At times, the views of some District Banks may differ from others. As a result, some District Banks may wind up using moral suasion somewhat differently than others.

COORDINATION OF TOOLS

This chapter and the one before it discuss the various monetary tools and their advantages and disadvantages in using them. These tools can be used individually as well as in combination with others.

The art is to use them in proper combination for the occasion so that their net advantages are maximized.

SUMMARY

Selective controls are used to influence the availability of credit in specific sectors. The major selective controls are interest rate ceilings, margin requirements, consumer credit and real estate credit.

Interest rate ceilings refer to the maximum rates banks are allowed to pay to depositors for savings and other time deposits. It is used primarily to stimulate the housing industry. As a stabilization tool, it has various pros and cons. Its pros are: (i) It is a good tool for affecting the availability of credit in the housing sector. (ii) It can be used to exert a direct influence on business spending. Its cons are: (i) It is discriminatory and causes waste. (ii) It makes it difficult to interpret monetary aggregates.

Margin requirements fix the maximum amount of a loan that can be given for purchasing or carrying of securities. It is used primarily to regulate fluctuations in stock prices. As a stabilization tool, its pros are: (i) It enables the authority to regulate the stock market credit without changing the overall policy. (ii) It is effective when high interest rates fail to discourage speculators from purchasing stocks on credit. Its cons are: (i) It is not effective where a stock market is not well developed. (ii) As margin requirements exist in the United States, they can be easily evaded.

Consumer credit control is used primarily to regulate credit for the purchase of consumer durables. There are arguments for and against its use as a stabilization tool. Those favoring its use claim that it effectively stabilizes prices of consumer durables by dampening demand through higher down payments and shorter repayment terms. It is especially useful, they claim, during periods of short supply caused by the diversion of raw materials to the production of defense goods. Critics claim that it is difficult to administer and that it discriminates against the lower and middle income groups whose need for credit to buy durable goods is the greatest.

Real estate credit curbs are used to slow the construction of new housing and other buildings, especially when construction material is in short supply. Its proponents make similar claims about its effectiveness as do those favoring credit controls on consumer durables. In addition, they claim, it is easy to administer because it is handled by a relatively few institutions under the control of the authorities. Its primary weakness stems from its denial of housing to those who need it most and who cannot afford the required down payment and repayment terms.

Moral suasion can be used to regulate general credit as well as credit in specific sectors. Unlike other tools, it can be used only by voluntary means. The main instruments of moral suasion are informal requests to member banks, publicity and direct contacts. Proponents of moral suasion claim that it is effective when backed by a threat of more positive action by the central bank if its advice is not heeded; when accompanied by a vigorous use of other tools; and in an emergency situation such as war. This tool is difficult to use where a large number of banks are involved. It works inequitably between those who are patriotic and those who are not. Furthermore, at times, some District Banks may view the problem differently and may pursue the policy somewhat differently than others.

FOOTNOTES

[1]Jimmie R. Monhollon, "Regulation Q: An Instrument of Monetary Policy," **Monthly Review: Federal Reserve Bank of Richmond** (July 1970), p. 6.

[2]Adrian W. Throop, "Monetary Policy: A New Emphasis in Regulations Affects Liability Management," **Business Review: Federal Resere Bank of Dallas** (November 1974), pp. 2-3.

[3]Milton Friedman, "Controls on Interest Rates by Banks," **Journal of Money, Credit and Banking** (February 1970), pp. 29-30.

[4]James M. O'Brien, "Federal Regulation of Stock Market Credit: A Need for Reconsideration," **Business Review: Federal Reserve Bank of Philadelphia** (July-August 1974), p. 24.

[5]David Eastburn (ed.), **The Federal Reserve On Record: Readings On Current Issues From Statements by Federal Reserve Officials** (Philadelphia: Federal Reserve Bank of Philadelphia, 1965), pp. 138-142.

[6]James A. Largay and Richard R. West, "Margin Changes and Stock Price Behavior," **Journal of Political Economy** (March/April 1973), p. 329; and Thomas G. Moore, "Stock Market Margin Requirements," **Journal of Political Economy** (April 1966), p. 166.

[7]Donald R. Hodgman, "Selective Credit Controls," **Journal of Money, Credit and Banking** (May 1972), p. 343.

[8]Eastburn, p. 143.

[9]**Ibid.**, p. 149.

QUESTIONS FOR REVIEW

1. Do selective controls affect the general availability of credit? Explain.
2. What is moral suasion? How is it used to regulate credit?
3. Explain how a reduction in margin requirements stimulates the economy.
4. Discuss the pros and cons of interest rate ceilings as a stabilization tool.
5. Explain why consumer credit control is not currently used in the United States.
6. Describe how real estate credit can be used to regulate the real estate sector as well as the economy.
7. Explain how a change in margin reqirements affects total credit.
8. Explain how interest rate ceilings for banks and nonbank thrift institutions are implemented in the United States.
9. Evaluate the effectiveness of moral suasion as an instrument of monetary control.
10. Explain why economists such as Milton Friedman and James Tobin recommend the removal of interest rate ceilings.

SUGGESTED FURTHER READING

1. Dill, Arnold. "Selected Credit Controls: The Experience and Recent Interest." **Monthly Review: Federal Reserve Bank of Atlanta.** May 1971, pp. 78-86.
2. Eastburn, David P. **The Federal Reserve on Record: Readings on Current Issues From Statements by Federal Reserve Officials.** Philadelphia: Federal Reserve Bank of Philadelphia, 1965.
3. Federal Reserve Bank of Boston. **Housing and Monetary Policy: Proceedings of the Monetary Conference, Melvin Village, New Hampshire: October 1970.** Boston, Mass.: Federal Reserve Bank of Boston, 1970.
4. Francis, Darryl R. "Selective Credit - No Substitute for Monetary Restraint." **Review: Federal Reserve Bank of St. Louis.** December 1969, pp. 13-17.
5. Friedman, Milton. "Controls on Interest Rates by Banks." **Journal of Money, Credit and Banking.** February 1970, pp. 15-32.
6. Hodgman, Donald R. "Selective Credit Controls." **Journal of Money, Credit and Banking.** May 1972, pp. 342-359.
7. Kaminow, Ira & O'Brien, James M. (ed.). **Studies in Selective Credit Policies.** Philadelphia: Federal Reserve Bank of Philadelphia, 1975.
8. Largay, James A. & West, Richard R. "Margin Changes and Stock Price Behavior." **Journal of Political Economy.** March/April 1973, pp. 328-339.

9. Mayer, Thomas. "Financial Guidelines and Credit Controls." **Journal of Money, Credit and Banking.** May 1972, pp. 360-374.
10. Melton, William C. "The Market for Large Negotiable CD's." **Quarterly Review: Federal Reserve Bank of New York.** Winter 1977-78, pp. 22-34.
11. Monhollan, Jimmie R. "Regulation Q: An Instrument of Monetary Control." **Monthly Review: Federal Reserve Bank of Richmond.** July 1970, pp. 2-8.
12. Moore, Thomas Gale. "Stock Market Requirements." **Journal of Political Economy.** April 1966, pp. 158-167.
13. Nadler, Paul S. "Regulation Q and Credit Control." **Bankers Magazine.** Spring 1970, pp. 17-25.
14. O'Brien, James M. "Federal Regulations of Stock Market Credit: A Need for Reconsideration." **Business Review: Federal Reserve Bank of Philadelphia.** July-August 1974, pp. 23-33.
15. Rao, D.C. "Selective Credit Policy: Is It Justified and Can It Work?" **Journal Of Finance.** May 1972, pp. 473-479.
16. Romans, J.T. "Moral Suasion as an Instrument of Economic Policy." **American Economic Review.** December 1966, pp. 1220-1225.
17. Ruebling, Charlott. "The Administration of Regulation Q." **Review: Federal Reserve Bank of St. Louis.** February 1970, pp. 29-40.
18. Silber, William L. "Open Market Rates and Regulation Q." **National Banking Review.** March 1967, pp. 299-303.
19. "The Structure of Margin Credit." **Federal Reserve Bulletin.** April 1975. pp. 209-220.
20. Throop, Adrian W. "Monetary Policy: A New Emphasis in Regulations Affects Liability Management." **Business Review: Federal Reserve Bank of Dallas.** November 1974, pp. 1-14.
21. Tobin, James. "Deposit Interest Ceilings as a Monetary Control." **Journal of Money, Credit and Banking.** February 1970. pp. 4-14.

CHAPTER XVI

Decision Making Process
In
The Federal Reserve System

The effectiveness of monetary policy depends as much on the decision making process as on the tools available for use, the experience and caliber of those who make or help to make the decision, the state of knowledge regarding the relationship of various economic variables and the degree of cooperation offered by the public. The process can make the difference between success and failure. A good decision making process uses all the information available at the time to reduce the chances of error, utilizes available expertise and shortens the time needed to reach a decision. This chapter describes the decision making process followed by the Federal Reserve in applying the monetary tools described in the two previous chapters.

DISCOUNT RATE

Action to change the discount rate is initiated by any of the District Banks and goes into effect upon approval of the Board of Governors. Each District Bank is required to establish its own rate every 14 days. The body within a district that establishes the rate is the board of directors. The board of each bank meets one or two times a month. An executive committee of the board, composed of four or more directors, sets the rate during interim periods in those cases where the board meets once a month. The boards of some District Banks, such as those in New York and San Francisco, meet twice a month, once in person and the other in a telephone conference call. Certain staff members attend the board meetings. Among them are the president, first vice president, research officers, secretary and assistant secretary.

The number of officers who may be invited to attend is usually limited. The suggestion to change the discount rate can come from the Board of Governors, the president of a District Bank, one or more of the directors, members of the research staff or a combination of these. The discount rate is often discussed in FOMC (Federal Open Market Committee) meetings, though the Committee has no responsibility for this tool. On a few occasions, the Board of Governors has met with all district presidents to discuss the discount rate, among other matters.

Preparations For Directors' Meetings

Preparations for meetings of directors of District Banks vary among districts. Some districts furnish directors certain types of reports prior to a meeting, while others don't. In almost all cases, directors are apprised of economic activity within their districts through periodic statistical reports and through special studies on a variety of topics.

The Minneapolis Bank, for example, sends its directors a summary of correspondence between the public and directors prior to each meeting. The purpose of the summary is to give the directors an overall view of their constituents' concerns with respect to the economy in general and the discount rate in particular.

In Cleveland, Boston, Philadelphia and Richmond, the research staffs prepare a review of current economic activity containing charts and tables and send it to directors prior to each meeting.

Occasionally, District directors get summaries or copies of communications received by the District Banks from the Board of Governors. For example, in the meeting of January 6, 1978, the Board of Governors felt that the discount rate should be raised to 6½% rather than 6¼%, which the Reserve Bank of Chicago requested. The Board asked its Secretary to convey the tenor of that discussion to the Reserve Bank of Chicago and to the Reserve Bank of New York whose directors were believed to be inclined toward the 6½% rate. The Board's staff also routinely keeps each district president informed about discount rate requests from various Reserve Banks that are awaiting a Board decision.

Procedure Used By District Directors To Reach A Rate Decision

Here is an outline of the procedure commonly followed in reaching a decision on the discount rate at a regular meeting of the board of directors of a District Bank:

   i. Research officers report on developments in domestic financial markets, and international exchange markets, loans to member banks and recent economic developments. Directors may ask questions during the presentations.

  ii. Wherever a representative of a branch board is permitted to attend a meeting of the district head office board (HOB), the representative either makes a formal presentation or makes comments in the "go around" (a period during the meeting when each person expresses his/her views on the subject under discussion). In either case, the branch representative conveys the branch board's views on business and economic conditions in the branch's area. (Table 16-1 shows Reserve Banks that have branches and their locations. Table 16-2 lists Reserve Banks that allow branch representatives to attend HOB meetings and those that don't.) A branch board representative is not present during a vote on the discount rate.

 iii. During the "go around", each director comments on such matters as retail sales, production, inventories and financial developments.

 iv. The president (or, in his absence, the senior vice president) presents his views along with his policy proposal, which he offers in the form of a motion. (In some cases, a motion for a discount rate action comes from a director.) This is followed by a general discussion.

  v. The proposal is put to a vote. The secretary communicates the decision along with the general feelings of the directors to the Board of Governors in Washington by an encoded telegram.

Role Of Branch Boards In Decision Making Process

There are three methods by which branch boards can provide input to HOBs in setting the discount rate. They are: (i) Joint meetings of HOB and branch boards (ii) Sending a representative to HOB meetings (iii) Submission to the HOB directors of the minutes of meetings of branch boards. All Reserve Banks do not use all of the

TABLE 16-1

FEDERAL RESERVE BANK BRANCHES

Reserve Banks	Branches
1. Atlanta	Birmingham Jacksonville Miami Nashville New Orleans
2. Boston	None
3. Chicago	Detroit
4. Cleveland	Cincinnatti Pittsburgh
5. Dallas	El Paso Houston San Antonio
6. Kansas City	Denver Oklahoma City Omaha
7. Minneapolis	Helena
8. New York	Buffalo
9. Philadelphia	None
10. Richmond	Baltimore Charlotte
11. St. Louis	Little Rock Louisville Memphis
12. San Francisco	Los Angeles Portland Salt Lake City Seattle

Source: 1 **Federal Reserve Bulletin** (August 1978), p. A73.

three methods—the Reserve Bank of Atlanta uses only one, while others use two or all three.

The HOB of District Banks having one or more branches, except the District Bank of Atlanta, meets with each branch board separately and/or with all branch boards together 1 to 4 times a year. (For more detail, see Table 16-2.) In these meetings, all members of the branch boards are free to express their views to the HOB.

The branch boards of those District Banks that allow branch representation at HOB meetings convey their views through representatives. (Among the ten District Banks having one or more branches, seven permit branch representation. For more detail, see Table 16-2.) Branch board representatives are usually selected on a rotating basis for each HOB meeting. Each branch director presents an economic report of his area at the meeting of his branch board, which is held one week prior to a HOB meeting. The selected branch representative summarizes the discussion at the HOB meeting. In other cases, the views of branch boards are presented by the branch manager. District Banks that do not permit branch representation obtain the views of branches at the HOB meeting from a manager of branches, who operates at the District Bank office.

Branch boards can also provide input to the HOB by submitting minutes of their meetings. Though all branch boards forward minutes of their board meetings to their respective head offices, only three (Reserve Banks of Chicago, Kansas City and Minneapolis) forward them to their directors on a regular basis. In all other cases, the head office forwards to its directors the minutes of a selected branch-board meeting or a portion of them.

Preparation For The Board Of Governors' Meetings

As mentioned earlier, a change in the discount rate becomes effective after approval by the Board of Governors. The Board typically considers discount rate requests once a week. The meeting is attended by the Governors and appropriate officers and staff.

The Board prepares for such a meeting by reviewing periodic memoranda, listing pending recommendations of various District Banks regarding the discount rate. Comments submitted by the directors of District Banks in support of their recommendations are also furnished to Board members. In addition, Board members gain an insight into conditions from periodic briefings (usually once a week) by their staff in which, among other things, current economic and financial developments are reviewed.

Procedure Used By The Board Of Governors To Reach A Decision

The procedure normally used by the Board of Governors to reach a decision about the discount rate is as follows: Staff members specializing in the area make presentations appropriate to the Board's needs in reaching a decision. Board members ask questions and, at times, for staff recommendations. Then, each Board member expresses his/her view on the issue. This is followed by a general discussion among members. At the conclusion of the discussion, a vote is taken. The vote constitutes the position of the Board.

From time to time, the Discount Policy Group, composed of senior officers of the Board, also presents its findings to the Board in its consideration of monetary policy. The major functions of the Group are:

i. To watch the operation of the discount function for general oversight and for uniformity among different Reserve Banks

ii. To determine international implications of discount activity and its impact on the domestic economy and the banking system

iii. To study operating and regulatory matters pertaining to the discount function

iv. To anticipate emergency situations that may call for larger amounts of credit at the discount window

v. To evaluate trends in types and volumes of discount window credit.

Generally a proposal relating to only one tool is before the Board at any single meeting. But that proposal is not considered in isolation; other monetary tools may be discussed or referred to. It is recognized that making a change in one tool might require concurrent or future alterations in one or more of the other tools to achieve a given objective.

OPEN MARKET OPERATIONS

The body that conducts open market operations is known as Federal Open Market Committee (FOMC). It is the key decision making body in the monetary policy area for the whole Federal Reserve System. It meets once a month. However, if the situation warrants, the FOMC holds interim meetings (usually by phone) to revise instructions. The principal people who attend meetings are: the Board of Governors, presidents of all Reserve Banks, Committee staff officers (secretary, assistant secretary, economist, associate economists,

TABLE 16-2

EXTENT OF INVOLVEMENT OF BRANCH BOARDS INTO THE DISCOUNT RATE DECISION MAKING PROCESS

Reserve Banks	Number Of Times HOB* Meets With Branch Boards	Number Of Branch Representatives Attend The HOB* Meeting	Is The Copy Of Minutes Of Branch Board Meetings Sent To HOB* Directors?
Atlanta	None	Five (One from each branch)	No
Boston	Not Applicable	Not Applicable	Not Applicable
Chicago	Twice a year in a joint session	One	Yes
Cleveland	Four times a year in a joint session	Two (One from each branch)	No
Dallas	Once a year in a joint session with all branch boards plus once a year individually with one branch board, selected on a rotating basis	Three (One from each branch)	No
Kansas City	Twice a year individually with each branch board	Three (One from each branch)	Yes
Minneapolis	Once or twice a year in a joint session	One	Yes
New York	Once a year in a joint session	None	No
Richmond	Once a year in a joint session with all branches plus once a year individually with each branch	None	No
Philadelphia	Not Applicable	Not Applicable	Not Applicable
St. Louis	Once a year in a joint session with all branch boards plus once a year individually with one branch board, selected on a rotating basis	None	No
San Francisco	Once a year in a joint session with all branch boards plus once a year individually with one branch board, selected on a rotating basis	Four (One from each branch)	No

*Head Office Board

etc.), and the FOMC Manager and deputy managers. Staff officers and the Manager and deputy managers are selected every year by the Committee at its first meeting on or after March 1 to serve until the following March. Officers are selected from the staff of the Board as well as from Reserve Banks. There is no fixed limit on the number of staff officers. If the need arises, the Committee can expand the list of staff officers or invite one or more other employees of the Federal Reserve System to a specific meeting.

Preparation For FOMC Meeting

Committee members normally do two things to prepare for a meeting: (1) Absorb all factual and analytical information received before the meeting. (2) Consult staff aides. Before each meeting, Committee members receive the following reports:

i. Green Book. Reviews the facts and implications of recent domestic and foreign economic developments including a statement showing how actual events seem to be conforming to or deviating from the most recent economic projection. It is prepared by the Board's staff. When significant deviations from the projection become evident, their implications for the longer run are evaluated and the forecast is revised. Roughly three times a year, or more frequently if unusual developments occur, the Committee is provided with a comprehensive economic forecast extending one to two years into the future. Between the major forecasting efforts, the previous forecast is updated before each monthly meeting. Since the economic forecast is a major input to the policy decision, it is based upon two independent efforts—one upon detailed projections of GNP components prepared by staff experts in the various areas and the other upon the MIT/Penn-Social Science Research Council econometric model. Results of both these methods are studied by senior members of the Board's research staff who then work out what is basically a judgmental projection of economic activity.

ii. Blue Book. Lays out several policy alternatives believed to be of special relevance to the Committee and their possible outcomes. It also is prepared by the Board's staff in consultation with the Manager of the System Open Market Account. Each alternative includes such things as operating targets expressed in ranges of annual growth of major monetary aggregates consistent with FOMC objectives. A given alternative may call for an annual growth rate of 4½ to 6½ percent for M-1A, 7½ to 10 percent for M_2, 9 to 11½ percent for M_3 and 5 to 8 percent for credit proxy. Credit proxy includes member banks' deposits and certain other liabilities subject to reserve requirements. (Other liabilities subject to reserve requirements and counted in the proxy are: (i) net liabilities of member banks to their foreign branches and to branches in U.S. territories and possessions, (ii) Eurodollars borrowed from foreign banks, (iii) loans sold by member banks to their affiliates and (iv) certain loans or participations in pools of loans sold under repurchase agreements to investors other than banks.) Operating targets consistent with a given alternative are expressed in ranges because it is believed that the Manager cannot hit a specific number exactly and conflict among different series of monetary aggregates may arise.

iii. Red Book. Analyzes district business and financial trends. It is prepared by one of the Reserve Banks on a rotating basis. It usually compares district developments with national trends and shows any significant differences that may be present between them.

iv. Reports on open market and foreign exchange operations prepared by the Manager. The former covers such things as securities transactions made since the previous meeting and comments on any special problem the Manager has encountered in carrying out the Committee's instructions, while the latter reports on foreign currency operatons.

The Board of Governors also gains insight from the Federal Advisory Council with whom it meets four times a year. (The Council, as discussed in Chapter XIII, consists of 12 members. The board of directors of each District Bank annually selects one member from its district.)

Before a meeting, each district president customarily meets with staff aides to review the state of the economy and to discuss the appropriateness of current monetary policy. Members of the Board of Governors attend briefings by Board staff experts. In addition, each district president gains an insight into the policy issue at meetings of the district boards of directors at which the topic is usually discussed. District presidents consult staff aides in the following manner: Several days before a FOMC meeting, the president holds a meeting with the staff of the bank's research department and senior officers. At that time, the Green Book and both reports of the Manager of open market operations are in. Discussion revolves around analyses of economic developments in their own district and their relation to national trends drawn from the Green Book, the Manager's reports and other sources focusing on the larger picture of the nation as a whole. From the discussion there emerges a consensus as to the direction of monetary policy. The senior officer summarizes the general opinion of the staff and gives his own view as to the appropriate direction of monetary policy in the days ahead. The president listens to suggestions and asks questions on key points. But he does not finalize his position because more information is needed. The FOMC meeting is usually held on Tuesday. The Blue Book arrives on Saturday (three days before the meeting). On Monday, each president and his associate (or number of associates in the case of the District Bank of New York) journey to Washington. Upon arriving at their hotel, they receive additional material covering developments in both domestic and foreign markets through Friday's close. In addition, they receive supplementary material to the Green Book that arrived the preceding Thursday. On Monday evening, the president and his associate (or associates) go over once again, in summation, the views expressed by staff aides in the light of the latest informaton. Then, and only then, the president finalizes the general position that he will support the next day before the Committee as a whole.

The quality of factual and analytical documents depends upon the experience and knowledge of the staff that prepares them. According to Sherman Maisel, the Federal Reserve has probably the best economic staff in the world. It surpassed all other agencies in its knowledge of the intricacies of the country's statistical system, and in its ability to collect and analyze data.[1]

Strategy and Tactics

The FOMC approach to monetary policy involves a two-stage decision process. The first stage involves the development of a long term plan for monetary policy based upon long term objectives, which is called "strategy." The second stage deals with the formulation of short term plans with an eye on long term objectives, "tactics."

In developing its strategy (policy stance), the Committee takes into account objectives for economic growth, employment and prices as well as the expected course of fiscal policy. It then sets targets of monetary aggregates and/or money market conditions to help achieve objectives. The Committee does not change its policy stance at every meeting or every other meeting. It moves slowly in establishing it and maintaining it for some months. (In response to the Congressional Joint Resolution of March 1975, the Chairman announces the FOMC's desired growth rate ranges for certain monetary aggregates for the next four quarters in a quarterly presentation to (alternately) the House and Senate Banking Committees.)

After the Committee establishes a policy stance, it proceeds to develop short term plans (tactics) to achieve the objective. If the policy stance is expressed in targets of certain monetary aggregates, the Committee will devise the best tactic it knows to hit those targets. In devising tactics, the Committee takes into account forces already in motion and their likely impact on the period immediately ahead. If monetary aggregates change unexpectedly, tactics are revised.

Procedure Used To Reach Decision

By the time Committee members gather in Washington, they are well prepared to deliberate. They have digested all of the reports provided prior to the meeting, have consulted their aides and, above all, have tentatively formed their general position.

To understand the logic behind each step used in arriving at decisions, it is necessary to know the Committee's general approach to a decision. First the Committee wants to thresh out the views of members as to the current state of the economy and prospects for the future. The differences in views on such matters may call for different policy actions. Second, the Committee sorts out the views of members as to the appropriate open market actions. Finally, it engages in a give-and-take discussion in an effort to synthesize individual views into a consensus. Following is a detailed description of each step taken by the Committee to reach its decisons:

   i. The Committee generally deals first with foreign exchange operations. The Manager (or deputy manager for foreign operations) reports on events in foreign exchange since the previous meeting. The Manager's information is up-to-the minute because he checks with officials involved in the operation at the New York Reserve Bank immediately before coming to the meeting. His report may include one or more recommendations. After discussion, the Chairman translates the consensus into a policy proposal on foreign exchange operations and puts it to a vote.

ii. The Committee then turns to domestic policy. On occasion, the Chairman may start by capsulizing his own views and he may share with the Committee some information that was not available previously.

iii. A Senior Board staff economist reports on economic and financial developments and their effects on the long term outlook. (Several times a year, these economists give detailed economic projections for the next year or so, which are based on explicit assumptions about fiscal and monetary policy during the period.) Members then put questions to the staff and/or bring to the attention of the Committee any significant new information they have about the economic and financial situation.

iv. The Manager (or deputy manager for domestic operations) highlights domestic open market operations and developments in financial markets since the previous meeting. He may have recommendations to make on technical operational matters. Here again, Committee members, if they wish, may ask questions and/or comment on any issue.

v. A senior Board staff member lays out the likely effects of adopting each of several alternatives governing open market operations. Normally, the effects of three alternatives are discussed. The three alternatives (A, B and C) discussed in the meeting of July 17, 1972 serve as an example. Alternative A: "To implement this policy, while taking account of the forthcoming Treasury financing, developments in capital markets, and international developments, the Committee seeks to achieve bank reserves and money market conditions that will support **somewhat faster** growth in monetary aggregates over the months ahead." Alternative B: "To implement this policy, while taking account of the forthcoming Treasury financing, developments in capital markets, and international developments, the Committee seeks to achieve bank reserves and money market conditions that will support **moderate** growth in monetary aggregates over the months ahead.'' Alternative C: ''To implement this policy, while taking account of the forthcoming Treasury financing, developments in capital markets, and international developments, the Committee seeks to achieve bank reserves and money market conditions that will support somewhat **slower** growth in monetary aggregates over the months ahead.'' Each alternative is documented with a set of intermediate operating targets along with its expected effect on key variables such as bank reserves, monetary aggregates, interest rates, etc.

vi. Then comes the time for the ''go around.'' The Chairman calls upon each Governor and each of the district presidents in turn for his/her views and recommendations. Since New York is the financial center of the U.S. and of the world and open market operations are conducted at the New York District Bank, its president often makes the first presentation. Comments are made on the economic outlook and how each member's views agree or differ from those of the staff and on what each member regards as an appropriate monetary policy in the circumstances.

vii. Toward the end of the meeting, members translate their general policy preference into specific recommendations for monetary growth rates and money market conditions. About once each quarter the Committee also reviews its longer-run (1-year) monetary objectives.

viii. In the end, the Chairman guides the Committee to a consensus. Generally, by the time each participant presents his/her views, a consensus has emerged. The Chairman translates the consensus into a directive and presents it to the Committee for final discussion. After the discussion, the directive, often with some amendments, is put to a vote. The approved directive gives broad instructions to the Manager about open market operations. In discussion (or in presentations), the freedom of expression is fully respected. Each Committee member has the right to vote in any way he wants without having to defend the action, but an individual's preferences for the directive can be deduced from his general policy views and a dissenter may, on occasion, amplify upon the specific reasons for his dissent. Staff members also have freedom of expression. A senior staff member once wrote, "It is worthy of note that no principal of the Committee intrudes onto staff domain by trying to influence any of the staff analyses or presentations; the proprieties of intellectual freedom are strictly observed."[2]

RESERVE REQUIREMENTS, INTEREST RATE CEILINGS AND MARGIN REQUIREMENTS

Since the decision making process with respect to reserve requirements, interest rate ceilings and margin requirements is substantially the same, they are discussed together. The Board of Governors has the responsibility for setting them. Meetings are attended by the Board of Governors and appropriate officers and staff.

Preparation For A Meeting

Whether the Board of Governors meets to review reserve requirements, interest rate ceilings or margin requirements, the staff in each case prepares reports in the form of memoranda and submits them prior to a meeting. Memoranda supply information and analyses relating to the use of the policy tool to be discussed. Memoranda may discuss alternative courses of action that the Board might take. Board members also benefit from periodic briefings about economic and financial developments by their staff since they are pertinent to the consideration of any tool. Briefings are usually held once a week.

Procedure Used To Reach Decision

The procedure commonly used to arrive at a decision is as follows:
   i. Oral presentations by staff economists in their respective areas of expertise related to the policy tool under consideration. Presentations are designed to provide information and analyses of alternatives that can help Board members in reaching their decision. Thereafter, Board members often ask

the staff questions or for amplification of certain points. The staff generally does not make recommendations. However, an exception can occur if a Board member specifically asks for recommendations.

ii. Presentation of findings by the Reserve Requirement Policy Group, if needed. The Group is composed of senior officers of the Board who represent several of its divisions. It considers questions of reserve requirements and rates as they pertain to the Board's responsibilities on monetary policy. In recent years, the concerns of this Group have been confined mainly to the issues of reserve requirements in relation to the burden of membership in the Federal Reserve System and of proposals regarding imposition of reserve requirements on foreign banks operating in the United States.

iii. The "go around," in which the Chairman calls upon each member to express his/her views on the issues at hand.

iv. General discussion, at the conclusion of which a vote is taken, with each Board member voting in turn. The result represents the decision of the Board.

As indicated in the previous chapter, the Board is required to consult the Federal Deposit Insurance Corporation (FDIC) and the Federal Home Loan Bank Board (FHLBB) to change interest rate ceilings (Regulation Q). Consultation generally takes place at a meeting of the Interagency Coordinating Committee On Bank Regulations, of which the Comptroller of the Currency is also a member. The Board of Governors may first meet to determine what views are to be expressed on behalf of the Board as a whole or of individual members in the coming meeting with the Chairmen of the FDIC and the FHLBB. Then, the vice chairman or any other member of the Board of Governors meets with the chairmen of the other two agencies, gives the Board's views and tries to develop a package that is acceptable to all. These representatives convey the substance of the meeting's discussion to their respective boards and senior staff members. Thereafter, the Board of Governors decides to approve that package, either as it is or with some changes. The representatives of the Board of Governors does not have to meet representatives of the other two agencies in person. The statutory function of "consulting" on Regulation Q can also be fulfilled by other means of communication such as written correspondence or by telephone.

Consultation with the FDIC and the FHLBB requires little time. For example, on January 20, 1970, the Board members met at 9:30 a.m. to determine their own views with respect to interest rate ceilings. At 10:30 a.m., its representative met with directors of the FDIC and the FHLBB and agreed on the course of action. At 3:10 p.m., the Board of Governors met again and approved the decision. Representatives of other agencies are not permitted in the meetings of the Board of Governors where monetary policy is to be discussed.

The Board is not required to consult with the Securities and Exchange Commission or any other Federal agency to change margin requirements. However, as a matter of practice, the Board does consider the views of others in arriving at its decision concerning this tool.[3]

MORAL SUASION

Since the Federal Reserve uses moral suasion infrequently and sparingly, neither a formal organizational structure nor formal procedural structure exists. It is usually used in the form of letters to banks, speeches and Congressional testimony. For example, on May 16, 1973, the Board sent a letter to 190 nonmember banks requesting them to adhere voluntarily to the action it had taken with respect to large certificates of deposit for member banks. (Under the Monetary Act of 1980, even nonmember banks and other depository institutions having transactions accounts and/or nonpersonal time deposits are required to comply with reserve requirements of the Federal Reserve.)

SUMMARY

The effectiveness of monetary policy depends, among other things, on the process used in reaching decisions. A change in the discount rate is usually initiated by a Reserve Bank and approved by the Board of Governors. The board of directors of each Reserve Bank has the responsibility for this tool. The boards of Reserve Banks meet once or twice a month. There is no set procedure as to the material furnished to directors prior to a meeting. Some Reserve Banks do not provide any written material at all. In a board meeting, the procedure normally used to reach a decision is as follows: Research officers make presentations. Directors ask questions and/or make comments, followed by the "go around" in which each director presents his/her views in turn. The president may propose a course of action or proposals may come from other directors. This is followed by a general discussion. The president then puts the proposal to a vote. The secretary communicates the Chairman to the Board of Governors, which meets to act on the action taken by a Reserve Bank.

The body that oversees the conduct of open market operations is the FOMC. It meets once a month. To prepare for a meeting, Board members absorb all the factual and analytical information provided ahead of a meeting and consult their staff aides. The material furnished in advance includes Green Book, Blue Book, Red Book and two reports from the Manager. The procedure generally used in the FOMC meeting is as follows: Foreign exchange operations are normally discussed first. The Manager reports on foreign operations. After a general discussion, recommendations are put to a vote.

The discussion of domestic open market operations starts with a presentation by a senior staff economist who reviews economic and financial developments. The Manager highlights domestic open market operations and developments in financial markets since the previous meeting. This is followed by a presentation of a senior staff member regarding the likely effects of adopting each of several alternatives. Thereafter, the "go around" begins. The Chairman calls upon each Board member and each president for his/her views. This is followed by a general discussion. After this, the Chairman guides the Committee to a consensus and formulates the proposal. After a brief discussion, the proposal is put to a vote.

The decision making process regarding reserve requirements, interest rate ceilings and margin requirements is more or less the same. Prior to a meeting, the Board's staff prepares memoranda which are submitted to Board members. Memoranda supply information and analyses relating to the use of the policy tool to be discussed and alternative courses of action that the Board might take. The procedure used to reach a decision in a meeting is as follows: the Board's staff economists make oral presentations in accordance with their area of specialization related to a policy tool under consideration. This is followed by a "go around," the Chairman calling on each member to express his/her views. This is followed by a general discussion. At the conclusion of the discussion, a vote is taken. The vote constitutes the position of the Board. In the case of interest rate ceilings, the Board is required to consult the FDIC and the FHLBB.

Moral suasion is adopted without a formal organizational or procedural structure. Whenever such a tool is used, it is pursued mainly by the Board of Governors in the form of letters to banks, speeches or Congressional testimony.

FOOTNOTES

[1]Sherman J. Maisel, **Managing the Dollar** (New York: W.W. Norton, 1973), p. 47.

[2]Edward A. Wayne, **Come to the F.O.M.C.** (Richmond, Virginia: Federal Reserve Bank of Richmond, 1967), p. 7.

[3]Letter from Norman Shupeck, attorney, The Federal Reserve System, Washington, D.C., November 7, 1974.

QUESTIONS FOR REVIEW

1. Why is it important to study the decision making process as it applies to monetary tools? Explain.
2. Discuss the process used in bringing about a change in the discount rate.
3. What are the different reports submitted to members of the FOMC prior to a meeting? In your judgment, does such a procedure help improve the quality of final decisions made by this body?
4. Explain briefly Green Book, Red Book, and Blue Book.
5. Evaluate critically the procedure followed in the FOMC meeting in arriving at a decision.
6. What is the name of the body that has responsibility over reserve requirements? What procedure does this body use in arriving at a decision?
7. Explain the role the Federal Deposit Insurance Corporation and the Federal Home Loan Bank Board play in the decision making process as it applies to interest rate ceilings.
8. Should the Security & Exchange Commission have any input in the formulation of policy about margin requirements? Why?
9. Evaluate the role of the Manager in the decision making process as it applies to open market operations.
10. Explain why the FOMC expresses targets in ranges rather than in specific numbers?

SUGGESTED FURTHER READING

1. Federal Reserve Bank of New York. **A Day at the Fed.** New York: Federal Reserve Bank of New York, 1977.
2. Friedman, Benjamin M. "The Inefficiency of Short-Run Monetary Targets for Monetary Policy." **Brookings Papers on Economic Activity: 2.** 1977, pp. 293-346.
3. Karekan, John H. and Miller, Preston J. "The Policy Procedure of the FOMC: A Critique," in **Prescription for Monetary Policy: Proceedings**

from a Seminar Series. Minneapolis, Minnesota: Federal Reserve Bank of Minneapolis, 1976, pp. 19-42.

4. Kimbrel, Monroe. **Inside the Federal Open Market Committee.** Atlanta, Georgia: Federal Reserve Bank of Atlanta, 1978.

5. Letter from Arthur F. Burns, Chairman of the Board of Governors, The Federal Reserve System, Washington, D.C., to 190 Nonmember Banks, May 16, 1973. (Xeroxed.)

6. Letters from Clement Van Nice, First Vice President, Federal Reserve Bank of Minneapolis, Minneapolis, Minnesota, August 4, 1978 and September 19 and 25, 1978.

7. Letters from Eric Hingst, Assistant Vice President, Federal Reserve Bank of Atlanta, Atlanta, Georgia, September 11 and 25, 1978.

8. Letters from F. Garland Russel Jr., Senior Vice President, General Counsel and Secretary, Federal Reserve Bank of St. Louis, St. Louis, Missouri, September 6, 18 and 25, 1978.

9. Letters from Joseph F. Morrissette, Manager, Bank and Public Relation Department, Federal Reserve Bank of Richmond, Virginia, September 18, 1978 and October 4, 1978.

10. Letter from Lawrence C. Mordock Jr., Vice President and Secretary, Federal Reserve Banks of Philadelphia, Pennsylvania, August 11, 1978.

11. Letter from Nancy M. Ferar, Economist, Office of the Staff Director for Monetary Policy, The Federal Reserve System, Washington, D.C., July 27, 1978.

12. Letters from Robert Smith III, Assistant Vice President and Secretary, Federal Reserve Bank of Dallas, Texas, August 17 and 31, 1978 and September 11 and 26, 1978.

13. Letters from Robert F. Ware, Assistant Vice President and Economist, Federal Reserve Bank of Cleveland, Cleveland, Ohio, July 24, 1978 and October 28, 1978.

14. Letters from Theodore E. Allison, Secretary of Board, The Federal Reserve System, Washington, D.C., August 25, 1978 and September 22, 1978.

15. Letters from Thomas E. Davis, Senior Vice President and Director of Research, Federal Reserve Bank of Kansas City, Kansas City, Missouri, July 28, 1978, August 21, 1978 and September 25, 1978.

16. Letters from Ward J. Larson, Senior Vice President, General Counsel and Secretary, Federal Reserve Bank of Chicago, Chicago, Illinois, September 18, 1978 and October 17, 1978.

17. Letters from William M. Burk, Senior Economist and Director of Public Information, Federal Reserve Bank of San Francisco, San Francisco, California, September 22, 1978 and October 5, 1978.

18. Meek, Paul. **Open Market Operations.** New York: Federal Reserve Bank of New York, 1978.

19. Poole, William. "The Making of Monetary Policy: Description and Analysis." **New England Economic Review.** March/April 1975, pp. 21-30.
20. The Federal Reserve System. **Federal Open Market Committee: Rules of Procedure (12CFRZ72): As Amended Effective February 19, 1975.** Washington, D.C.: The Federal Reserve System, n.d.
21. The Federal Reserve System, Freedom of Information Office. FOI: Discount Rates, January 6, 1978. (xeroxed.)
22. The Federal Reserve System. **The Federal Reserve System: Purposes and Functions.** Washington, D.C.: The Federal Reserve System, 1974.

CHAPTER XVII

Problems of Monetary Policy

Despite the fact that monetary policy in the United States is used intensively and, by and large, effectively, it is not without problems. Its major problems are:

    A. Lags
    B. Imperfect knowledge
    C. Conflicts among goals
    D. Changes in payment system
    E. Attrition of membership
    F. Growth in Eurodollars
    G. Discriminatory effects

LAGS

It takes time to cool off an overheated economy, and to stimulate it when depressed. The worst is that lags are not only substantially long but also fairly unpredictable. There are three types of lags in monetary policy: (1) recognition lag, (2) policy lag and (3) outside lag.

Recognition lag is the time required to recognize the problem, that is, the point at which policymakers are convinced that the economy has changed in such a way as to require a change in policy. It takes time to recognize the problem because of the delays in compiling, aggregating and analyzing data. Many analysts are not satisfied with one piece of information. They want to see supporting evidence from several economic series over some time before they make a recommendation. According to Mark Willes, U.S. policymakers take about three months to recognize the need for a change in policy.[1]

Policy lag is the time between recognition and structuring and implementing a new policy. It occurs because of the time required to work out the details of a new policy and to go through the administrative procedure to implement it. Sometimes, political considerations force policymakers to delay the change. Policy lag in the U.S. monetary policy is believed to be close to zero because of the autonomous nature of the Federal Reserve System and of the relatively small and homogeneous group of policymakers.

Outside lag is the elapsed time between institution of a policy and its impact on the economy. Though Keynesians and Monetarists are divided on the length of outside lag, both recognize its existence. Keynesians say that it takes about 12 quarters (as evidenced by the FRB/MIT model) before the full effect is realized. Monetarists claim that the full effect is realized within 4 quarters (as evidenced by the St. Louis model). Keynesians believe that a long lag occurs because consumption and investment expenditures are affected by long term interest rates. It takes time for long term rates to change in response to a change in the money stock. After long term rates are changed, it takes time before industry and business purchase capital goods, people buy houses, and local and state governments float bonds to initiate new construction projects. Outside lag also creates problems for policymakers. If it is too long, a new policy may produce a substantial effect at the time it is no longer needed or when an entirely new policy is needed to remedy the situation. This problem can be solved by forecasting, enabling policymakers to take corrective action ahead of time. But, at the present time, our ability to forecast is far from perfect.

IMPERFECT KNOWLEDGE

Despite a tremendous amount of research, there are still many unknowns in economics. It is not precisely known how the economy works and how different variables are related to each other and to the economy. Economists still debate how the effect of a change in the money stock is transmitted to GNP; whether the relation between the money supply and GNP is stable or unstable; the speed and size of a response to a monetary action; how much a given change in the money supply affects prices and output; how inflation is caused and disseminated; how inflationary expectations are formed; and so on. Since our knowledge about the economy is not perfect, our policy prescriptions to cure its ills have to be less than perfect. This is why different groups of economists recommend different policy prescriptions. One group recommends rules and the other discretion in conducting monetary policy; one advocates the use of monetary aggregates as targets and indicators and the other, monetary aggregates and money market conditions; and one suggests the use of only monetary policy for stabilization purposes and the other, of both fiscal and monetary policies.

Because of imperfect knowledge, policymakers have problems in setting targets, as well as in hitting them. The problem of projecting in advance the changing relationship between money and the economy makes it difficult to determine what targets are needed to achieve a given objective. The difficulty of hitting targets stems from the fact that the money supply is affected not only by policy variables (discount rate, etc.), but also by nonpolicy variables (float, etc.). Over a long period of time, policy variables have an important influence on the money supply. But over short periods, nonpolicy variables cause slippages. Often these slippages are enormous.

True, we do not have perfect knowledge. But, we are not completely ignorant either. We have learned a lot during the recent past. Every economist now recognizes that the money supply has an important effect on the economy. Everyone now admits that inflationary expectations, among other things, contribute to inflation, and inflation cannot go too far unless accommodated by an increase in the money supply. Everyone recognizes lags in the effect of monetary policy, though their estimates vary. Officials of the Federal Reserve claim that they now have the ability to hit the target of Federal funds rate, averaged over a one week period, and of money stock averaged over six month period, with a small error.

CONFLICTS AMONG GOALS

Another problem is caused by the presence of conflicts among various ultimate goals. Full employment, for example, conflicts with price stability and balance-of-payment equilibrium. Such conflicts make it impossible to achieve different goals simultaneously. Policymakers must sacrifice one or more goals to accomplish another. Full employment conflicts with price stability because when the economy moves toward full employment, rising costs and aggregate demand put an upward pressure on prices. In recent years, unemployment has been recognized as a social rather than individual failing. This forces policymakers to pursue an expansionary rather than contractionary policy, making it difficult to deal with the problem of inflation.

The goal of full employment conflicts with balance-of-payment equilibrium because a high level of employment tends to increase imports and decrease exports. Imports rise because high employment is generally accompanied by increases in domestic prices. The greater affluence resulting from a higher level of employment also increases the purchases of imported articles. Exports decline because domestic products become less competitive in international markets due to higher prices. Other things remaining constant, an increase in imports and decrease in exports worsen the balance of payments.

CHANGES IN PAYMENT SYSTEM

In recent years the payment system in the United States has changed in two important ways: (1) Payments accounts have been extended to new institutions. (2) Savings accounts can be used for third party payments. In 1980, the Federal Reserve, in the light of new developments, redefined monetary aggregates. These changes may temporarily affect the ability of the Federal Reserve to regulate the economy. Since many old monetary aggregates cannot be reconstructed to make them historically consistent, past relationships between policy instruments and monetary aggregates and between monetary aggregates and ultimate targets cannot be effectively used. It will take time before new relations are established. Without the adequate knowledge of the relationship between monetary instruments and monetary aggregates, the authority cannot control monetary aggregates effectively. If the relationship between monetary aggregates and ultimate targets is not known, the authority will have problems in determining appropriate targets of monetary aggregates to achieve ultimate objectives.

Extension of Payments Accounts

The major payment accounts extended in recent years are: (i) NOW accounts, (ii) credit union share drafts, (iii) thrift-institution checking accounts and (iv) money-market mutual funds.

NOW Accounts
A NOW account is an interest bearing deposit on which withdrawal

can be made by a negotiable order. As of 1978, mutual savings banks, savings and loan associations and commercial banks in Massachusetts, New Hampshire, Maine, New York, Vermont, Rhode Island and Connecticut were permitted to offer such accounts.

The Federal Reserve can make good use of past relationships between monetary instruments and monetary aggregates if old monetary aggregates can be reconstructed in such a way so that they are historically consistent. NOW accounts make it difficult to do that. NOW accounts draw funds both from demand and savings deposits. Since it is not known how much funds came from demand deposits and how much from savings deposits, the old M_1 cannot be reconstructed to make it historically consistent. The old M_1 will be overestimated if all NOW accounts are added, and underestimated, if they are not. NOW accounts also create a problem in reconstructing the old M_2 because some funds might have moved from thrift savings accounts. According to Carl M. Gambs, NOW accounts are not yet large enough to create a serious problem.[2] If they are legalized for the entire nation, they would create serious complications.

Credit Union Share Draft

Many credit unions now offer the facility of transferring funds with a check-like instrument called a share draft. Share draft accounts are usually interest bearing. Customers, unlike NOW or regular checking accounts, receive a statement rather than cancelled checks.

Share draft accounts present precisely the same problem as NOW accounts. Since share drafts are a substitute for demand deposits, their exclusion results in an underestimation of old M_1 and M_2. Adding them to demand deposits does not make them historically consistent because some of these funds might otherwise be in regular savings accounts at thrift institutions. Though at the present time share draft accounts do not present any problem because of their small size ($72 million in July 1976), there is clearly room for considerable expansion.

Thrift Institution Checking Accounts

State chartered mutual savings banks and savings and loan associations in Connecticut, Maine, Rhode Island and New York have the authority to offer checking accounts as do state chartered savings and loan associations in Illinois. The exclusion of these deposits from old M_1 and M_2 underestimates their growth magnitudes. Adding them to demand deposits would not be satisfactory because some of these funds might have otherwise remained at savings accounts at thrift institutions.

Money Market Mutual Funds

Money-market mutual funds were a financial innovation of the 1970's. These funds primarily hold portfolios of short-term corporate and government securities and banks' large CDs. With these funds, small investors, like large ones, can obtain high returns at low transaction costs. Since 1974, an increasing number of these funds has allowed funds owners to redeem their shares by writing a check. Generally, they can write a check for any amount in excess of $500. These funds also make it difficult to reconstruct old monetary aggregates that are historically consistent because of the problem of determining how much money came from demand deposits and how much from time deposits.

Use Of Savings Accounts For Third Party Payment

A number of regulatory changes in recent years have made it possible for individuals to use savings accounts for third party payments, further complicating the problem of reconstructing certain monetary aggregates to make them historically consistent. The main changes in this direction are: (i) bill paying services, (ii) telephone transfers, (iii) automatic transfers to cover overdrafts and (iv) electronic-funds transfer method.

Bill Paying Services

In 1975 savings and loan associations and commercial banks were permitted for the first time to offer bill paying services from savings accounts. These services serve as partial substitutes for checking accounts.

Telephone Transfers

The Federal Reserve, also in 1975, allowed member banks to transfer funds from savings to checking accounts on the basis of telephone authorization, applicable only to nonbusiness accounts. This action followed telephone transfers services already in use by some thrift institutions and nonmember banks. Though telephone transfers are not widely used at the present time, their use clearly creates problems in reconstructing old M_1 and M_2 that are historically consistent.

Automatic Transfer To Cover Overdrafts

In 1978 the Federal Reserve permitted member banks to cover overdrafts or to insure maintenance of a minimum balance in checking accounts by automatically transferring funds from savings accounts to checking accounts. In the same year, the Federal Deposit Insurance Corporation approved a regulatory change to allow other banks and mutual savings banks to offer automatic transfers. This service is available only to individuals, not to businesses, government agencies or nonprofit institutions. It further adds to the problem of developing data of old M_1 and M_2 that are historically consistent.

Electronic Funds Transfer

The Federal Home Loan Bank Board permits member savings and loan associations to make payments from savings accounts through an electronic transfer system. Banks, in some states, are also allowed to offer this service. Institutions which offer the service set up remote service units in public places such as airports and supermarkets to allow customers to make transfers without visiting the institution. This service also creates the same problem of reconstructing certain monetary aggregates.

ATTRITION OF MEMBERSHIP

The attrition of membership in the Federal Reserve System is also weakening monetary management. At the end of 1977, member banks held less than 73 percent of the total commercial bank deposits, down about 8 percentage points over an 8-year period.[3] The attrition is occurring because member banks are at a serious disadvantage relative to other depository institutions. Most nonmember banks and thrift institutions may hold their required reserves in the form of earning assets or in the form of deposits, such as correspondent balances, that would be held in the normal course of business. Member banks, in contrast, are required to keep their reserves entirely in nonearning assets (cash in bank vault and on deposit at the District Bank).

The attrition in membership will weaken monetary management because an increasingly smaller share of the nation's deposits will remain under the direct control of the Federal Reserve. With member bank attrition, policymakers will find it difficult to pursue a restrictive monetary policy during inflationary periods because discount window funds would not be available to many banks for smooth and orderly adjustments to their lending and investment policies.

The attrition in membership will also make it more difficult to predict the relationship between the money supply and reserves provided by the Federal Reserve because a larger fraction of the nation's deposits will become subject to different reserve requirements set by different states. Moreover, fewer banks affiliated with the Federal Reserve System means that fewer institutions can be influenced by its changes in reserve requirements. This instrument has not been actively used, fearing that it may worsen the membership problem if reserve requirements are raised. However, in 1980 the Congress legislated "Depository Institutions Deregulation and Monetary Control Act" that required all depository institutions, having transactions accounts or nonpersonal time deposits, to adhere to the reserve requirements of the Federal Reserve. This may very well halt the further withdrawal of membership.

GROWTH IN EURODOLLARS

The growth in Eurodollars has also complicated the task of monetary management. Eurodollars are deposits denominated in U.S. dollars at banks outside the United States, including foreign branches of U.S. banks. The depositor may be a U.S. resident or a foreigner who has earned dollars directly or has bought them on the foreign exchange market. Typically, a Eurodollar deposit is a large round sum of $1 million to $50 million but, in the form of CDs, deposits may be as small as $20,000. While deposits can be made for any standard maturity from call to one year or more, the majority are placed for three months or less.[4] Eurobanks turn these deposits into earning assets by lending them to borrowers seeking dollars or other currencies. (Dollars can be used for other currencies because they can be easily converted on the foreign exchange market.)

The Eurodollar market complicates the task of monetary management because it enables domestic banks to counteract the effect of monetary policy by borrowing from or lending to such a market. If the Federal Reserve pursues a restrictive policy, banks can lessen its effect by borrowing from the Eurodollar market. During severe credit stringency in the latter part of 1966, in 1969 and early 1970, and, to a lesser extent, in 1973-74, U.S. banks obtained funds from this market to make business loans. Similarly, if the Federal Reserve follows an expansionary policy, banks can reduce its effect by utilizing available funds in expanding their overseas activities rather than for loans that might expand business activities at home.

Many economists believe that although the growth in Eurodollars has made the task of the Federal Reserve more difficult, it has not reduced its ability to control the money supply.[5] The Federal Reserve has offset the effect of Eurodollar transactions on the money supply by applying marginal reserve requirements on Eurodollars held by U.S. banks.

DISCRIMINATORY EFFECTS

Another problem of monetary policy is its discriminatory effects on different groups of borrowers. These, at times, restrict policymakers from taking certain courses of action, or put some pressure on them to do something to help those who are hurt unfairly by a policy decision.

The impact of a restrictive policy falls heavily on home buyers, state and local governments, small businessmen and low income families. Home buyers are hurt because a restrictive policy causes a decline in the amount of money available for mortgages due to disintermediation that occurs as market interest rates rise far in excess of the maximum rates banks and thrift institutions are allowed to pay on time deposits. However, the Federal Reserve, in 1978-80, weakened the process of disintermediation resulting from its restrictive action by allowing banks to pay interest rates on a certain type of CD equal to the rate earned on the most recently issued 6-month Treasury bill. The flow of funds for housing stops when market rates exceed ceilings on mortgage loans set by certain states. The flow of funds for FHA (Federal Housing Authority) and VA (Veterans Administration) guaranteed loans for housing also stop when market rates exceed the limits set by these agencies. However, at such times, Federal agencies such as the FNMA (Federal National Mortgage Association) and the FHLMC (Federal Home Loan Mortgage Corporation) relieve some of the pressure by diverting funds from other uses into the mortgage market. (The FNMA sells its securities to obtain funds to purchase FHA and VA guaranteed loans, as well as conventional loans. The FHLMC sells securities to the public and uses the proceeds to purchase mortgages from Federally insured savings and loan associations. Specifically, the FHLMC engages in purchases and sales of FHA and VA guaranteed loans, participates in conventional loans, and purchases conventional loans outright.)

High interest rates have an adverse effect on state and local government expenditure because: (i) An increase in interest rates raises the cost of financing. Construction projects of state and local governments depend heavily on borrowed funds and are, therefore, affected by the cost of financing. (ii) State and local governments have to abandon and/or postpone some of their projects if and when market rates go over their own legal interest rate ceilings.

The impact of a restrictive policy falls more heavily on small businessmen than on large ones. When funds are in short supply, banks are more inclined to lend to their large and steady customers than to small and risky ones. Moreover, unlike small companies, large companies can raise funds directly from the market by floating their own issues and, in some cases, by borrowing from the Eurodollar market.

The belief that a tight money policy hurts low income families more than medium and high income families hinges on the premise that the low income group buys more consumer durable goods on credit than the other groups. The high cost of borrowing and less availability of installment credit make it difficult for low income people to purchase such products.

Small banks are also unevenly affected by a restrictive policy because they find it more difficult to obtain necessary funds than large banks. The latter, with their ingenuity and resources, manage to avoid, at least for awhile, the adverse effect of a restrictive policy. In the past, large banks have at times met their customers' demand for loan by liquidating large blocks of their security holdings, by tapping nondeposit sources such as the Eurodollar market, Federal funds market and discount window, and by selling a portion of their loan portfolios to their holding company affiliates, subsidiaries and foreign branches.

In addition, there are many other problems confronting the monetary authority. It can restrain credit expansion more effectively than it can stimulate it. It can control the supply of money and not the demand for it. Above all, problems are complex and constantly changing and our knowledge is never complete.

SUMMARY

The major problems for monetary policy are: (1) lags, (2) imperfect knowledge, (3) conflicts among goals, (4) changes in payment system, (5) attrition of membership, (6) growth in the use of Eurodollars and (7) discriminatory effects.

Lags present a problem for monetary policy because they are not only long but also fairly unpredictable. Among all lags, outside presents the most difficulty.

Another problem is the imperfect knowledge about relationships among various economic variables, making it difficult for policymakers to come up with the right policy every time.

Changes in the payment system in recent years have also created a problem. Payment accounts have been extended to many new institutions. In some cases, savings accounts can be now used for third party payments. These changes have altered the relationships between monetary aggregates and ultimate objectives. Furthermore, they are increasing the deposits of those institutions that are not within the domain of the Federal Reserve.

The continuous attrition of Reserve membership is weakening monetary management because it is reducing the share of the nation's deposits controlled by the Federal Reserve. The growth in the Eurodollar market is causing a problem because it makes it possible for domestic banks to counteract the effect of monetary policy by borrowing from or lending to such a market.

Discriminatory effects of monetary policy create problems for policymakers because they, at times, restrict them from taking a certain course of action, or put pressure on them to do something to help those who are hurt unfairly.

FOOTNOTES

[1]Mark Willes, "Lags in Monetary and Fiscal Policy," **Business Review: Federal Reserve Bank of Philadelphia** (March 1968), p. 5.

[2]Carl M. Gambs, "Money - A Changing Concept in a Changing World," **Monthly Review: Federal Reserve Bank of Kansas City** (January 1977), p. 7.

[3]G. William Miller, Chairman, Board of Governors of the Federal Reserve System, Statement before the Committee on Banking, Finance and Urban Affairs, House of Representatives, July 27, 1978, **Federal Reserve Bulletin** (August 1978), p. 636.

[4]Jane Sneddon Little, "The Impact of the Euro-dollar Market on the Effectiveness of Monetary Policy in the United States and Abroad," **New England Economic Review** (March/April 1975), p. 4.

[5]Geoffrey E. Wood and Douglas R. Mudd, "Do Foreigners Control the U.S. Money Supply?" **Review: Federal Reserve Bank of St. Louis** (December 1977), p. 11.

QUESTIONS FOR REVIEW

1. What do we mean by lags in monetary policy? How do they present problems for policymakers?
2. Outline briefly the changes that have taken place in our payment system during the 1965-1975 period.
3. Explain how the introduction of savings accounts for third party payments presents a problem for policymakers.
4. Explain how the extension of payment accounts to many new institutions presents a problem for our monetary policy.
5. "Since our knowledge about the relationships of various economic variables is not perfect, any monetary action is likely to do more harm than good to the economy." Comment.
6. What are the principal conflicts among different goals? How do they present problems in policy making?
7. Explain how the Eurodollar Market functions. In what ways does it cause problems for monetary policy?
8. Explain why the Federal Reserve is interested in having all depository institutions under its control.
9. Evaluate critically discriminatory effects of a restrictive monetary policy.
10. Describe how different Federal agencies work to relieve somewhat the adverse effect of a tight money policy on the housing industry.

SUGGESTED FURTHER READING

1. Brimmer, Andrew F. "Multi-national Banks and the Management of Monetary Policy in the United States." Paper presented before the Eighty-Fifth Annual Meeting of the American Economic Association, Toronto, Ontario, Canada, December 28, 1972. (Mimeographed.)

2. Davidson, Philip H. "Structure of the Residential Mortgage Market." **Monthly Review: Federal Reserve Bank of Richmond,** September 1972, pp. 2-6.
3. Federal Reserve Bank of Boston. **Housing and Monetary Policy: Proceedings of the Monetary Conference.** Boston, Massachusetts: Federal Reserve Bank of Boston, 1970.
4. Gambs, Carl M. "Money - A Changing Concept in a Changing World." **Monthly Review: Federal Reserve Bank of Kansas City.** January 1977, pp. 3-12.
5. Gibson, William E. "Eurodollars and U.S. Monetary Policy." **Journal of Money, Credit and Banking.** August 1971, pp. 647-665.
6. Hamburger, Michael J. "The Lag in the Effect of Monetary Policy: A Survey of Recent Literature." **Monthly Review: Federal Reserve Bank of New York.** December 1971, pp. 289-298.
7. Lawler, Patrick J. "Today's Monetary Policy Affects Tomorrow's Economy." **Voice: Federal Reserve Bank of Dallas.** September 1978, pp. 1-10.
8. Little, Jane Sneddan. "The Impact of the Eurodollar Market on the Effectiveness of Monetary Policy in the United States and Abroad." **New England Review.** March/April 1975, pp. 3-19.
9. Massaro, Vincent G. "Eurodollars and the U.S. Money Supply." **The Conference Board Record.** September 1971, pp. 46-48.
10. Mayer, Thomas. "The Lag in Effect of Monetary Policy: Some Criticism." **Western Economic Journal.** September 1967, pp. 324-342.
11. Stevens, Neil A. "A Mortgage Futures Market: Its Development, Uses, Benefits, and Costs." **Review: Federal Reserve Bank of St. Louis.** April 1976, pp. 12-19.
12. Warburton, C. "Variability of the Lag in the Effect of Monetary Policy, 1919-1965." **Western Economic Journal.** June, 1971, pp. 115-133.
13. Willes, Mark H. "Lags in Monetary and Fiscal Policy." **Business Review: Federal Reserve Bank of Philadelphia.** March 1968, pp. 3-10.
14. Winningham, Scott. "Automatic Transfers and Monetary Policy." **Economic Review: Federal Reserve Bank of Kansas City.** November 1978, pp. 18-27.
15. Wood, Geoffrey E. and Mudd, Douglas R. "Do Foreigners Control the U.S. Money Supply?" **Review: Federal Reserve Bank of St. Louis.** December 1977, pp. 8-11.

INDEX

INDEX

INDEX

INDEX

INDEX

INDEX